De

"The Parish Pantry (Spizarnia Kosciol)"
Keepsake Edition

"Spizarnia Kosciol — The Parish Pantry," Keepsake Edition, is dedicated to the memory of the Polish pioneers who founded the St. Teresa of Avila Catholic Church after helping to settle and build the community of Harrah, Oklahoma.

With aspirations for a better life, with faith in God, and with a dream of farming their own land and building their own community, they journeyed to Harrah. They tilled the fertile new land to plant their crops — the seeds of hope and prosperity. The parish and the community today are possible because of their labors, their commitment and their vision.

May the faith and pioneering spirit of these Polish settlers be a cherished heritage that lives on in the members of St. Teresa's parish.

"The Parish Pantry"

(Spizarnia Kosciol)

Keepsake Edition

A collection of Polish recipes and other favorites from Harrah, Oklahoma

© Copyright 1996

by Court Christ the King, #1586, of The Catholic Daughters of the Americas
St. Teresa of Avila Catholic Church
1576 N. Tim Holt Dr., Harrah, Oklahoma 73045

ISBN 0-9619314-1-8
Library of Congress Card Catalog Number: 96-070267

Printed in the United States of America
TOOF COOKBOOK DIVISION

STARR ★ TOOF

670 South Cooper Street
Memphis, TN 38104

Appreciation

The members of the CDA Cookbook Committee would like to express their appreciation to:

- The members of the Catholic Daughters of the Americas (CDA), the parish and the community who shared their treasured recipes with us to make this a successful endeavor;

- Rosalie Marino for sharing her original Polish paper cutting work of art with us to illustrate this book;

- Dallas artist Patrick Nesbitt for the cover design, his artistic interpretation of the traditional "wycinanki" folk art style;

- Harrah artist Juanita Maxey for the wonderful pen and ink sketches of St. Teresa's, today and yesterday;

- Harrah resident Mary Beebe, retired English teacher, for proofreading this book;

- The members of the parish and the community who submitted recipes for this Keepsake Edition of "The Parish Pantry (Spizarnia Kosciol)". This book would not have been possible without their contributions;

- The many people who purchase this book. Profits from the sale of this book will be used by the CDA to fund the many parish and community service projects it sponsors;

- and, the volunteers of RSVP, Inc., the Retired Senior Volunteer Program, who, under the direction of Elizabeth Patterson, RSVP, Inc. executive director, were a tremendous help in preparing the text of the book. Volunteers Barbara Brimm, Betty Miller, June Buckley and Carol Walsh worked countless hours to retype the original book. These volunteers shared their special skills and gift of time in the community-spirited manner that has built RSVP, Inc., a United Way agency, a successful reputation over its many years of operation in our community.

About the CDA

The Catholic Daughters of the Americas (CDA) is a national organization of Catholic women that fosters the purposes of unity, faith, charity, service and fellowship.

Unity

The CDA was founded in 1903 in Utica, New York, with 60 charter members. The organization grew rapidly. Within 10 years, there were 206 courts, or local chapters, in 32 states with more than 16,000 members. By 1923, membership had surpassed 170,000 members in 45 states and courts had been added in Panama, Puerto Rico, Cuba and Canada. Those figures have been roughly maintained through the decades to the present, with the members representing 1,569 courts.

In Oklahoma today, there are 876 members that belong to 16 courts throughout the state.

Court Christ the King Court #1586 was instituted in Harrah, Okla., at St. Teresa's October 28, 1951. Today the court has more than 50 members. The unity of the national organization allows all members to have an effective voice in international, national, state, civic and moral issues. The collective voice of the CDA can speak out against poverty, war and all forms of social injustice and can speak for christianity. The organization is involved in overseas relief to starving families and children.

Charity

A portion of the CDA local dues are forwarded from the local courts to assist in the national and international projects. The members of the Harrah court also lend support to national programs that work for youth and the Catholic bishops and against abortion and pornography.

On the local level, the Court maintains a food closet that serves the community. The members prepare food baskets each Thanksgiving for area families in need. A favorite project in recent years has been the Community Christmas Toy Store, which the CDA members support each year. The group also helps families year-round by specific cases of need.

Community

In addition to helping individuals and families in need, the CDA members are involved in other areas of community service. The members make and contribute more than a thousand popcorn balls to the annual community Halloween party. They sponsor an annual essay and poetry contest open to all students in the public school system. The CDA is a steady participant in the annual Harrah Day activities and in the town's Polish Festival.

Service

The CDA members are involved in numerous activities that revolve around service to the parish. They sponsor a weekly coffee time after the 10 a.m. Sunday mass. They host breakfasts annually for First Communion and the graduating senior class in the Confraternity of Christian Doctrine (CCD) Education program. The graduation breakfast also honors all high school and college graduates in the parish district. In addition to providing gifts for the children enrolled in the CCD program and organizing an annual Christmas party for them, the CDA members provide refreshments and are the helping hands for many parish special events.

Fellowship

The members share in a number of activities that are designed around meetings of the court. Standing programs include the "Heart Speaks to Heart," "Community," and "Continuing Life" programs that encourage service to the church and to the community in all courts across the Americas. The CDA regular meeting is held at 7 p.m. on the first Sunday of the month in the parish hall.

Faith

In all their works, the CDA members are united by their faith. The power of prayer is the most important tool the CDA has in carrying out its work. Praying the rosary, for the deceased members of the CDA and for the priests and for religious vocations are central to the purpose of the CDA.

CDA Act of Consecration	Lord Jesus, I give you my hands to do your work; I give you my feet to go your way; I give you my eyes to see as you do; I give you my tongue to speak your words; I give you my mind that you may think in me; Above all, I give you my whole life that you may grow in me, So that it may be you, Lord Jesus, who works, loves, and prays in me. Amen.

A History of St. Teresa of

In essence, the history of the St. Teresa of Avila Catholic Church is the history of Harrah, Okla., for the church was founded by ten Polish families who came to this area just outside of the eastern boundary of the Oklahoma Land Run of 1889 to establish their homes and to farm.

They came by covered wagon from Marche, Arkansas, where many Polish immigrants had begun settling as early as 1877. They had been lured to Marche by word of low land prices, but the land proved sandy and rocky, and crops did poorly.

Ready to try their luck elsewhere, Oklahoma Territory beckoned, with news of unassigned lands available to be claimed. The land encompassing Harrah was the western edge of property owned by the Pottawatomie and Shawnee Indian tribes. In July 1890, the two tribes ceded this western real estate back to the government under the Dawes Act.

This cleared the way for the second Oklahoma Land Run, September 22, 1891, in territory just to the east of the Unassigned Lands that had been settled by the "89ers". The men came ahead of their families in 1891, and by speed of horse and fleetness of foot, the Polish people staked their claims along the North Canadian River in what is now part of Oklahoma County. Their families followed, many coming in 1892.

They first lived in dugouts, tilled the land, and some of the men worked on the emerging public roads to pay the government for filing fees and taxes owed on their new 160-acre farms.

United in their Polish heritage and Catholic faith, the newcomers began meeting in each other's homes to pray the rosary and sing hymns. Eventually, a circuit-riding priest would come once, and sometimes twice a month to offer mass.

In 1896, a new railroad was being planned for Oklahoma Territory that would follow the grade of the Canadian River at the point where Harrah is situated today. A railroad station was established and named Sweeny Switch after the railroad agent, E. W. Sweeny. A post office was eventually located there.

In 1898, resident Louis Navarre sold 40 acres of his land to Frank Harrah, a merchant who developed and platted the original townsite along either side of the railroad. On October 27, 1898, the name was changed from Sweeney, Oklahoma Territory, to Harrah, O.T.

In 1897, one of the non-Polish members of the parish community, John Beal, donated land to build a church. The members donated labor to build the church on the site of the present-day cemetery. The church burned March 13, 1923, when smoldering charcoal left unattended sparked the fire that left some 200 parishioners without a church building.

Avila Catholic Church

A temporary church was immediately constructed and was later used as a school building. Plans for the present-day church were soon underway and it was completed in time for the first mass to be celebrated on December 24, 1925.

The church operated a school from the late '30s to the mid '60s. It was staffed by the Carmelite sisters of Villa Teresa in Oklahoma City. The school was originally housed in the building that had been built to temporarily serve as the parish church after the destruction of the original church. A wood frame building constructed in 1938 for a church house was also used.

The school prospered along with the town and on July 5, 1956, ground was broken for the present-day parish hall and classrooms.

Although the school was closed, a vibrant Confraternity of Christian Doctrine program has grown steadily with the parish. In March 1983, under the direction of Father Gerard Nathe, O.S.B., an educational building was constructed debt-free.

Today, under the direction of Father James Murphy, O.S.B., the church continues to grow. A number of parish organizations are active in projects that serve both the parish and the community.

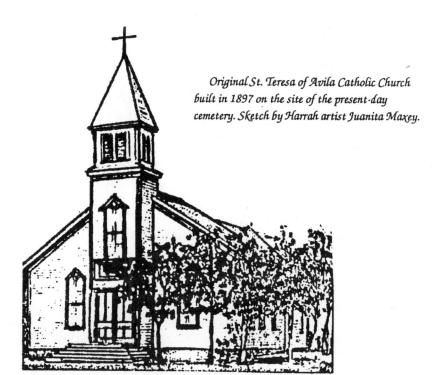

Original St. Teresa of Avila Catholic Church built in 1897 on the site of the present-day cemetery. Sketch by Harrah artist Juanita Maxey.

Masses

Sunday	8:00 a.m.
	10:00 a.m.
Monday	7:30 a.m.
Tuesday	7:30 a.m.
Wednesday	6:30 p.m.
Thursday	7:30 a.m.
Friday	7:30 a.m.
Saturday Vigil	5:30 p.m.
Polish Mass	6:00 p.m.,
	Third Sunday of the Month

Peace be with you

Organizations

At St. Teresa of Avila Catholic Church

- **The Catholic Daughters of the Americas**
  Court Christ the King #1586
  Meets the first Sunday of each month, 7 p.m., Parish Hall

- **The Confraternity of Christian Doctrine (CCD) classes**
  Meets Wednesday, 7-8 p.m. and Sundays, 9-10 a.m.

- **The Altar Society**
  Meets the first Sunday of the month at 2 p.m.

- **The Knights of Columbus**
  Meets the first Sunday of the month at 7 p.m.

- **The Polish Club**
  Meets last Sunday of the month at 2 p.m.

- **The Choir**
  Practices Wednesdays at 7 p.m.

- **Inquiry Class**
  Meets Mondays at 7 p.m.

- **Youth Group**
  Meets twice a month.

Wycinanki

(Vih-chee-non-kee)

"Decorative Paper Cut-Outs"

The polish folk art of decorative paper cutouts belongs to the most beautiful of folk arts in the world. It is the official national art of Poland. That is why the colorful Wycinanki was chosen to illustrate this cookbook. Additional designs have been included in this Keepsake Edition of "Spizarnia Kosciol – The Parish Pantry."

In this folk art, the individual paper cutouts were made by hand, without drawing, with sheep shearing scissors. They were used twice a year for decorating the walls and ceiling beams in peasant cottages — once before Christmas and then before Easter. These cutouts were usually placed over a door. The cutout skill and the charm of the decorative paper cutouts adorning the peasant cottages were a criterion of the resourcefulness and good taste of the housewife.

Illustrating the divider pages of the recipes are the decorative paper cutouts of "Kurpiowskie," Kurpie, from the area of the former Green Forest. Out of the many regional types, the Kurpie cutouts distinguish themselves by their unique character. The one-color decorative paper cut-outs such as "stylized lilies" are a symmetrical arrangement of plain and zoomorphic themes and present a particularly high artistic level.

Apart from them, multi-colored decorative paper cutouts were often produced that were put together in their final composition by a layering, or paste-up technique. The cutout of the roosters used on the cover of this cookbook is an example of this layering technique.

In the district of Kurpie, similarly as in other regions, the decorative paper cutouts appeared in the middle of the 19th century. At the beginning of the 20th century, they belonged to the declining fields of folk art. Reactivated after the World War II, the art lived to see a remarkable resurgence. In present times, many Polish artisans are engaged in the production of the paper cutouts, and often continue a family tradition in their style. The talents of the modern Polish woman present a review of the various local varieties and capture the characteristics of the individual periods of the development of the decorative paper cutout.

In another variation of the Wycinanki art, chandelier-like ornaments made from colored paper are hung from the ceiling for the Christmas celebration. They are known as pajaki, or spiders, because of their spreading effect that resembles a spider's web. Feathers and beads are sometimes added for a special effect.

In making the elaborate cutouts, the paper is folded and cut for the basic pattern. Then other colors are pasted on with a paste of egg-white, flour and water. Great lengths are taken to make these as intricate and elaborate as possible.

Easter

Polish Easter Traditions

Preparations for a Polish Easter are involved. There are the religious fasts and sacrifices made in observance of the 40 days of Lent that begins with Ash Wednesday and last until Easter Sunday. There is the obligation to examine one's soul and go to Easter confession, known as the Rite of Penance. There are preparations in the home to be made. Polish homemakers plan a spring cleaning that is completed by Palm Sunday. New clothing for Easter is made or purchased. The home is decorated with care. With these preparations done, Easter week is devoted to attending church.

Food represents the laboring of hands and Polish women labor prior to Easter to prepare the makings of a sumptuous feast. It is a tradition that Polish women do not cook or work on Easter Sunday, because it is a holiday for the housewife, too. The breads are baked and ready, the meats have been prepared, eggs have been colored and relishes and pickles are ready from earlier labors. There is enough for everyone and everyone is encouraged to help themselves. No turkeys are baked, no potatoes are mashed, and the day is not spent in the kitchen. Easter Sunday is a time to celebrate Christ's resurrection at mass and to enjoy the company of friends and family.

The holiday feasting begins on Easter morning. The feast consists mainly of cold dishes such as ham, roast pork loin, sausages of all types, hard-boiled eggs with various sauces, relishes such as horseradish, pickles, pickled mushrooms and beets, vegetable salads and potatoes in sour-cream. Sausages and roast pork complete the offerings.

The desserts are the delight of the table. They include the traditional Easter Babka; sernik, which is cheesecake with raisins; beautiful towering tortes and mazureks.

It is an old Polish custom that a little white sugar lamb be placed at the middle of the table as the symbol of Jesus. A little red banner and sugar flowers usually adorn the lamb. "Lambs" shaped from butter or pastry are also used. Traditionally, next to the lamb stood a bowl of colored eggs and hyacinths. Wine, homemade cordials, or nelewka, which are made by combining one part of fruit syrup with three parts of vodka, sparkled in bottles on the table.

Pussy willows and other flowers such as hyacinths, the traditional Polish Easter flower, decorate the laden table.

Palm Sunday

Following the 40 days of Lent that begins with Ash Wednesday, Palm Sunday marks the beginning of the Easter season for Roman Catholics.

In Poland Palm Sunday is sometimes called Flower Sunday. Everyone attending church enters bearing a palm. If actual palms are unavailable, pussy willow or pine branches are sometimes substituted. The priest blesses the palms during the mass. These consecrated palm fronds are thought to have protective powers and are kept in the home for protection from misfortune. Burning a small piece of the palm during threatening weather is believed to offer divine protection. This rite of the Easter season is very much a part of the traditional Palm Sunday observance at St. Teresa's, too.

In Poland, the week between Palm Sunday and Easter is devoted to daily prayer and attending church. Houses are cleaned and decorated in anticipation of the holiday. Shares of the specially-prepared sausages and other meats and colored eggs are taken to neighbors and friends and to the less fortunate.

Swiecone
The Blessing of the Easter Fare

On Holy Saturday, the evening vigil mass before Easter Sunday, the blessing of the food – or Swiecone – is performed during the mass. It is a custom still practiced at St. Teresa's today.

Foods representing part of the Easter Sunday meal are placed in a basket and brought to church for the blessing. Much care is taken to prepare the basket. The baskets are lined with the finest linen and are often kept for this purpose only. In early Poland, it was the custom for many families to pass these special baskets down to the next generation.

The baskets may be filled with ham, sausages, colored eggs, babka and slices of cakes or breads that are representative of the Easter meal. The priest says a special blessing over the food and then it is sprinkled with Holy Water that has been consecrated earlier during the vigil.

The Sharing of an Easter Egg

It is a tradition that the Easter meal begin with the sharing of an egg, preferably one that was blessed at Swiecone, the blessing of the food at the Vigil Mass the Saturday night before Easter Sunday.

The lady of the house cuts an egg into a few more pieces than there are people present for the meal (should friends or neighbors drop in). Before everyone is seated, a plate holding the wedges of egg is passed to each person by the head of the household or another important family member or guest. Each person takes a piece of the egg to share and expresses wishes for long and happy lives and a prosperous year for everyone. The egg is symbolic of new life or new beginnings.

Easter Sunday Menu

Appetizers

Deviled Eggs
Marinovannye Griby - Russian Pickled Mushrooms *
Ogorki Kwaszone - Dill Pickles *
Peach Pickles *
Pickled Beets *

Salads

Pudding Fruit Salad*
German Potato Salad

Main Dishes

Brisket
Homemade Salami *
Kielbasa - Polish Sausage *

Side Dishes

Gourmet Potatoes
Cabbage Casserole

Breads

Babka *
Bohemian Rye Bread *

Desserts

Mazurka Cake *
Polish Easter Cake *

See Index for Recipes
* Make ahead

Easter Egg Dyes
A Natural Tradition

The beautiful art of Polish, Ukrainian and other East European dyed Easter eggs is well known. The patterns and colors are beautiful. How did our ancestors dye eggs before the convenience of the small color tablets we purchase in stores today? They used the natural roots, berries, nuts and grasses available to them.

These dyes may be made in your own kitchen just like our pioneering ancestors did. The subtle colors achieved from the natural dyes can be fun and beautiful. You can never be quite sure of the color you'll get, but that's part of the fun of this tradition.

Here are some common natural ingredients and the approximate colors they will render. Some will require a mordant, which is a chemical that fixes a dye such as vinegar, to bring out a color:

Light Yellow
    Boil about 1 cup of safflower with 1 teaspoon of vinegar.

Yellow
    Boil orange Marigold flower petals.

Golden Yellow
    Use turmeric and a teaspoon of vinegar.

Greenish Yellow
    Use yellow Marigold petals.

Orange
    Use the skins from yellow onions.

Ruddy Red
    Use the skins from red onions.

Dark Brown
    Use walnut hulls.

Light Green
    Use moss, preferably taken from under a stone.

Blue/Lavender
    Use red cabbage with a tablespoon of alum.

Gray/Purple
    Use cranberries with a teaspoon of vinegar.

Salmon
    Use sandlewood.

Blue/Purple
    Use blueberries.

Purple
    Use blackberries.

Light Lavender
    Use raspberries.

Polish Onion Skin Eggs

10 eggs   **Alfalfa for green eggs**
2 c. onion skins, finely packed

   Place eggs in single layers in large saucepan. Add cold water to cover eggs and onion skins. Bring to boil; simmer until eggs are of desired color, at least 10 minutes. Take off heat. Remove eggs to wire rack to cool. Rub eggs with a little salad oil. Pat dry on paper towels. Strain onion mixture. Reuse to color additional eggs.

Rosie L. Klimkowski

Patterned Eggs

Eggs   **White vinegar**
Paper towels   **Vegetable oil**
Tongs or egg dippers   **Dyestuffs for colors desired**

For patterned eggs:
Cheesecloth, cut into 8" squares   **Fresh herb leaves such as parsley,**
Rubber bands   **dill or cilantro.**

   Hard-cooked eggs are called "jajki". The natural coloring process is a part of the cooking procedure for the eggs.
   Use vinegar on a paper towel to wipe each egg to remove the waxy covering sometimes put on store-bought eggs. Allow the eggs to dry.
   Put about one cup of the dyestuff for every two cups of cold water in a pan. You will need a separate pan for each color you wish to make.
   Place the raw eggs into the pan and bring the water to a boil. Turn the heat down and allow the water, dyestuff and eggs to simmer for about 10 minutes.
   Run the cooked, dyed eggs under slightly cold water to cool. When the eggs are cooled, you can add a shine to the eggs by wiping them with vegetable oil that has been applied to a paper towel.
   For the patterned eggs, place leaves from the herb flat against the egg. Wetting the leaves will help make them stay in place. Use as many leaves as you desire. The leaves will leave a pattern and the dyestuff will color the background. Wrap cheesecloth around each egg to hold the leaves in place. Secure with a rubber band. Boil the bound eggs.

Pisanki
Decorated Easter Eggs

The art of beautifully-decorated eggs — pisanki — has been traced as far as the eleventh century. In Poland, decorating the eggs was often a social occasion usually organized by the young girls of the village.

The beautiful pisanki are painstaking works of art. Colors are applied one color at a time. Areas that are not to be colored receive a layer of wax that is applied using a needle or a tiny metal tube such as the end of a shoelace. The waxed areas will not be colored when the egg is dipped. The wax on those areas of the design may then be melted away and the colored areas waxed and the egg dipped in a new color for a multi-colored design. This process is repeated until the design that is desired is complete.

In earlier days in Poland, a gift of an Easter egg from a girl to a boy was a sign that his attentions would not be unwelcome.

Hors d'oeuvres

Hors d'oeuvres have a very important place in the Polish cuisine. This is what is prepared and served on all festive occasions. Hospitality was always considered sacred in Poland. Slavs believed that "a guest in the house is God in the house."

Foods are prepared weeks and days in advance so that the holiday can be devoted to church, family and friends. The delicacies are left on the table where everyone can help his or herself. There is plenty for everyone.

Egg Tips

To hard cook eggs, cover with cold water, bring to simmering over medium heat. Turn down temperature to low heat and cook for 10 or 15 minutes.

When cooking a large quantity of eggs such as for Easter, after bringing the water to a boil, set the pan off of the heat, keep the lid on the pot and let it stand until cool. When water is cold, eggs will be firmly cooked.

Egg yolks turn dark when cooked too long or cooked at high temperature.

To determine whether an egg is fresh, immerse it in a pan of cool, salted water. If it sinks, it is fresh; if it rises to the surface, throw it away.

Fresh eggs' shells are rough and chalky; old eggs are smooth and shiny.

To determine whether an egg is hard-boiled, spin it. If it spins, it is hard-boiled; if it wobbles and will not spin, it is raw.

Egg whites won't run while boiling or poaching if you'll add a little vinegar to the water.

Eggs will beat up fluffier if they are allowed to come to cool room temperature before beating.

For baking, it's best to use medium to large eggs. Extra large eggs may cause cakes to fail when cooled.

Egg shells can be easily removed from hard-boiled eggs if they are quickly rinsed in cold water first.

For fluffier omelets, add a pinch of cornstarch before beating.

For a never fail, never weep meringue, add a teaspoon of cornstarch to the sugar before beating it into the egg whites.

Once your meringue is baked, cut it cleanly using a knife coated with butter.

A meringue pie may be covered with wax paper or plastic wrap with no fear of sticking, if you'll first grease the paper with oleo.

Dyngus Day
On Dyngus Day, Everybody's Polish

Celebrated the Monday after Easter, Dyngus Day can only attempt to be described as a welcoming of spring, a celebration of the demise of winter, and the petitioning for a good planting season to bring a bountiful harvest — all rolled into one rollicking day that in former times in Poland had many elaborate customs for both men and women, particularly the young and marriageable.

Now a national holiday in Poland, Dyngus Day can be traced back to the 10th century where it was a pagan rite of spring before Poland was converted to Christianity.

The Slavic word "dyngus" means "sprinkling." The word can also be traced to Germanic roots with meanings to "come to an agreement, to evaluate" and to the 16th century in "coming to the service of another," to "bringing a case before court" or to "bicker over a price" or "to ransom." In early Poland, they bickered with nature through a practice of switching each other with pussy willow branches and with the pouring of water to make themselves pure and ready for the coming year. The custom of pouring water is an ancient spring rite of renewal or cleansing, purification and fertility.

In the merriment of Dyngus Day, one could buy, or ransom, his way out of the switchings or punishments of the day with certain acts or promises. The punishment suffered throughout the Dyngus Day is called "oblewanki", or drenching with water. Boys and girls are quick to plan ways to douse each other with water, sometimes making elaborate plans for both ambush and escape. The younger boys would march in a procession through the village from cottage to cottage making a lot of noise, singing songs and demanding ransoms — goodies left from the Easter table. The girls made their own rounds in the village singing and carrying a fresh evergreen branch which was decorated with ribbons and flowers and known as the "gaj". It is a sign of promise and good fortune.

The more genteel of the village replace the dousing with symbolic sprinkling and often with the spraying of perfume. The water is also supposed to evoke the rains which will aid the spring planting and is symbolic of health and good harvests.

The early Catholic Church took these rites of pouring water and associated them with the sprinkling of baptism, thus "baptizing" the rites and turning them into a more meaningful rite that marked the celebration of the new church year.

In the early Catholic Church, baptisms were performed only during the Easter season. The Polish Prince Mieszko I was baptized on the Monday after Easter in 966 A.D., thus Dyngus Day evolved into a celebration of thanksgiving that the first king of Poland was baptized into Christianity and that, thus, the Roman Catholic Church was established in Poland.

May Day in Poland

For Roman Catholics, each day of the year is named after a great soul that has lived – a saint. The first day of May honors St. Philip and St. Jacob the Apostle, known as the patron of marriageable girls. May Day in Poland began as a spring celebration that combined the elements of welcoming spring, mating rites and games and of pulling practical pranks much like April Fool's Day in America.

On the eve of May Day, the boys would make small scarecrows or straw figures they called filipki, or "Little Philips." They would throw them on rooftops and down chimney flues and would incorporate them into various other pranks. They left them at cottages to tease the girls of late marriages or spinsterhood.

More popular was the placing of a majek, or "Little May" in front of the home of a favored girl. The majek was a tall, smooth pole, (what is more commonly known as a Maypole,) that had been decorated with ribbons and flowers at the top. The parents of the girl chosen to be crowned or honored with the placing of the maypole, were expected to open their home for dancing and singing.

For modern-day Catholics, the first day of May is a holy day in honor of the Blessed Virgin Mary, the mother of Jesus and queen of heaven. All Catholics are obligated to participate in the May Day mass. The entire month of May is dedicated to special prayers and celebrations honoring the Blessed Mother.

Wigilia
Christmas Eve Supper

Preparations for Christmas were a welcomed diversion from the cold days of winter that came after the harvest was over in Poland. The house was decorated, outdoor festivities were planned and ornaments for the tree were made. The tree was trimmed with paper chains, apples and nuts wrapped in gold or silver foil, gingerbread figures, bright ribbons, beads and paper flowers. Paper cutouts adorned the walls.

The Polish call the Christmas tree podlaznik or podlazniczka for "sad orchard." It was the tradition that the evergreen be hung point-down from the ceiling in a place of honor in the home. If it was a small tree, it might be hung over the table where the Christmas feast would be served.

The important meal of the Polish Christmas holiday is Wigilia, Christmas Eve supper. It is traditionally meatless, but is still very opulent. The Christmas Eve meal is served in courses. All should represent the produce of the land in the prior year. The common "sweet" at the end of the meal is a compote of stewed dried fruit. Poppy seeds are always included as a symbol of peaceful sleep; and honey, too, for sweetness and contentment.

Traditionally, the table for the Christmas Eve supper is set with the finest linen in the home. A white tablecloth is always used for the Christmas Eve supper and no one is supposed to leave the table during the meal. It adds dignity to the evening. Blades of straw are placed under the tablecloth to commemorate Christ's birth in a manger.

It is customary to set an extra place setting for a possible guest or beggar, because no one is turned away in the night preceding Christ's birth. To the Poles, "a guest in the house is God in the house." It is considered good luck to have an unexpected guest for Christmas Eve dinner.

The extra place is also for loved ones who are far away. It is a sign that they are with their families in spirit.

Christmas

Like Easter, Christmas is an extended celebration. The observance begins on Christmas Eve and continues to the Feast of Epiphany on January 6, the day the Three Wise Men visited the Holy Child.

The idea of a gift-bearing Santa Claus is not a part of the Polish tradition, although the idea has become more often incorporated into the celebration as a result of media exposure.

In Poland, there is the tradition of St. Nicholas who appears on December 6 as the patron of good children. The saint, impersonated by a tall, bearded man wearing a cloak and carrying a miter, visits the homes where celebrations of St. Nicholas are in progress and asks the children questions about their catechism — the Church teachings about Christianity. Small toys are rewards for correct answers. Although the tradition of celebrating the feast day of St. Nicholas is similar, there is no connection to the western Santa Claus.

Christmas Day

Christmas Day is very peaceful in Poland. People rest, visit relatives and friends. Not much cooking is done. Meals are served cold or reheated.

Christmas Dinner usually consists of cold turkey with cranberry sauce, and vegetable-potato salad. A clear, hot borscht in cups follows with breadsticks. Sometimes the meal is a goose with cabbage and baked potatoes. If company is expected there will be an elegant torte, honey cake and cookies. Coffee is made very strong and served in demitasse cups. Bowls of nuts and dishes with candies are placed on tables.

Little Star

According to Polish tradition, the festivities of the Christmas Eve meal did not begin before the first star appeared in the evening sky. Children would eagerly watch the sky to be the first to see the first star, which commemorates the star of Bethlehem. The formal name for the Christmas Eve holiday is Boze Narodzenie — the Nativity — but it is informally called Gwiazdka by children and adults alike, meaning "Little Star."

Polish Wedding Customs

In early-day Harrah, a wedding in the Polish community was not only the celebration of one of the seven sacraments of the church, it was a much-anticipated social event. It was a day-long occasion that was marked by plenty of food, lively music, dancing, ceremonial observances, and the chance to visit with relatives and friends.

It was most common for a wedding to be held in the morning, followed by a luncheon at the family home of the bride or groom, or wherever they would be living as a newly-married couple. Weddings were never held on a Friday — a day of fasting and penance, or on Saturday or Sunday, when regular masses were held. A wedding mass was required and was held on a weekday, commonly around 10 a.m. so as not to interfere with the regular noon mass. The celebration festivities usually lasted until midnight. Weddings were not held at night.

Veronica Kupczynski of St. Teresa's and her husband, Maximillian, who is now deceased, were married November 5, 1930. She describes their wedding as a very typical and wonderful occasion and remembers the fun they had on the wedding days of family and friends.

"The ushers and bridesmaids would meet at the bride's house before going to the church for the wedding mass," Mrs. Kupczynski said. "It was the custom to have a blessing, usually given by an older man in the family." When they returned from church, another blessing would be given at the home in which they would live.

The bride and groom usually chose a "starosta" — either the best man or an older man in the family — for the wedding celebration. The starosta was sort of an official emcee and social director for the day's festivities. He would have several bright colored ribbons about 18 inches long pinned to his lapel so the guests would recognize his role. The starosta made customary speeches before the couple left for the church and after lunch. Before leaving for church, he would ask "Who's going to interfere with this wedding?" Those at the home would sing a short, lighthearted little song that admonished the bride to behave herself.

One custom involved the starosta asking, upon returning from the church and entering the home where the couple would live: "Who built this house?" He would then stumble around the room as if the floor was slanted or crooked. "How in the world did they ever climb these steps?" he would ask. A little song, which Mrs. Kupczynski can still sing in Polish, was sung by the crowd. The playful ceremony showed that the couple would have their "ups and downs" in life, she said. The starosta would announce lunch by telling them that if the bride and groom and guests don't get enough to eat, it's their own fault because the cooks have plenty and there are more kettles in the kitchen. Often a toast was made by the "druzki," the best man.

A couple of days ahead of the wedding, several ladies would start cooking pies and cakes for the event. Roast pork, fried chicken, baked ham, sauerkraut and potatoes, vegetables, fruit pies and other desserts awaited the crowd in abundance. The morning of the wedding, at least two women would stay at the home to complete the preparation of the meal. A common custom was to meet the newly-married couple at the door upon their return with glasses of wine.

Music for the occasion was commonly provided by someone with a violin accompanied by a guitar player. Music and dancing went on most of the day. After supper, the drusba presided over a traditional dance with the bride. The men would line up and pay a dollar for a short dance with the bride — usually no more than a quick turn-around.

In another custom often practiced, a china plate was placed on the table. The men would throw silver dollars, which were often more common than paper money in early times, at the plate. If they broke the plate, they got to dance with the bride again. The bride and groom kept the silver dollars as a nest egg for their new life together. Mrs. Kupczynski recalls that she and her husband received $150.

Nowadays, a wedding celebration at St. Teresa's includes the groom in the customs. Not only do the men line up to dance with the bride — usually receiving a shot of whisky or wine for their dollar, but the women also line up to dance with the groom. They usually receive gum or a similar treat for their dollar. A band is usually hired for the occasion and following the evening wedding, everyone enjoys finger foods, and dancing, with the Polka still remaining the most popular dance.

Mrs. Kupczynski said another custom was to remove the bride's veil after supper, which usually was the job of the maid of honor, "the druzka." Everyone would gather around the bride and sing a playful song in which the bride was begging them not to remove the veil. In the song, everyone was surprised when a frog jumped out from under the veil. The rite signified that the bride was no longer a young maiden, but now an old married woman with responsibilities.

Mrs. Kupczynski still has her veil, which was made by her sister-in-law. The thin, gauzy net headpiece, now yellowed with age, has a poufy cap that was starched to stand up. It was not customary for a bride to carry a bouquet. She wore her flowers in her hair. Between the gatherings of the cap were small openings where fresh flowers and stems of greenery were inserted to form a halo of flowers. The veil barely touched the floor.

On the Sunday following the wedding, it was customary for the couple to invite just their closest family for a dinner after mass, followed by another day of celebration, including the musicians and dancing.

Traditional
Polish Costumes

The varied terrain of Poland unofficially divides the country into six regions that have evolved their own distinctive styles that are mostly reflected in the traditional costumes.

There is Mazaosze or Mazovia in the center of Poland; Malopolska, or "Little Poland," on the country's upper Vistula; Wielkopolska, or "Great Poland," on the middle Oder and Warta; Pomorze, or Pomerania, on the shore of the Baltic Sea; Slak, or Silesia, on the upper Oder; and Podhale, the Carpathian and sub-Carpathian area.

The typical costume includes a "shirt," which is a combination blouse and petticoat. A full skirt is worn over this. Married women usually wear a kerchief, head-covering or cap. The elaborate head-dresses and flower wreaths are usually worn by the young girls. Aprons are worn in all regions and are considered basic, not an addition to the dress. They are usually of embroidered lace.

Men are also fond of elaborate head dresses such as hats with plumes and feathers. In the country, a man tucks his trousers inside his boots.

Mozovia

In Mozovia, the Mazurs are famous for their rainbow-colored stripes. The colorful fabrics are used for both men's trousers and for women's skirts. The skirts of red, yellow, green and orange stripes are stiffly lined and tightly gathered. Aprons are of embroidered lace. "Serduszek," or vests of richly-embroidered velvet are works of art. The men wear greatcoats of dark blue.

Little Poland

The costumes of Little Poland are considered the most representative of the Polish culture. The men wear the flaring red coat of the Hussars with a hat of the Hussar Army that typically sports a peacock feather. Ornamental belts are a common accessory to the costumes. The women love beautiful embroidered blouses of white-on-white to set off their billowing starched skirts of flowery designs. The bodice is elaborately trimmed in gold or silver embroidery. Many strands of wooden beads are worn and colored ribbons hang to the edge of the skirt. Red boots that are often laced in green complete the costume.

Pomerania

The traditional costumes of Pomerania are not often seen. The women wear high-neck blouses that are worn under black bodices embroidered in gold and laced with a colored ribbon. The skirts are red or white with a white apron. The men wear long, dark blue coats with shoulder capes.

Great Poland

In Great Poland, girls are seen in native costumes that feature a combined vest and skirt coat in white that laces and is worn over a black skirt. A white, turban-shaped, large round hat that is tied with lacy cloth in a big bow under the chin.

Silesia

In Silesia, the German influence is evident in the traditional costumes. The men's costumes sport fur caps, blue jackets with bright buttons and leather pants. The women top their traditional costume with a cap of starched white lace and muslin that looks somewhat like a gardening bonnet with a squared crown and broad floppy brim.

Carpathia

The mountaineers of the Carpathian region love finery which incorporates a lot of white that is set off by bright accents. The men wear a tight white wool trouser with wide striped seams. The pants are bound around the ankles. The front is embroidered with an ornament in bright red and blue. They wear heavy white embroidered blouses and a broad, leather belt — sometimes as wide as a foot — that is accented with brass studs. Their embroidered vests are elaborate and ornate. They make their own leather moccasins that are gathered around the edges with a thong. A small, black felt hat sporting an eagle or falcon feather tops off the costume. A large brooch is worn on the chest and the men carry a long-handled axe that doubles as walking stick.

In this group, the women's costumes are less ornate, but not by any means plain. They wear full skirts and dark velvet "surduszeks" that are adorned with many spangles. Their lacy white blouses have elaborately embroidered sleeves. They wear necklaces of multi-colored beads with many strands. They wear either the soft leather moccasins of the region or high, dark boots laced over white stockings. Married women cover their heads with a flowered kerchief.

Being Polish Is

In The Heart

Poland has been completely wiped off the map three times in recorded history. Poland was sheltered in the hearts of a determined people who believed that to be Polish was as much a way of living as it was a place.

Lovers of Freedom

For 123 years, the Poles remained a nation without a country. The first Partitioning of Poland was in 1772 when Russia, Prussia and Austria each claimed a portion of Poland. The Second Partitioning came in 1745 when Russia seized more land. The third Partitioning came in 1795 and wiped Poland off the map. The ideals of liberty and democracy remained strong among the Polish people and helped bring about Poland's rebirth in 1918.

Polish Patriots in America

Two Polish patriots played key roles in helping America secure its freedom. A brilliant young Polish nobleman, Thaddeus Kosciuszko, had been educated in military academies in Warsaw and Paris. When the War of Independence began in America, he left Poland and came to America to offer his services to General George Washington. Other Polish patriots who believed in the ideal of individual freedom and liberty followed Kosciuszko, including Casimir Pulaski, who became a brigadier general in the American Revolutionary Army.

Pulaski died in battle in 1779 while leading a cavalry charge at Savannah, Ga. Kosciuszko was responsible for blocking entrance to the Hudson River to keep the British fleet from sailing upstream to New York and dividing American forces in two. Kosciuszko later persuaded Thomas Jefferson to set up a military academy at West Point.

After the Revolutionary War, Kosciuszko returned to Poland in 1792 to find the country in danger of being divided again. He gathered together an army of peasants and took up the fight, but in 1793, was shot from his horse and taken prisoner by the Russians. Poland was seized.

Kosciuszko was released from prison in 1796, but was not allowed to return to Poland, which by then was under Russian rule. He went to France and worked for freedom for Poland, but there was no hope. He died in exile in Switzerland in

1817, and the Russians allowed his body to be returned to Cracow (Kracow). It was 100 years later, in 1917, that America's President Woodrow Wilson addressed Poland in one of his Fourteen Points, stating that the Allies were fighting the war in order to secure the right of self-determination for all nations and that Poland must be free again. In 1918, as World War I ended, Poland declared its independence.

Independence was again short-lived. In 1939 Poland was invaded by Germany from the west and shortly after aslo by the Soviet Union from the east. Despite a strong underground resistance, Poland eventually was dominated by the Soviets and a Communist regime was established to run the country. This was never accepted by the Poles. In 1980, the resistance had grown over the years and finally emerged in the form of an independent trade union called Solidarity. Their protests moved the country and even the world. On December 29, 1989, a government based on democracy was established and Poland became a democratic legal state called the Republic of Poland.

The Polish have strong Christian beliefs. Their love of God, love of country and love of freedom is a fitting legacy to people of Polish descent in America.

The Legend of the

Ice Flowers

Catholics believe that they can pray to the Holy Mother just as a child would confide in his or her earthly mother. Mary will even plead for them with God, just as a mother intercedes for her children when the father is stern in his justice.

The Queen of Heaven is honored with flowers, which she loves. Flowers are loved by the Polish as a sign of God's love for the world.

The legend of the Ice Flowers has it that Mary protects not just her children, but also the neglected flowers. This is why the "ice flowers" form on frosty windowpanes on very cold days. It is believed that these are the ones that did not have a chance to bloom during the summer. According to the legend, these are the flowers that were first created for the evergreen trees.

The legend relates that when the Lord created the world, the last thing he did was to send the flowers to earth. He had so many that he couldn't send them all. There were fruit trees and all other flowering plants, but the needle-bearing trees such as pines, spruce, hemlock and firs were left without blossoms.

In order to console them, He told them that summer is not the only season on earth. There would be a winter, too, when snow-white clouds would cover the fields and all the other trees would be naked and bare. Only the evergreens would remain fresh and green for the beauty of the forest and the happiness of man.

So, the Lord took care of the trees, but there were still the little flowers left — the ones that should have bloomed on those trees. It is told that Mary then said: "Oh, Lord, let those flowers go to the dwellings of men and stay with them the whole winter."

The Lord was very pleased. Since that day, those flowers adorn the window panes of houses, like millions of tiny stars. Nothing can happen to those flowers for the whole winter long. When the warm air during the day erases them, they hover in the air and come back at night. This was the Lord's will, through the intervention of Mary.

The Parish Pantry (Spizarnia Kosciol), Keepsake Edition

Table of Contents

Heritage at the Hearth

In 1984, lifetime Harrah resident, Aline Honea, now deceased, called one morning to say she was sorting through her recipes and had pulled out the ones that had served her best over the years — her favorites that had become holiday traditions for her family. Her daughter, who was my aunt, had died a few years before, and so, she wanted to hand them down to someone close to the family that would appreciate them.

Her telephone call set off a cultural alarm. How many more residents of Harrah age 80 and older were there — especially the descendants of the Polish settlers? The members of the Catholic Daughters began talking about this and asking: "Is anyone writing down some of their recipes? The effort to do this became "Spizarnia Kosciol — The Parish Pantry." It was released in 1987.

Our Catholic Daughters group was truly blessed by the project. We heard from many wonderful people of Polish descent across Oklahoma and the United States. The profit was used for many good projects in the parish and the community. Almost a decade later, requests for the book were still being received, so a new edition was proposed.

We hope this revised edition will bring about a special joy of sharing, too. With "Spizarnia Kosciol — the Parish Pantry, Keepsake Edition" the collection continues. We have added 128 recipes to the original book. We hope you enjoy the cultural favorites we have included and that you find our modern-day recipes to be ones that add something special and new to the menu for the enjoyment of your family and friends. Consider the recipes in this book as our offer of hospitality to you, for in the Polish culture, "a guest in the house is God in the house."

— "Smacznego!" (bon appetit!)
Judy Seikel, cookbook project chairperson

The Cookbook Committee

Beth Patterson	Barbara Brimm
Rosalie Marino	Kay Brown
Barbara Dull	Kathy Small
Diana Hanna	Rosalie Jorski Cook
Evelyn Saxton	Pat Hopcus

and a special thanks to the members of the CDA, the parish and the community who shared their special recipes.

Appetizers,
Beverages,
Pickles

Amaretto Sour

1 (12 oz.) can pink lemonade	Amaretto
1 (12 oz.) can water	

In blender mix lemonade, water and ice. Add ½ can of Amaretto to mixture. Serve with ice or frozen.
Delicious!

Vicki Dimmer

Brandy Slush

1 (12 oz.) can frozen orange juice concentrate	2 c. tea (made with 2 tea bags)
	1 qt. brandy
1 (12 oz.) can frozen lemon juice concentrate	7 c. water
	2 c. sugar

Bring water and sugar to boil and let cool. Mix remaining ingredients with syrup and freeze. Fill tall glass ¾ full with slush; add club soda. Use your favorite garnish.

Bonita (Konop) Yox

Peach Fuzz

3 large peaches	1 (6 oz.) can filled with vodka or rum
5 to 6 ice cubes	
1 (6 oz.) can frozen lemonade	

Place ingredients in blender until peaches and ice are of a fine texture. Pour into glasses.

Mary Keller

A toast!

"Na zdrowie" (pronounced: nah zdrovyeh) means "to your health" and is said both for "cheers" as a toast and as "bless you" when someone sneezes.

Strawberry Daiquiris

1 (12 oz.) can frozen lemonade
1 (12 oz.) can frozen limeade
2 qt. 7-Up (diet or regular)

1 (16 to 20 oz.) pkg. frozen
   strawberries (in sugar)
2 c. rum

Mix and refrigerate, covered, overnight. Add more 7-Up when serving, if desired.
Enjoy.

Vicki Dimmer

Hot Buttered Rum Batter

1 lb. powdered sugar
1 lb. margarine, softened
1 lb. brown sugar

2 tsp. cinnamon
1 tsp. nutmeg
1 qt. vanilla ice cream, softened

To serve:

Coffee cup of hot water

1 jigger rum

Mix powdered sugar, brown sugar, cinnamon and nutmeg in a large bowl. Cream together softened ice cream and softened butter. Mix creamed ingredients into dry ingredients. Mix with hand mixer until fluffy. This can be kept on hand, stored in the freezer. To serve: Put 1-2 Tbsps. of the mixture into steaming hot mugs of water along with 1 jigger of rum.

This makes a large amount. Recipe can be cut in half. If you have batter left from entertaining and you don't want to store it in the freezer, you can add some baking powder and flour to make a soft cookie dough. Place by tablespoons on ungreased cookie sheets and bake.

Judy Seikel

New! Cytrynowka – Lemon Vodka

Rind of 1 lemon, sliced
2 tsp. sugar

1 qt. vodka

Cut the lemon rind thin so it's almost transparent. Add the lemon rind and sugar to the vodka. Let stand for four days, then strain. Serve ice cold.

Rosalie Cook

 Judy's Bloody Mary Mix

1 qt. tomato juice	Dash of Tabasco
1 (6 oz.) can frozen lemonade	Juice of ½ lemon
4 beef bouillon cubes	Salt and Pepper
⅓ c. Worcestershire sauce	Water

Mix the 6 oz. can of lemonade concentrate with 1½ juice cans of water. Add 1 cup of the lemonade mixture to the quart of tomato juice (store the rest). Dissolve the bouillon cubes in 1 cup of water and then add this to the tomato juice mixture. Add the Worcestershire sauce and a dash of Tabasco. Add the lemon juice. Salt and pepper is mixed in 2-to-1 ratio and added to taste. I mix 1 jigger (a jigger equals 1½ ounces) of pepper with 2 jiggers salt. Use about 1 jigger of the mixture and store the rest. Add to tomato mixture.

Judy Seikel

Dandelion Bloom Wine

1 qt. dandelion blooms	3 lb. sugar
1 gal. hot water	1 pkg. dry yeast
1 lemon, sliced	

Break stems at the base of the blossom when picking dandelions. Drench blooms in large container to remove bugs or sand. Add dandelion blooms and all other ingredients to the gallon of hot water and bring to a boil. Let the mixture ferment in a jug. When it quits bubbling, it is through working and is ready to bottle.

Doyle Miller

New! Krupnik – Fire Vodka

1 c. honey	1 Tbsp. cinnamon
½ c. water	½ tsp. cloves
1 tsp. vanilla	1 tsp. grated lemon rind
¼ tsp. nutmeg	2½ c. vodka

Combine the honey with water, vanilla, spices and lemon rind. Bring to a boil, cover and simmer five minutes. Add the vodka, heat, and serve immediately in juice glasses.

When my daughter, Cathy Webster, Pat Hopcus and I visited Krakow in 1994, we became friends with a family that invited us to their home. They served this hot wine before dinner.

Rosalie Cook

New! Grape Wine

2 12 oz. cans frozen grape juice
4 c. sugar

1 tsp. dry yeast dissolved in warm
water

Mix all together well and put in a gallon jug. Fill with warm water and stir well. Put a toy balloon on the neck of the jug and poke a hole in the balloon with a needle.

Let stand three weeks until balloon fills with gas and then becomes deflated. Then wine is ready. Do not move it while fermenting. The cheapest brand of juice makes the best wine.

Marjorie Magott

Twenty-One-Day Wine

1 qt. Cranapple juice
1 qt. Welch's grape juice
1 qt. water

3 ½ c. sugar
¼ tsp. dry yeast

Add all ingredients in a 1 gallon glass jug in the order listed. Do not mix or stir. Add small balloon on top of jug mouth. Store in a dark place for 21 days. Balloon will go up and down.

Judy Seikel

Bohemian Tea

3 lemons
3 Tbsp. Lipton black tea
2 c. boiling water

2 c. sugar
Ice

Squeeze juice of 3 lemons and set aside. Slice rinds of 2 lemons into thin strips. Combine tea and lemon rind with boiling water. Let stand 15-20 minutes. Strain and add lemon juice and sugar. Add water and ice to make 1 gallon.

The Cookbook Committee

🐦 *New! Instant Hot Spiced Tea*

2 c. Tang orange drink mix
1 c. instant tea
2 tsp. cinnamon
1 tsp. cloves

2 small tubs Crystal Light
    lemonade mix

Mix thoroughly. Use two teaspoons to one cup of hot water. If this is not sweet enough, one-half cup of sugar may be added.

Sue Nickel

🐦 *Tang Tea*

2 c. Tang orange drink mix
1 large env. lemonade mix
1 c. sugar

½ c. instant tea
1½ tsp. cinnamon
1½ tsp. cloves

Mix ingredients well. Makes about 1 quart. Add 1 tablespoon of mix to 1 cup of hot water.

Can be used with diluted cranberry juice for hot punch.

Suzanne Visnieski

🐦 *Banana Punch*

2 pkg. cherry Kool-Aid
1 pkg. orange Kool-Aid
1 large can pineapple juice
3 bottles 7-Up (8 oz.)
1 small can crushed pineapple

3 c. sugar
Juice of 4 lemons
1½ qt. water
3 beaten, mashed bananas

Freeze overnight. Add 1 small can crushed pineapple and extra bananas before serving if desired.

Vicki Dimmer

To Remove Tea and Coffee Stains

Baking powder will remove stains from tea or coffee cups.

 Punch

1 c. sugar (more or less)
2 pkg. (small) raspberry Kool-Aid
1 can pineapple juice

1 qt. ginger ale
1 qt. strawberry soda
Grenadine syrup for color

Mix sugar, Kool-Aid and pineapple juice until sugar is dissolved. Add ginger ale and strawberry soda. (Add more sugar if needed and then grenadine syrup for sweeter taste and more color.)

Fern Koelsch

Strawberry Punch

8 scoops strawberry Kool-Aid
    (presweetened)
1 (12 oz.) can frozen lemonade
1 (12 oz.) can frozen strawberries,
    pureed

1 (46 oz.) can unsweetened
    pineapple juice
½ gal. water
3 qt. ginger ale

Mix all ingredients, except ginger ale. Freeze in milk carton. Before serving, remove mixture from freezer. Pour room temperature ginger ale over frozen mixture. Mix and serve.

Sally Balkenbush

New! Tropical Cream Punch

1 14 oz. can Eagle Brand milk
1 2-liter bottle of club soda.
1 12 oz. can frozen concentrated

Welch's Orchard Passion Fruit
juice

In punch bowl, mix milk and juice well. Gradually add club soda and stir. Serve over ice. Makes three quarts.

Kathy Small

 New! Hot Cocoa Mix

8 qt. box Carnation powdered milk   **1 lb. box Nestle's Quick cocoa mix**
8 oz. jar dry coffee creamer   **1 c. powdered sugar**

Mix well. Use ⅓ cup dry mix to 1 cup of boiling water.

Sue Nickel

Hot Buttered Cranberry Punch

¾ c. brown sugar   **½ tsp. allspice**
¼ tsp. salt   **2 (1 lb.) cans jelled cranberry sauce**
½ tsp. cinnamon   **1 qt. pineapple juice**
¾ tsp. cloves   **Cinnamon sticks**
4 c. water   **Butter or margarine**
¼ tsp. nutmeg

Bring sugar, 1 cup water and spices to a boil. Crush cranberry sauce with a fork. Add rest of water and beat with rotary beater until smooth. Add pineapple juice and simmer 5 minutes. Keep steaming hot over hot water.

To serve, ladle punch into mugs. Add pats of butter or margarine. Serve with cinnamon sticks for stirring. Makes 2½ quarts.

Rosalie Marino

New! Wassail

(Hot Spiced Fruit Punch)

2 quarts apple cider or apple juice   **¼ c. lemon juice**
2 c. orange juice   **1 stick whole cinnamon**
1 c. pineapple juice   **1 tsp. whole cloves**

Combine ingredients in large pan and simmer.
This recipe is basic and amounts of juices can be adjusted to personal taste. Many times I omit the lemon juice. I make this so often during the holidays that I don't even measure anymore.

Diana Hanna

🐦 Wassail

"Be thou well."

½ gal. apple juice or cider
½ c. honey
2½ c. pineapple juice
1 can frozen lemonade or ¼ c.
    lemon juice

2 sticks cinnamon or 2 tsp.
    cinnamon
2 whole cloves
Dash of nutmeg

Simmer and stir with peppermint sticks.

Rosalie Marino

🐦 Artichoke Dip

1 (14 oz.) can artichoke hearts,
    drained and chopped
1 c. mayonnaise

1 (4 oz.) can green chili peppers,
    chopped
1 can grated parmesan cheese

Combine the ingredients into an 8-inch round baking dish. Bake at 350° for about 20 minutes or until heated through. Serve warm with tortilla chips and bread sticks. Makes about 2½ cups.

Mary Keller

🐦 **New!** Zesty Artichoke Spread

1 large can artichoke hearts
1 c. parmesan cheese
1 c. mayonnaise

dash of garlic salt, worcestershire
    sauce, and hot sauce

Drain and chop artichoke hearts. Combine all ingredients and spoon into lightly greased, 1-quart casserole dish. Bake at 350° for 20-25 minutes or until lightly browned and bubbly. Serve with crackers.

Diana Hanna

Cream Dip Spread

2 (8 oz.) pkg. cream cheese
2 tsp. Worcestershire sauce
2 tsp. Accent

8 green onions, chopped
2 pkg. pressed beef or ham, chopped
Olives (optional)

Cream together cheese, Worcestershire sauce, Accent, onions and chopped beef. Add green or black olives if desired. Serve with chips or crackers.

Fern Koelsch

Mary's Mexican Dip

16 oz. can refried beans
½ packet taco seasoning mix
6 oz. can avocado dip
18 oz. container sour cream
4½ oz. chopped ripe olives

2 large diced tomatoes (cherry)
1 small onion
1 (4 oz.) can chopped green chilies
1½ 2 c. shredded cheese

In order, spread the ingredients in a pan. Serve.

Mary Horn

Mexican Dip

8 oz. cream cheese
10 oz. bean dip
8 oz. sour cream
Cheese, shredded
½ c. chopped green onions

Tabasco to taste
Salt to taste
¼ c. Cheddar cheese, shredded
¼ c. Monterey Jack cheese

Mix all ingredients together and bake 20 minutes at 350°. Use 8-inch round baking dish. Decorate with avocado.

Mary Keller

🐦 Five-Layer Taco Spread

1 large can refried beans
1 small jar medium picante sauce
5 large avocados, mashed
1 to 2 tsp. lemon juice
6 green onions, diced
Salt and pepper to taste

1½ Tbsp. Miracle Whip salad
   dressing
1 pt. sour cream
2 large tomatoes, chopped
2 c. sharp cheddar cheese
1 c. black olives, sliced

    In a large casserole-type dish, layer the ingredients as follows. First layer: Mix refried beans and picante sauce and spread into dish. Second layer: Mix avocados, lemon juice, onions, salt, pepper and salad dressing together. Third layer: Spread the sour cream. Fourth layer: Chopped tomatoes (more tomatoes can be used). Fifth layer: Spread grated cheese and olives. Chill.

Joyce Nowakowski

🐦 New! Tortilla Snacks

1 8 oz. pkg. cream cheese, (room
   temp.)
2 chopped green onions

½ small can chopped olives
½ small can green chilies

    Mix ingredients and spread on flour tortillas. Roll up and slice about ¼-inch thick. Chill. Serve with picante sauce.

Diana Hanna

🐦 Shrimp Dip

3 (8 oz.)pkg. cream cheese
1 c. mayonnaise
½ c. finely chopped celery

2 small finely chopped green onions
1 lb. tiny shrimp, cooked
Lemon juice to taste

    Soften cream cheese and mix with mayonnaise. Add other ingredients and mix well. Chill.

*   I serve this with Triscuits, but you may use any crackers of your choice. This is better if it is made the day before it is served.*

Sally Balkenbush

🐦 Shrimp Dip

1 can tomato soup (no water)
3 small pkg. cream cheese
2 cans drained small shrimp
1 stalk chopped celery

1 bunch chopped green onions
¼ c. warm water
1 pkg. Knox unflavored gelatin

Mix gelatin in warm water. Set aside. Heat soup to boiling and melt cream cheese in soup. Let set 15 minutes. Mix remaining ingredients. Refrigerate 30 minutes until cool. Pour into mold. Let stand 2-3 hours until set.

Brenda Spaeth

🐦 Shrimp Dip

1 can deveined shrimp, drained
1 (8 oz.) pkg. cream cheese
½ c. mayonnaise

½ c. chopped celery
¼ c. chopped onion
1½ Tbsp. lemon or lime juice

Mix all ingredients and serve with chips or crackers.

Evelyn Saxton

🐦 Shrimp Dip

12 oz. Philadelphia cream cheese
½ c. Hellmann's mayonnaise
3 stalks celery

5 green onions (use stalks)
1 lb. shrimp (fresh)
Zatarain's crab boil

Mix together cream cheese and mayonnaise in large bowl. Chop celery, onions and mix in the cheese mixture. Boil fresh shrimp for 20 minutes in Zatarain's crab boil (can be bought in grocery store). Drain and cool. Rinse with cold water. Peel shrimp and cut into pieces. Add shrimp to the sauce. Refrigerate and serve with party crackers of your choice.
   Very good!

Cindy Garrett

🐦 Spinach Dip

1 pkg. frozen, chopped spinach
1 c. sour cream
1 c. Hellmann's mayonnaise
½ c. green onion tops

½ tsp. dill weed
½ tsp. salt
1 tsp. Beau Monde seasoning
1 tsp. lemon juice

Mix all ingredients and let stand, covered, in the refrigerator for 24 hours before serving. Serve with fresh vegetables.

Joyce Nowakowski

🐦 Spinach Dip

1 pkg. frozen spinach, thawed
1 c. mayonnaise
½ c. fresh green onions, chopped
½ c. chopped parsley (less if
   desired)

1 tsp. salt
1 tsp. Accent
1 tsp. dill seeds
Juice of 1 lemon

Squeeze water from spinach. Add remaining ingredients. Good with relish tray.

Ina Wiedemann

🐦 Vegetable Dip

16 oz. cream cheese, softened
3 oz. sour cream
Diced onion
Diced green pepper

Dash of black pepper
1 jar dried beef, cut in small pieces
Enough milk to cream ingredients

Serve with vegetables or crackers.

Barbara Dull

 *Vegetable Dip*

½ pt. Miracle Whip
½ c. Catalina salad dressing
1 onion, grated

Savory salt
Tabasco sauce

Mix all ingredients and chill. Use seasonings to taste.

Pat Bacon

 *Fruit Dip*

1 small jar marshmallow cream
1 block cream cheese

Fresh strawberries

Mix marshmallow cream and cream cheese. Dip strawberries into.

Karen Kuhns

 *Cocktail Crackers*

2 (12 oz.) bags small Zesta crackers
1 tsp. lemon pepper
1 tsp. garlic salt
1 tsp. dill weed

1 pkg. Hidden Valley Original
    salad dressing mix (dry)
⅔ c. oil

Mix all seasoning and dressing mix with oil. Pour over crackers. Mix well.
Good as snack, in a salad or soup. Will keep if stored in airtight container for
weeks.

Sue Nickel

Sugared Grapes

Dip wet grapes in granulated sugar and keep refrigerated until ready to add to the dish
at serving time.

Frosted Grapes

Dip grapes in slightly beaten egg whites and then coat with sugar. Let dry on wax paper.

Oyster Cracker Snacks

2 pkg. oyster crackers
1 c. oil
1 pkg. original Hidden Valley
   dressing

½ tsp. garlic salt
1 tsp. lemon pepper
1 tsp. dill weed

Mix well and pour over the 2 packages of crackers in a large bowl or paper bag. Shake well. Be careful not to stir much or you will break the crackers. Store in a covered container.

Joyce Rugg

Oyster "Hidden Valley Ranch" Crackers

2 pkg. oyster crackers
1 c. light corn oil
1 tsp. garlic salt
2 tsp. lemon pepper

2 tsp. dill weed
1 small pkg. Hidden Valley Ranch
   original dressing mix (mix with
   buttermilk pkg.)

Mix seasonings and oil together well. Pour over crackers and stir until well coated. Put in tight container. Shake 2 or 3 times a day for 2 days. Makes 1 gallon Ziploc bag. Freezes well.

Sally Balkenbush

Mandarin Munchies

6 Tbsp. soy sauce
6 Tbsp. margarine, melted
2 tsp. ground ginger
1 tsp. onion powder
1 tsp. garlic powder

1 tsp. celery seed
½ tsp. ground red pepper
2 cans (5 oz.) chow mein noodles
2 c. unsalted peanuts
4 c. Cheerios

In a large bowl, combine soy sauce, margarine, ginger, onion and garlic powders, celery seed and red pepper. Mix in noodles, peanuts and cereal. In 15"x10" baking pan, spread out the mixture evenly. Bake in preheated 250° oven for 15 minutes. Turn off oven. Let set for another 15 minutes. Cool. Store in tightly covered containers. Makes 3 quarts.

Joyce Nowakowski

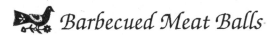 New! Deviled Eggs

6 hard-boiled eggs
½ tsp. salt
½ tsp. dry mustard
¼ tsp. pepper

3 Tbsp. salad dressing or
mayonnaise
Optional: 1 tsp. vinegar or ¼ tsp.
Worcestershire sauce.

Shell eggs and cut in half lengthwise. Remove the yolks and place in small mixing bowl. Mash the yolks with a fork. Blend in seasonings and stir until smooth. For fluffy filling, yolk mixture can be beaten with a mixer. Fill egg whites. For professional-looking deviled eggs, put yolk mixture in a pastry bag and use a fluted tip to pipe the filling into the cooked egg white.

For garnish, use sliced radishes, sliced olives or sprigs of fresh dill.

The Cookbook Committee

Barbecued Meat Balls

1 lb. (good) ground meat
1 egg
½ tsp. salt

½ c. evaporated milk
2 Tbsp. shortening
½ c. crushed Fritos

Sauce:

½ c. catsup
¼ c. water
2 Tbsp. vinegar

1 Tbsp. prepared mustard
2 Tbsp. brown sugar
2 Tbsp. Worcestershire sauce

Mix meat ball ingredients well. Form into balls, about as large as a quarter. Brown on all sides over moderate heat.

Mix all ingredients for sauce. Heat and pour over meat balls. Cook 30 minutes over low heat, turning often. The Fritos give these meat balls an unusual taste. Serve hot.

Helen C. Nixon

Sausage Balls

1½ lb. sausage
10 oz. grated Cheddar cheese

3 c. Bisquick

Mix together. Make into small balls. Place on greased cookie sheet and bake 20 minutes at 400°.

Carolyn Miles

Swedish Meat Balls

1½ lb. ground beef
1½ c. Pepperidge Farm herb
  season stuffing
1 c. light cream
1 green pepper, chopped
½ c. chopped onion

1 egg
¼ c. parsley, finely chopped
1½ tsp. salt
¼ tsp. ginger
Dash of pepper
Dash of nutmeg

Sauce:

1 can Ocean Spray cranberry sauce
1 bottle chili sauce

2 oz. La Victoria hot red chili relish
Salsa jalapeno

Soak herb stuffing in cream 5 minutes. Cook onion and green pepper in 1 tablespoon butter till tender. Mix all together and beat vigorously until fluffy, about 5 minutes on medium, then 8 minutes by hand. Chill and shape into small balls.

Sauce: Mix all ingredients and pour over meat balls. Bake 30-40 minutes at 350°. Can be made and frozen, cooked later.

Vicki Dimmer

Stuffed Mushrooms

12 large mushrooms
2 Tbsp. butter
1 medium onion, chopped fine
3 Tbsp. Parmesan cheese
½ c. Ritz crackers, chopped fine

(or poultry stuffing)
Dash of garlic salt
Dash of pepper
⅓ c. white wine

Remove stems of mushrooms. Chop the stems. Wash and drain the mushroom caps. Melt butter. Add remaining ingredients, except wine. Stuff the caps with the mixture. Put in shallow pan. Pour on wine. Bake 25 minutes at 325°.

Marty Janowiak Casteel

🕊 Studzienina (Zimne Nogi)

Jelled Pig's Feet

Pig's feet
Salt
Pepper
Garlic

Onion
Pickling spices
Hot pepper
All seasoning as desired

Clean feet of hair by searing over open flame. Cut into 3 or 4 pieces. Clean feet thoroughly. Select a cooking pot large enough to cover feet well and fill with cold water. Add spices and bring to a boil. Cook slowly approximately 2 hours or until tender. Add more water if needed during cooking. Cool and refrigerate. Skim off fat and serve with vinegar or hot pepper sauce.

Mrs. Frank Hopcus (Mary)

🕊 Jellied Pigs' Feet

2 fresh pigs' feet
2 fresh or smoked pork hocks
2 stalks celery, cut in halves
4 bay leaves
8 whole black peppercorns
2 cloves garlic

1 tsp. instant chicken bouillon
  granules
8½ c. water
1 tsp. salt
Lettuce
Wine vinegar

Clean pigs' feet. Rinse well with water. In large saucepan, combine pigs' feet, pork hocks, celery, bay leaves, peppercorns, garlic and chicken granules (if desired). Add water. Bring to a boil. Reduce heat. Simmer, covered for 2 hours. Skim off foam. Add salt. Simmer covered, 2 hours more. Remove pigs' feet and hocks. Cool. Strain broth through fine strainer. Remove skin and meat from pigs' feet and hocks. Discard skin and bones. Chill broth until partially set. Fold in meat. Pour into 2 (4 cup) molds. Refrigerate until firm. Unmold onto lettuce-lined plates. Garnish with parsley and cherry tomatoes if desired. Serve with wine vinegar. Serves 8.

Rosie Lee Klimkowski

Marinated Carrots

2 lb. carrots
1 c. sugar
1 tsp. prepared mustard
1 Tbsp. Worcestershire sauce
1 onion, chopped

½ c. salad oil
¾ c. vinegar
1 (10½ oz.) can tomato soup
1 sweet green pepper

Slice carrots crosswise making "coins". Cook in salted water until just crisp and tender; drain. Mix with beater the salad oil, sugar, vinegar, mustard, soup and Worcestershire sauce. Pour over hot drained carrots. Stir in pepper and onion. Refrigerate.

Katie Magott

Chili Sauce

1 gal. tomato juice or 6¼ ripe
    tomatoes (peel and core before
    measuring)
⅔ c. chopped white onions
1½ c. sugar
1 tsp. grated nutmeg
¾ tsp. Tabasco sauce

½ tsp. curry powder
2 c. vinegar
5 tsp. salt
2 tsp. ginger
1 tsp. cinnamon
1 tsp. mustard

Put tomatoes and onions through food chopper. Add all other ingredients and simmer 2 hours or until thick. Stir frequently to prevent scorching. When sauce is of desired consistency, pour into sterilized jars and seal at once. If desired, ¾ tsp. of red pepper may be used instead of the Tabasco sauce.

Louise Olive

Chamomile Tea...

"This European custom was brought from Poland by my mother, Frances Kupczynski Magott, in 1914. Known as a midwife among relatives and friends, Frances raised chamomile, an herb, to make tea for the newborn baby and mother.
The tiny daisy-like flowers were gathered in the morning and dried until needed. Chamomile is a mild relaxer and soothes the nerves."

Mrs. Bill (Martha) Hopcus

🐦 Chrzan Z/burakami

(Horseradish With Red Beets)

16 oz. can red whole beets
2 Tbsp. sugar
2 Tbsp. white vinegar

4 oz. jar prepared white horseradish
Salt and pepper to taste

Grate beets; add remaining ingredients. Mix together and refrigerate. Will keep for several days. This can be used as a dip or relish with ham or Polish sausage (kielbasa).

Mrs. Frank Hopcus (Mary)

🐦 Picante Or Hot Sauce

16 c. chopped fresh tomatoes
4 c. chopped onions
1 c. sugar
1½ c. white vinegar
½ c. jalapeno peppers

⅓ c. pickling salt
1½ Tbsp. chili powder
2 tsp. white pepper
2 tsp. ground cumin
1 tsp. alum

Mix all ingredients in a large kettle. Bring to a boil. Reduce to simmer and cook 1½ hours, uncovered. This will need to be stirred frequently to keep from sticking. Ladle into jars and seal. Makes 8-10 pints.

Fern Koelsch

🐦 Taco Sauce

12 tomatoes or 2 (16 oz.) cans
6 jalapeno peppers
3 medium onions

¼ c. vinegar
2 tsp. sugar
Dash of salt

Peel tomatoes if using fresh tomatoes. Combine all ingredients in a saucepan. Cook 2 hours on low heat. Pack into pint jars. Process 8 minutes at 5 pounds pressure in canner. After opening, add 1 can tomato sauce to each pint. Mix well and refrigerate. Delicious with chips or tacos!

Julie Guild

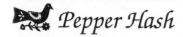

Pepper Hash

12 large green peppers
12 large red peppers
4 hot red peppers

1 qt. vinegar
2 Tbsp. salt
2 c. sugar

Remove seeds and grind all peppers coarse. Cover with boiling water and let stand 15 minutes. Drain; cover again with hot water and let it come to a boil. Drain and add vinegar, salt and sugar. Cook 15 minutes and seal in jars. Use like relish or garnish for meats.

Suzanne Visnieski

Texas Jalapeno Peppers

Jalapeno peppers, sliced
1 Tbsp. sugar
1 Tbsp. peppercorns
¼ tsp. alum powder
1 qt. vinegar
1 tsp. salt

⅔ c. olive oil
¼ tsp. turmeric
Bay leaves
Garlic cloves
1 large chopped onion

Wear rubber gloves when preparing. Slice the peppers. Combine all the ingredients, except peppers and garlic, in kettle and bring to boil. Add the jalapeno peppers. Return to simmering stage. While simmering, pack in hot jars and seal. Put 2 cloves of garlic in each jar before sealing. Be sure tops of jars are wiped clean as the oil will deteriorate the rubber.

Mary Jo Jorski

Tomato Chutney

6 lb. ripe tomatoes
½ lb. onions
4 tsp. whole allspice
1 tsp. cayenne pepper

1 Tbsp. salt
1¼ c. vinegar
2 c. brown sugar

Peel and quarter tomatoes and put them in large pan together with the peeled and thinly-sliced onions. Add the allspice, tied in cheesecloth and the cayenne and salt. Cook over gentle heat until the mixture is pulpy, then stir in the remaining ingredients. Simmer until thick. Put in sterilized jars and seal.

Patti Visnieski

Nana's Chow-Chow

3 qt. onions
1 gal. green tomatoes
1 gal. cabbage
3 qt. vinegar
3 qt. sugar
½ c. salt

1 c. green hot peppers (optional)
2 Tbsp. ground cloves
2 Tbsp. allspice
3 Tbsp. cinnamon
3 Tbsp. turmeric

Combine all ingredients and cook 30-45 minutes (until it changes color). After cooked, add 3 tablespoons turmeric. Pour into hot jars and seal.

Greg Winters

To Correct Over-Salting or Over-Sweetening

If you've over-salted soup or vegetables, add cut raw potatoes and discard once they have cooked and absorbed the salt.

A teaspoon each of cider vinegar and sugar added to salty soup or too-sweet vegetables will also remedy the situation.

If you've over-sweetened a dish, add salt.

Zucchini Squash Relish

12 c. squash
4 medium onions
2 green bell peppers
1 red bell or pimento
5 Tbsp. canning salt

2½ c. sugar
2 c. vinegar
2 Tbsp. turmeric
2 Tbsp. celery seed

Chop vegetables. Mix with salt. Let set overnight. Drain. Rinse. Bring to boil the sugar, vinegar, turmeric and celery seed. Add vegetables. Bring to boil for 4 or 5 minutes. Seal in hot jars.

Rosalie Jorski

Zucchini Relish

12 c. squash, chunked
2 small cans pimento or 2 red
   peppers, chopped
2 green peppers, chopped
4 c. onions, chopped
5 Tbsp. salt

2½ c. vinegar
4½ c. sugar
1 tsp. turmeric
2 tsp. celery seed
2 Tbsp. pickling spice (in a bag)

Put all vegetables through food chopper or processor. Mix vegetables and salt and let stand overnight. Drain liquid off the next day. In large saucepan, mix vinegar, sugar, turmeric, celery seed and pickling spice. Bring to rolling boil, then add vegetables and boil 5 minutes. Pour into clean, hot pint jars. Seal and process in water bath for 5 minutes. Makes approxmately 6 pints.

LouAnn Spaeth

🐦 *New!* Cold Beets in Mustard Dressing

1 1 lb. can whole beets
1 Tbsp. olive oil
1 Tbsp. vinegar
1 tsp. dijon mustard

Salt, to taste
Pepper, to taste
½ tsp. dried thyme and basil, mixed

Drain the beets and put them in a bowl.

In a jar, put all ingredients except the beets. Shake to mix well.

Pour the marinade over the beets in a bowl and allow them to marinate at room temperature for 10-15 minutes. Store in jar and refrigerate.

Serve cold as an hors d'oeuvre.

Judy Seikel

🐦 *New!* Beets in Sour Cream-Bacon Sauce

6 fresh beets, medium
2 strips bacon
1 Tbsp. flour
½ c. sour cream

Salt, to taste
Pepper, to taste
Sugar, to taste
Vinegar, to taste

Wash unpeeled beets thoroughly. Cook in microwave oven until tender. When cool enough, peel and chop coarsely. Set aside.

Fry bacon in skillet until crisp. Remove bacon from skillet. Add flour to bacon fat in skillet and stir until smooth and light brown. Crumble bacon and add to sauce in skillet along with the sour cream. Add beets and stir. Add salt, pepper, sugar and vinegar to a sweet-sour taste. Allow to simmer a minute. Serve with roast beef or wild game.

Judy Seikel

New! *Marinovannye Griby*

(Russian Pickled Mushrooms)

1 c. red wine vinegar	*2 tsp. salt*
2 whole cloves	*2 cloves garlic, peeled and crushed*
½ c. cold water	*1 lb. small mushrooms*
5 whole peppercorns	*1 Tbsp. vegetable oil*
½ bay leaf	

In a medium-sized stainless steel or enameled saucepan, combine the vinegar, cloves, water, peppercorns, bay leaf salt and garlic. Bring to a boil over high heat. Add the mushrooms and reduce the heat to low. Simmer uncovered for 10 minutes, stirring occasionally.

Cool to room temperature. Remove the garlic clove. Pour the entire mixture into a 1-quart jar. Slowly pour the vegetable oil on top. Cover the jar tightly with plastic wrap and secure with a rubber band.

Marinate the mushrooms in the refrigerator for at least a week.

Judy Seikel

Homemade Sauerkraut

40 lb. cabbage	*Handful caraway seed*
Scant c. sugar	*Smidgeon of dill seed (optional)*
Scant c. salt	

Remove outer leaves from cabbage. Halve heads and remove hearts. Shred cabbage with kraut cutter over large tub or dishpan. Add sugar, salt and seed. Mix with hands until juicy. Pack loosely in jars. Add juice about level with top. Add 1 or 2 hearts to each jar. Put lids on jars as tightly as possible. Store in basement or similar area. Set jars on newspapers and cover with same in case juice leaks out while sauerkraut is working. Do not disturb jars if they leak. Sauerkraut will still be okay. Allow 4-5 weeks. Makes about 15 quarts. Rule of thumb: 10 pounds cabbage to make 1 gallon sauerkraut.

Frances Rychlec

 # Kapusta

(Sauerkraut)

5 lb. green cabbage   **1 tsp. salt per jar**

Shred cabbage (a little more coarse than for slaw). Pack into pint jars tightly. Add 1 tsp. salt to the top each jar. Pour boiling water over cabbage to fill jar. Screw the lid tight and put into a pan or on several layers of newspapers to catch the overflowing juices as cabbage works during fermenting process. Allow 2-3 weeks in a warm room to attain desired sauerkraut flavor. No additional water will be needed. After about 3 weeks, tighten lids again and store for use. Yields approximately 7 pints.

Mrs. Frank (Mary) Hopcus

 # New! Kraut

8 lbs. cabbage   **1 Tbsp. sugar**
¼ c. pickling salt   **1 Tbsp. dill seed**

Cheese cloth   **One gallon crock or jar**

Shred about 8 lbs. cabbage. Mix well with ¼ cup pickling salt, 1 Tbsp. sugar and 1 Tbsp. dill seed. Put into one gallon crock or glass jar. Pack well, cover with cheesecloth and weight down. Set on the kitchen counter for about a week or 10 days. If there is not enough juice, boil some water, let cool and pour over kraut to cover. If a scum forms on cloth, rinse it off.

This can be left in the jar in the refrigerator. Screw on lid tightly.

Pauline Piotrowicz

Sauerkraut for the soul...

"Mama always made cabbage rolls and Golimpki for the holidays. There was always homemade bread and sauerkraut and pork. We always enjoyed the holiday foods. Now, our kids want the same foods. Now I make homemade sauerkraut, too."

Rosie L. Klimkowski

New! Grandmother's Pickled Okra

1 qt. water
1 pt. white vinegar
½ c. plain salt
¼-½ tsp. celery seed (to taste)
½ tsp. mustard seed

⅛ tsp. alum
½ tsp. dill seed
2 slices garlic
¼ tsp. horseradish
Pepper, small amount

To make 7 pints:
Wash okra and stand in pint jars, stems down.
Heat the water, vinegar and salt to boiling and pour over okra in jars.
Put the seasonings in each jar and seal jars. Allow three weeks to work off.
(As deciphered from notes made by my mother.)

Judy Seikel

Aunt Clara's Cucumber Pickles

13 c. water
2 c. vinegar
1 c. salt
Dill

Garlic
Hot peppers
Cucumbers or tomatoes

Put dill, as much as preferred, 1 hot pepper and 1 button of garlic in bottom of jar. Pack in cucumbers or tomatoes. Put dill on top. Fill jars with water, salt and vinegar which has been boiled. Seal.

Mrs. A.J. Murphy (Father James' mother)

Dill Pickles

Fresh dill weed
Garlic buds
Grape leaves
4 qt. water

1 c. white vinegar
1 c. canning salt
Cucumbers

Pack whole cucumbers into ½ gallon jars, including several buds of garlic, sprigs of dill and several grape leaves. Mix vinegar and canning salt into water and bring to a good boil. Pour into jars over cucumbers. Store and let set a month or two before using. Enough for about 8 quarts.

Frances Wyskup

Dill Pickles

Cucumbers
Dill
Garlic
3 qt. water

1 qt. vinegar
1 c. canning salt
8 qt. jars

Wash cucumbers. Pack in 8 quart jars. Add buds of garlic and dill. Bring the water, vinegar and salt to a boil. Pour in jars and seal while hot. Do not use iodized salt.

Rosie Skropka

Grandma Hattie's Pickles

Use green cukes (medium size)
⅔ c. salt
3 qt. water (or more)
3 qt. cucumbers, sliced thinly
1 pt. onions, sliced thinly

3 pt. vinegar
3 c. sugar (or less)
1½ Tbsp. celery seed
3 Tbsp. mustard seed
1 Tbsp. turmeric

Soak 3 quarts sliced cukes and 1 pint sliced onions overnight in salt water. Use ⅔ cup salt to 3 quarts water. Drain. Soak in clear water 15 minutes. Add sugar and seasonings to vinegar and bring to a boil. Add cukes. Bring to a boil a second time and boil for 3 minutes. Put in pints and seal.

Judy Seikel

Kosher Dill Pickles

20-25 (4-inch) cucumbers
Water to cover Qt. jars (6-8)
3-4 tsp. alum
6-8 cloves garlic (optional)
Approx. 16 heads dill

6-8 hot red peppers (optional)
1 qt. cider vinegar
¾ c. salt
3 qt. water
6-8 grapes leaves

Wash cucumbers. Let stand in cold water overnight. Pack into hot sterilized jars. To each quart, add ½ tsp. alum, 2 heads or more dill, 1 clove garlic if desired and 1 hot red pepper if desired. Combine 1 quart cider vinegar, salt and 3 quarts water. Heat to boil. Pour over cucumbers. Put a grape leaf over the top of the cucumbers and seal. Makes 6-8 quarts.

Frances Rychlec

Polish Pickles

25 (4-inch) cucumbers
2 cloves garlic per jar
2 heads fresh dill per jar
1 small hot pepper per jar

1 c. pickling salt
3 qt. water
1 qt. cider vinegar

Wash cucumbers and pack in hot quart jars. To each quart and garlic, dill and pepper. Combine salt, water and vinegar. Bring to a boil. Fill jars within ½ inch of top with boiling mixture. Adjust lids. Process in boiling water bath for 15 minutes. Start timing as jars are placed in water. Makes 5 quarts.

Fern Koelsch

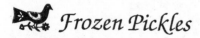

Ogorki (kiszone)

Polish Dill Pickles

3½ qt. water
2 c. vinegar
½ c. salt
½ tsp. dill

1 tsp. pickling spice
1 bud garlic
Cucumbers

Wash cucumbers removing all sand and dirt. Combine water, salt, vinegar and bring to a boil. Place equal amounts of dill, garlic and pickling spice in quart jars. Cut cucumbers diagonally or place whole cucumbers in jars, then pour boiling hot mixture over cucumbers and seal immediately.

Polly Lane

Frozen Pickles

1 gal. cucumbers
2 c. sugar
1 c. vinegar

Water to cover 3 medium sliced
onions (optional)

Slice cucumbers thin. Let onions and cucumbers stand 2 hours. Drain and rinse. Add sugar and vinegar. Add enough water to cover. Pack in containers and freeze.

Frances Rychlec

 # Ogorki Kwaszone

Dill Pickles

½ bu. firm cucumbers
1 c. salt
3 gal. water
Dill

Garlic (optional)
16 c. water
1 c. vinegar
¾ c. salt

Make brine of 1 cup salt and 3 gallons of water. Soak cucumbers in brine overnight. Drain and wipe dry. Fill quart jars with cucumbers, a sprig of dill and ½ bud of garlic. Boil the 16 cups of water, vinegar and salt. Pour boiling water over cucumbers. Seal immediately.

Dora Lee Kusek

Seven-to-Nine-Day Sunshine Dill Pickles

Medium size cucumbers
Grape leaves
Fresh dill weed
Garlic

Red peppers (optional)
¼ c. salt
5 c. water
1-5 c. vinegar

In the bottom of each jar, place 2 grape leaves, 2 pieces of dill and 1 or 2 cloves of garlic. Add red pepper if desired. Mix salt and from 1-5 cups of vinegar, according to how sour you prefer pickles and 5 cups of water. Bring to a boil. Pack cucumbers into jars. Pour solution over cucumbers. Seal jars and set in the sun for 7-9 days.

Minnie Nowakowski

Sweet Dill Pickles

Firm dill pickles
1 c. brown sugar

1 c. vinegar
½ tsp. pumpkin pie spice

Fill a pint jar of dill sliced pickles. Boil sugar, vinegar and spice together. Pour over pickles. Let stand in ice for 2 or 3 days. Stir before serving.

Anelia Block

Bread & Butter Pickles

25-30 medium cucumbers
8 large white onions
½ c. canning salt
8 c. cider vinegar
8 c. sugar
4 Tbsp. mustard seed

2 tsp. turmeric seed
1 tsp. cloves (whole)
1 tsp. celery seed
Enough water to cover cucumbers
  and onions

Wash and slice cucumbers as thin as possible. Stir onions and push into rings. Combine with cucumbers and salt. Add water and let stand 3 hours. Drain. Combine vinegar, sugar and spices in large kettle and bring to a boil. Add cucumbers/onions and heat completely, but don't boil. Pack while hot in jars and seal. Hot bath for 25 minutes.

Rhdonda Dean, Yukon, OK

Hot Sweet Pickles

1 gal. sour pickles
5 lb. sugar
1 (2 oz.) bottle Tabasco

5 small cloves fine chopped fresh
  garlic

Slice pickles as thin as you possibly can or use the food processor. Layer back in the pickle jar the pickles, sugar, garlic and Tabasco. Keep layering until you have used all ingredients. Let stand on cabinet for 5 days turning at least twice a day.

Sally Balkenbush

Grandma Hattie's 14-Day Sweet Pickles

2 gal. cucumbers
2 c. salt
1 gal. boiling water (times 4)
1 Tbsp. powdered alum
5 pt. vinegar, boiling

6 c. sugar
½ oz. celery seed
1 oz. cinnamon stick
1 c. sugar (times 3)

Into a clean stone jar, put 2 gallons of cucumbers, washed and sliced lengthwise. Dissolve 2 cups salt in 1 gallon of boiling water and pour while hot over cukes. Cover and weight down cukes and let stand for 1 week. On the eighth day, drain, then pour 1 gallon of boiling water over them and let stand 24 hours. On the tenth day, drain again and pour 1 gallon clean boiling water over and let stand 24 hours, then drain.

For the pickling mixture, combine the boiling vinegar, 6 cups sugar, celery seed and cinnamon stick. Pour over the pickles. Let stand. For 3 mornings, drain off the mixture, reboil and add 1 additional cup of sugar each morning. With the fourth day, or last reheating, pack into jars. Pour hot liquid over them and seal.

Judy Seikel

Lime Sweet Pickles

7 lb. medium cucumbers
2 c. lime
2 gal. water
2 qt. vinegar
4½ lb. sugar

1 Tbsp. salt
1 Tbsp. celery seed
1 Tbsp. whole cloves
1 Tbsp. mixed pickling spice

Slice cucumbers ½ inch thick. Cover with mixture of lime (purchased from hardware store) and water. Soak 24 hours. Rinse thoroughly. Cover with fresh water and soak for 3 hours. Drain well. Mix vinegar, sugar, salt, celery seed, cloves and pickling spice. Pour over cucumbers in solution 40 minutes. Pack in sterilized jars and seal.

Fern Koelsch

64

Lime Pickles

8 lb. chunked or sliced cucumbers
2 c. slack lime
2 gal. water
2 qt. white vinegar
1 Tbsp. salt

9 c. sugar
1 Tbsp. celery seed
1 Tbsp. pickling spices
1 Tbsp. whole cloves

Cover cucumbers and soak 24 hours. Stir every now and then. Remove from lime solution and wash 4 or 5 times. Now soak 4-5 hours in clear, cold water. Drain and cover with hot syrup mixture of vinegar, salt, sugar, celery seed, pickling spices and cloves (tie spices in bag). Let cucumbers stand overnight in syrup. Next morning, simmer 30 minutes in hot syrup. Can.

Frances Rychlec

Nine-Day Pickles

Cucumbers
1 c. salt
1 gal. water
1 c. vinegar
3 Tbsp. alum
3 qt. water
1 qt. vinegar at least

2 c. sugar at least
1 stick cinnamon at least
Mixed pickling spices
Celery seed
2 c. sugar
1 c. vinegar

Wash cucumbers. Combine 1 cup salt and 1 gallon water. Put the cucumbers in this combination (salt brine). Let stand 3 days. Rinse off brine and let stand 3 days in cool water. Slice cucumbers into chunks. Slowly simmer in 1 cup vinegar, 3 tablespoons alum and 3 quarts water for 2 hours. Make sure there is enough liquid to cover.

Make hot syrup. To each quart vinegar, add 2 cups sugar, 1 stick cinnamon, mixed pickling spices and quite a lot of celery seed (make enough syrup to cover cucumbers and tie spices up in bag). Drain off cucumbers. While still hot cover with the hot syrup.

For over 2 mornings, pour syrup off and boil, adding 1 cup sugar and ½ cup vinegar. Pour over cucumbers. On the third morning, heat in syrup and put in sterilized jars. Seal.

Frances Rychlec

 Peach Pickles

1 qt. good cider vinegar
4 pt. white sugar

2 oz. stick cinnamon
2 oz. whole cloves

Put all on and boil into a thick syrup, then drop peaches and cool through. Put in jars and seal.

Our Lady's Cathedral Cookbook
Circa 20s or 30s

Pickled Beets

Young beets
Beet liquid
Vinegar (red)

Sugar
Pickling spices

Ingredients are measured by amount of beet liquid used to cover beet pieces. i.e. 1 cup liquid, 1 cup sugar, 1 cup vinegar, 1 tsp. spices. May be doubled or tripled depending on amount of liquid used.

Select young beets. Important tip: Cut off leaves leaving 2 inches of stems on beet top. Also leave on the beet root. Wash beets thoroughly but do not break skin. Boil beets in water until tender. Drain, saving the red water. Cool beets; peel and cut into small pieces. Put cut up beets in a pot. Add sugar, vinegar, liquid from beets and pickling spices (pick out the red peppers). Let come to a boil. Pour into jars and seal. Beets in jars should be covered by juice.

Mrs. Frank Zayonc

Ripening tricks

Ripen green fruits by placing in a perforated plastic bag. The holes allow air movement, yet retain the odorless gas which fruits produce to promote ripening.

To hasten the ripening of garden tomatoes or avocado, put them in a brown paper bag, close the bag and leave at room temperature for a few days.

You'll get more juice from a lemon if you'll first warm it slightly in the oven.

Pickled Okra

1 qt. white vinegar
¼ c. salt
2 or 3 hot peppers
1 c. water

2 pieces garlic
½ tsp. dill
Small okra

Pack small okra in jars. Pack peppers, garlic and dill in each jar. Bring salt, vinegar and water to boil and pour into the jars. Seal and leave for 6 weeks before eating.

Babe Gelnar, Granite, OK

Red Cucumber Rings

2 gal. cucumber rings, ¼-inch
   thick, peeled and seed out
2 c. lime
2½ gal. water or enough to cover
4 c. vinegar, divided

1 Tbsp. alum
1 bottle red food coloring
12 c. sugar
12 sticks cinnamon
3 pkg. (6¾ oz.) red hots

Mix lime and water. Place cucumbers in enamel pan or crock. Pour lime mixture over; cover and let stand 24 hours. Drain and wash through several waters. Let set in clear water overnight. Drain and cover with vinegar (1 cup), alum, food coloring and water to cover. Simmer 3 hours. Drain and make a syrup of vinegar (3 cups), water (3 cups), sugar, cinnamon and red hots. Heat until sugar and red hots are dissolved. Let boil and pour over cucumbers. Let stand overnight. Drain syrup into pan. Reheat and pour over cucumbers for 3 days. On fourth day, reheat, pack in jars and seal. Process in water bath for 5 minutes.

LouAnn Spaeth

Pickled Hot Peppers

Hot peppers
2 parts vinegar
1 part water
1 or 2 pieces garlic, cut
2 tsp. oregano (for ½ gal.)
3 pieces onion

5-6 pieces carrot (or more if
   desired)
Salt to taste (about 5 heaping tsp. to
   ½ gal.)
Celery, green peppers, or other
   vegetables may be added as desired.

Wash hot peppers and pack in jar intermixing with the other vegetables. Use this liquid cold. Close or seal well.

Eugene Marshall, O.S.B.

🐦 Pickled Peppers

4 qt. long red, green or yellow
peppers (Hungarian, banana or
other varieties)
1½ c. salt
2 cloves garlic

2 Tbsp. prepared horseradish
10 c. vinegar
2 c. water
¼ c. sugar

Cut 2 small slits in each pepper. Wear rubber gloves to prevent burning hands. Dissolve salt in 4 quarts water. Pour over peppers and let stand 10-18 hours in a cool place. Drain and rinse and drain thoroughly. Combine remaining ingredients; simmer 15 minutes. Remove garlic. Pack peppers in hot glass jars, leaving ¼" head space. Pour boiling hot pickling liquid over peppers, leaving ¼" head space. Adjust caps. Process ½-pints and one pints 10 minutes in boiling water bath. Yields about 8 pints.

Eugene Marshall, O.S.B.

🐦 Squash Pickles

8 c. sliced squash
2 c. onions, sliced
2 c. bell pepper, sliced

3 qt. ice water
⅔ c. salt

Syrup:
3 c. sugar
2 c. vinegar

2 tsp. mustard seed
2 tsp. celery seed

Slice squash thin and soak in ice water mixed with salt for 1 hour. Pour off brine and make syrup. To make syrup, mix sugar, vinegar, mustard and celery seed. Bring to a boil. Drop in sliced onions, sliced bell peppers and squash. Bring to a boil, but do not cook. Put in hot jars and seal. No need for hot water bath.

Pauline Johnson

Borscht

1 lb. fresh beets	*1 Tbsp. fresh, frozen or canned*
1 small onion	*lemon juice*
1 qt. water	*2 eggs*
1 Tbsp. salt	*Sour cream*
1 Tbsp. sugar	

Peel beets and onion and cut into chunks. Put in a saucepan with water and cook 1 hour. Drain (save liquid) and work vegetables through grinder or blender. Season with salt, sugar and lemon juice in a separate bowl, beat eggs. Add hot beet liquid and beat soundly for approximately 1 minute. Stir in ground beet mixture and chill. Serve with a dollop of sour cream on top. Serves 6.

Louise Wyskup

To Freeze Corn

15 c. corn, removed from cob	*¼ c. pickling salt (scant)*
¾ c. sugar	*5 c. ice water*

Mix all ingredients together. Pack in freezer containers and freeze.

Cora Rudek

Corn Fritters

1 c. flour	*1 tsp. melted shortening or*
1 tsp. baking powder	*vegetable oil*
1 tsp salt	*1(16 oz.) can whole kernel corn,*
½ c. milk	*drained*
2 eggs	

Blend dry ingredients in a bowl. Mix eggs, milk and melted shortening together and add to the dry ingredients, stirring until smooth. Add drained corn and mix well in saucepan, heat about 1 inch of fat or vegetable oil to 375°. Drop corn mixture by spoonfuls into hot fat.

Frances Wyskup

🐦 To Freeze Green Beans

4 qts. green beans, snapped
8 c. water

8 beef bouillon cubes
1 tsp. onion salt

To serve:

2 tsp. sugar
1 Tbsp. vinegar
3 slices bacon, fried

1 medium onion, chopped
1 Tbsp. flour

Mix water, bouillon cubes and onion salt in large pot and bring to a boil. Add beans. Bring to boil again and boil for 12 minutes while covered. Remove from heat; remove cover and set pot in ice water to cool. Stir occasionally. Fill freezer containers with beans. Cover with liquid. Freeze.

To serve: Thaw and heat beans. Dissolve sugar in vinegar and pour over heated beans. Fry bacon. Remove bacon from skillet. Add chopped onion to bacon fat and saute. Add flour and stir until it thickens. Crumble the bacon in the sauce. Pour over the beans and serve.

Cora Rudek

🐦 Dumplings With Sauerkraut

2 c. flour
4 tsp. baking powder
½ tsp. salt

1 egg, well beaten
2 tsp. margarine
¾ c. milk

Mix ingredients and shape into small balls or push dough off from tablespoon into simmered sauerkraut. Cover and let cook 15 minutes. Do not lift lid. Dumplings will double in size.

Elizabeth Hawkins

French Green Beans

1 can french green beans	1 c. slivered almonds
½ tsp. salt	Paprika for color
1 (2 oz.) chopped mushrooms	Parmesan cheese to taste
¼ lb. grated cheese	

Sauce:

2 Tbsp. oleo	1 tsp. chili powder
2 Tbsp. flour	1½ c. milk

Cook sauce until thick. In greased casserole pan, put layers of green beans, mushroom, cheese and almonds and white sauce. Top with buttered crumbs, paprika and sprinkle with Parmesan cheese. Bake 30 minutes at 325°.

Fern Koelsch

Four Bean Casserole

½ lb. diced bacon	1 Tbsp. oil
2 chopped onions	1 (16 oz.) can drained kidney beans
½ c. brown sugar	1 (16 oz.) can drained pork and
⅓ c. vinegar	beans
1 tsp. garlic powder	1 (16 oz.) can drained baby butter
1 tsp. salt	beans
1 tsp. dry mustard	

Fry bacon and drain. Cook onions in the oil. Add the bacon, sugar, vinegar, salt, garlic and mustard. Simmer, covered for 10 minutes. Drain the bacon mixture and mix well. Bake 1 hour at 350°.

Karen Kuhns

Green Bean Bake

2 cans green beans
1 can cream of mushroom soup
⅓ c. milk

1 tsp. soy sauce
1 can onion rings
Pepper to taste

Cook and drain beans. Blend soup, milk and soy sauce until smooth. Stir in beans and ½ onion rings. Pour in casserole dish. Bake at 350° for 25 minutes. Top with remaining onion rings. Bake 5 minutes longer.

Susan Schirf

Stuffed Artichokes

1 c. bread or cracker crumbs
½ c. Parmesan cheese, grated
2 eggs. beaten
1 tsp. salt

¼ c. fresh, chopped parsley
6 prepared artichokes
1 tsp. butter or margarine

To prepare artichokes, remove outer hard leaves, cut bottom to even. Soak artichokes in water for ½ hour. Drain. Prepare stuffing by mixing all ingredients, except butter. Stuff each artichoke with about ¼ cup of mixture or that each artichoke has the same amount of stuffing. Stand up artichokes in a pan large enough to almost cover them with water. Place 1 tsp. butter on each artichoke. Cover with lid. Bring to a boil, then reduce heat to a simmer until leaves are tender, adding more water if necessary.

Orsola Wheeler
Mary Mahan

Fruit of our labor...

"Mama and us kids always made polish kielbasa and hickory smoked it. She made head cheese and kiska (rice and blood) good. It was a holiday specialty. She canned everything we grew in the garden to put away for the winter months. These canned foods were always a delicious part of our holiday meals."
Rosie L. Klimkowski

🐦 Vegetable Hot Dish

1 (10 oz.) pkg. frozen broccoli
1 (10 oz.) pkg. frozen cauliflower
1 (9 oz.) pkg. frozen green beans
1 medium onion, chopped fine
1 c. cubed American cheese

2 (10½ oz.) cans cream of
* mushroom soup*
Salt
Pepper

Arrange vegetable in a 9"x9"x2" square baking dish or casserole. Pour large pieces on bottom. Sprinkle with salt and pepper. Heat soup with cheese until cheese is melted. Pour over vegetables so soup will run down into dish. Bake in a 375° oven about 50 minutes.

Martha Greenlee

🐦 **New!** Sweet & Sour Vegetables

1 20-24 oz. package frozen mixed
* vegetables*

Cook until thick and cool:
1 c. water
1 c. sugar
2 Tbsp. flour

¼ c. vinegar
1 tsp. salt
1 Tbsp. mustard

Add to cooked vegetables:
1 green pepper
1 red onion

1 c. celery

Cook mixed vegetables according to directions on package and cool.
Pour sauce over vegetables and cover. Refrigerate 24 hours before serving.

Kristi Kretchmar

No-Tears Onion Cutting

You'll shed fewer tears if you'll cut the root end off of the onion last.

No more tears when peeling onions if your place them in the deep freeze for four or five minutes first.

Slicing onions can be a "tearful" job. Before peeling, pop onions in a warm oven for five minutes. Peel and cut them dry to eliminate "onion hands." Rub mustard powder on your fingers to rid them of lingering odors.

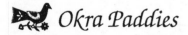 Vegetable Sauté

1 (4 oz.) can sliced mushrooms
1 (16 oz.) pkg. Bird's Eye broccoli,
cauliflower and carrots.

2 Tbsp. butter or margarine
¼ tsp. garlic salt
Water

Drain mushrooms, measuring liquid. Add water to liquid ½ cup. Saute mushrooms in butter in skillet until lightly browned. Add vegetable mixture, garlic salt and measured liquid. Bring to a full boil over high heat, stirring occasionally. Reduce heat; cover and simmer 5 minutes or until vegetables are tender. Makes 5 servings, 70 calories each.

Carol Brookes

New! Baked Vadalia Onions

4 med. Vadalia onions
4 Tbsp. butter

4 Tbsp. chicken bouillon granules

Peel onions to prepare for baking. Core each onion, but do not cut through the bottom. Using one tablespoon of bouillon granules and one tablespoon of butter, or to taste, for each onion, pour half a tablespoon of granules into each cored onion. Place a tablespoon of butter in each cored onion. Top each onion with the remaining half tablespoon of bullion allotted for each. Place in microwavable dish, cover with plastic wrap and cook for about 10 minutes, or until onions are tender.

Vadalia onions are seasonal and usually available during the early summer months.

Judy Seikel

Okra Paddies

1½ c. flour
½ c. corn meal
1 egg

2 c. milk
1 c. okra, sliced ¼" or ½" thick

Beat egg. Add milk along with dry ingredients, then add cup of okra. Form into paddies. Deep-fry in shortening. Serve hot. Salt and pepper to taste. May add onions or celery to batter if desired.

Eugene Marshall, O.S.B.

 Zucchini Patties

1 egg
½ c. Bisquick mix
Small amount grated onion

½ c. Parmesan cheese
½ c. zucchini, grated

Mix ingredients. Form into patties. Fry.

Frances Rychlec

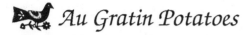 Au Gratin Potatoes

10-12 medium red potatoes
¼-½ lb. Cheddar cheese
½ pt. whipping cream

Onion salt to taste
Pepper to taste

Cook potatoes with jackets until almost tender. Cool. Remove jackets and grate coarsely a layer of potatoes into a buttered, shallow baking pan. Add a layer of cheese, Add onion, salt and pepper after each layer if desired. Repeat until dish is full. Pour whipping cream over all. Top with cheese. Bake, uncovered, at 350° for 50-55 minutes. For crisper potatoes, use large, 11"x14" pan.

Joyce Nowakowski

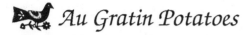 Bohemian Potato Dumplings

4½ c. mashed potatoes or rice
1½ tsp. salt
½ c. Cream of Wheat (uncooked)

3 eggs, slightly beaten
2 c. flour

Stir all ingredients together. Put dough on bread board and knead in more flour. Shape into oblong roll and cut into 2-inch dumplings (about 24). Drop into boiling water for 10-12 minutes. Do not put too many in pot at one time. Serve with melted butter, gravy or honey.

Bonnie (Konop) Yox

Kartoflane Kluski

(Raw Potato Dumplings)

2 c. raw potatoes

1 tsp salt

2 eggs

1½ c. bread crumbs

Grate potatoes fine and drain off brown liquid. Add the beaten eggs, salt, crumbs and flour to make stiff dough. Drop into boiling water from wet spoon. (Dumplings should be about 1½ inches long and ½ inch in diameter when cooked.) They are done as soon as they float to top.

Dora Lee Kusek

Potato Dumplings

3 c. mashed potatoes (hot)

½ c. bread crumbs

2 egg yolks

½ c. flour

Marjoram

2 egg whites

Salt

Pepper

Mix potatoes and bread crumbs. Add egg yolks. Stir in flour and pinch of marjoram. Salt and pepper to taste. Beat egg whites until stiff and fold in. Place on a floured board and roll to pencil thickness. Cut into 2-3 inch strips. Drop these into boiling, salted water. Boil until dumplings float to top. Drain and serve in soup. Maybe served on platters covered with chopped, crisp bacon.

Willie Wajda

Cooking Potatoes

Potatoes will bake in a hurry if they are boiled in salted water for 10 minutes before popping into a very hot oven.

A leftover baked potato can be re-baked if you dip it in water and bake in a 350° oven for about 10 minutes.

A thin slice cut from each end of the potato will speed up baking time as well.

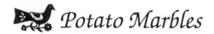 Potato Dumplings

6 c. grated potatoes
4 c. flour
2 tsp. salt

½ lb. salt pork, diced
1 onion, diced

Mix potatoes, flour and salt together. Mixture should be firm enough to shape into a 3-4 inch ball. Mix salt pork and onion together and press 1 tsp. of the mixture in center of potato mixture. Keep a pan of water handy in which to dip hands. Place dumplings in boiling water and boil gently for 1½ hours. Drain well and serve with butter. Serve leftovers by slicing dumplings and frying them in butter.

Minnie Nowakowski

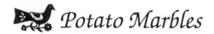 Potato Marbles

4 large potatoes
1 tsp. finely-chopped parsley
⅛ tsp. salt

⅛ tsp. pepper
1 egg, beaten

Preheat oven to 325°. Peel and boil potatoes until they are tender. Mash with electric beater or potato masher. Add parsley, pepper and salt. Mix well. Make into balls about the size of marbles. Lay a tiny sprig of parsley on each ball. Arrange balls on greased cookie sheet. Bake until light brown. Serves 6-8.

No leaven may be eaten or used in cooking during the Jewish Feast of Passover. Leaven include cereals, baking powder, yeast and baking soda.

Mary Canfield

Gourmet Potatoes

6 medium potatoes, cooked and
  diced
10 oz. sharp Cheddar cheese, grated
1 bunch green onions chopped (6
  or 8)

1 pt. dairy sour cream
1 tsp. salt
2 Tbsp. butter and ⅓ c. bread
  crumbs, combined

Mix first 5 ingredients well and turn into buttered 8"x"13 inch pan or casserole. Sprinkle top with buttered bread crumbs and bake at 300° for 45 minutes. Serves 6.

Pauline Haynes

New! Creamed New Potatoes

6-8 small new potatoes
1 chopped onion
Salt

Pepper
2 Tbsp. cornstarch
½ c. cream

Wash and scrape potatoes. Cook potatoes in salted water until nearly done. Drain off most of the liquid. Add chopped onion, salt and pepper and cook until onion is tender. Mix cornstarch in the cream. Stir in cornstarch and cream and cook until done.

Bill Hopcus
in memory of mother, Mary Hopcus

The calm of palms...

"Blessed palm leaves were used for protection from storms. Mama would burn a two or three-inch piece of palm in a saucer on the stove and say the Our Father and Hail Mary. Meanwhile, Daddy lit the lantern and we ran to the storm cellar until the storm passed. The next day, Mother buried the ashes from the blessed palm next to the house. Also, all blessed items that were discarded were disposed the same way. Mother didn't want blessed items to be walked on.

The standard joke was people who rarely come to church during the year, always came Palm Sunday to get their palm to protect from storms all year"

Mrs. Bill (Martha) Hopcus

New! New Potato Casserole

1½ lb. unpeeled new potatoes
1 medium onion, finely chopped
  (about ½ c.)
½ lb. cooked ham, cut into ½"
  cubes

¼ tsp. salt
¼ tsp. pepper
½ c. milk
½ c. whipping cream

Preheat oven to 400°. Scrub new potatoes under running water. Do not peel. Cut into ½" cubes and place in a large bowl. Stir in onion, ham salt, pepper, milk and cream until thoroughly blended. Turn mixture into well-buttered, shallow two-quart baking dish.

Bake uncovered 45 minutes to one hour, stirring twice during the beginning of baking, or until potatoes are soft and starting to brown. Serve from baking dish. Makes four servings.

Becky Spaeth

Potato Dish

3 or 4 potatoes
1 can mushroom soup
3 slices bacon
1 scant c. onions
1 bell pepper

Salt to taste
Pepper to taste
Celery seeds to taste
1 can pimentos
¼ lb. cheese

Chop bacon and fry. Mix all ingredients together well, but the cheese. Sprinkle cheese on top. Bake 30 minutes at 300°.

Ruby Hornbeck

Stuffed Baked Potatoes

6 medium potatoes, baked
⅓ c. cream
2 Tbsp. butter

1 (8 oz.) container, sour cream
   onion dip
¾ c. grated cheddar cheese

Cut baked potatoes in half lengthwise. Carefully scoop out potato meat and in large bowl, mash potatoes well. Add cream and butter. Add onion dip. Spoon mixture back into shells. Top with the grated cheese. Bake at 325° until cheese is melted, about 15 minutes.

Victoria Seikel

Stuffed Potatoes

6 large potatoes
3 Tbsp. butter
1 onion, chopped
1 c. mushrooms

½ c. bread crumbs
2 egg yolks
Salt
Pepper

Peel potatoes. Place in baking dish and bake at 350° for about 30 minutes. Cut off cap at one end of potato. Scoop out center. This is to be filed with the mushroom stuffing.

Stuffing: Fry onion and mushroom in butter. Add bread crumbs, egg yolks and seasoning. Fill potatoes. Replace cap and place in buttered baking dish, cap side up. Bake for 30 more minutes at 350°.

Willie Wajda

New! Fanned Baked Potatoes

4 med. baking potatoes	2-3 Tbsp. melted butter
1 tsp. salt	4 Tbsp. grated Cheddar Cheese
2-3 Tbsp. chopped fresh herbs	1½ Tbsp. Parmesan cheese
or dried herbs	Paprika, optional

Select smooth, evenly-shaped potatoes.

Fresh herbs such as parsley, chives, thyme or sage make these special although dried herbs that are on hand are quick and good, too.

Scrub and rinse the potatoes. On a cutting board, cut the potato crosswise into thin slices down the length of the potato, but don't cut all the way through. Use the handle of a spoon along the underside of the potato as a guide to keep from cutting through the potato with your knife. The potato slices can then be fanned out.

Fan the potatoes slightly and place them in a baking dish. Sprinkle with salt and herbs. Drizzle with the butter.

Bake the potatoes at 425° for about 50 minutes. Remove from oven and sprinkle with cheeses. Sprinkle lightly with paprika, if desired. Bake potatoes for another 10-15 minutes until lightly browned and cheeses are melted. Check potatoes with a fork to make sure they are tender.

Judy Seikel

Sweet Potato Casserole

3 large sweet potatoes, boiled in	1 tsp. lemon juice
skins, peeled and mashed	2 eggs
½ c. brown sugar, packed	½ small can evaporated milk
1 tsp. vanilla	

Topping:

½ c. brown sugar, packed	½ stick oleo, softened
½ c. flour	1 c. chopped pecans

Preheat oven to 400°. Mix ingredients. Put in greased casserole dish. Mix ingredients for topping together and top. Bake 30 minutes. Do not overbake, or pecans will burn.

Becky Spaeth

New! Apple/Sweet Potato Casserole

2 lbs. sweet potatoes   1¼ lbs. Winesap apples

Sauce:

⅔ c. brown sugar   1 Tbsp. lemon juice
1 Tbsp. butter   1 tsp. cinnamon
½ c. apple cider   ½ tsp. ginger
3 Tbsp. maple syrup

Boil apples and potatoes until ⅔ done. After they cool, peel apples and potatoes; quarter and slide ¼" thick.

Alternate potato and apple slices in baking dish. Pour hot sauce over them and bake for 30 minutes at 350° degrees.

Lila Dilis

New! Sweet Potato Casserole

3 c. mashed sweet potatoes (about a   ½ c. melted butter
    40-oz. can, drained)   ½ c. sugar
2 eggs, beaten   1 tsp. vanilla

Topping:

1 c. brown sugar   ½ c. flour
⅓ c. melted butter   ½ c. chopped pecans

Mix all ingredients for potato casserole. Spread in a 9"x13" greased baking dish.

Mix all ingredients for the topping. Sprinkle topping on top of potato mixture. Bake 25 minutes at 350°.

Suzan (Russell) Schirf

🐦 Tater Tot Casserole

¼ c. margarine
1 small chopped onion
1 lb. hamburger
3 Tbsp. flour
1 can drained corn

1 can mushrooms
1¼ tsp. salt
1(13 oz.) evaporated milk
1 pkg. tater tots

Preheat oven to 400°. Brown onion in margarine. Add flour, salt and can of milk. Stir until thickened. Brown the hamburger and add to the thickened mixture with corn and mushrooms. Stir thoroughly, spoon into casserole. Arrange tater tots in single layer on top of casserole. Cover and bake for 40 minutes or until bubbly and hot in center.

Minnie Nowakowski

🐦 Best Yet Way To Cook Rice

1 c. regular uncooked rice
2 c. boiling water

1 tsp. salt
1 Tbsp. oleo

Measure rice in dish that has a tight fitting cover. Stir in boiling water, salt and oleo. Cover and bake at 350° for 25 minutes. Do not lift lid during cooking. Keeps well in refrigerator for several days, just add a little water and heat.

Barbara Dull

🐦 Broccoli Casserole

½ stick oleo
1 c. onion
1 box chopped broccoli

1 can cream of mushroom soup
1 small jar Cheez Whiz
1 c. cooked rice

Melt oleo in skillet. Add chopped onions and saute until clear. Add package of thawed broccoli. Stir thoroughly. Add soup and simmer. Add Cheez Whiz and simmer. Add rice. Stir and continue to simmer. If too thick, add a small amount of water. Put in casserole dish. Bake 25-30 minutes at 350°.

Suzanne Visnieski

Broccoli Casserole

2 c. instant rice cooked
½ c. chopped celery
½ stick butter
1 can cream of mushroom soup

10 oz. fresh or frozen broccoli
½ c. chopped onion
1 (8 oz.) jar Cheez Whiz

In a saucepan on low heat, melt butter. Stir in Cheez Whiz and mushroom soup, chopped broccoli, celery and onions. Stir together. Mix rice with broccoli mixture and pour cheese mixture on and mix all together in 8"x8" pan. Bake at 350° for 45 minutes.

Gerry Roller

Broccoli Elegant

1 ½ c. water
6 Tbsp. water, divided
1 (6 oz) pkg. corn bread stuffing
   mix
1 large bunch fresh broccoli,
   cleaned, split lengthwise into
   serving size spears
2 Tbsp. flour

1 tsp. chicken bouillon granules
¾ c. milk
1 (3 oz.) pkg. cream cheese,
   softened
¼ tsp. salt
4 green onions, sliced
1 c. shredded Cheddar cheese
Paprika

Mix water, ¼ cup of the margarine and the packet of seasoning mix from the corn bread stuffing mix in a saucepan and bring to a boil. Remove from heat and stir in the corn bread stuffing crumbs. Let stand 5 minutes. Spoon stuffing around the inside edge of a lightly greased 13"x9"x2" baking dish, leaving a well in the center. Place broccoli in well and set aside. Melt 2 tablespoon margarine and add flour, stirring until smooth. Cook 1 minute, stirring constantly, until thick and bubbly. Add cream cheese and salt and stir until smooth. Stir in onion. Spoon mixture over broccoli. Sprinkle with cheese and paprika. Cover with foil and bake in a 350° oven for 35 minutes. Remove foil and bake 10 more minutes to brown. Serves 8.

Judy Seikel

 New! *Kapusta i Pomidor*

(Cabbage & Tomatoes)

Half head chopped cabbage
4 large tomatoes, chopped
4 onions, chopped
2 Tbsp. sugar

Salt to taste
1 Tbsp. vinegar, more or less
1 Tbsp. butter.

Cook all above until done.

Leon Magott
in memory of grandmother Mary Chwalinski Magott

Cabbage Casserole

1 head cabbage
Water to cover
Salt
Pepper
Your favorite cheese

Cream of celery, cream of
   mushroom or cream of chicken
   soup
Crushed crackers or bread crumbs
Butter or oleo

Wash a nice firm head of cabbage. Shred into thin slices. Drop in boiling water just until it wilts. Drain in colander. Season with salt and pepper. Layer in casserole dish with grated cheese and soup. Top with crackers or crumbs. Top with dabs of butter or oleo. Bake at 350° for 45 minutes or until nice and brown on top.

Mickey Wyskup

Corn Starch or Flour?
   Corn starch has twice the thickening quality of flour. For 1 Tbsp. of corn starch, you would use 2 Tbsp. of flour.

Cabbage Casserole

1 small head cabbage
1 c. grated cheddar cheese
½ c. milk
1 can cream of chicken soup
1 Tbsp. butter

Salt
Pepper
Cracker crumbs
Canned onion rings (optional)

Cook cabbage until glazed in a small amount of water. Drain. Add butter, salt and pepper to taste. Stir in cheese soup and milk. Pour over cabbage in casserole. Cover with cracker crumbs and bake at 300° approximately 1½ hours. You may also top with canned onion rings.

Sally Balkenbush

Carrot-Celery Casserole

8 carrots, peeled and cut into
    1-inch pieces
4 stalks celery, cut into 1-inch
    pieces
4 slices bread, toasted and cut in
    cubes

Salt
Water
4 Tbsp. sugar
1 c. white sauce
Velveeta cheese

Cook carrots in salted water for 5 minutes. Add celery and sugar and cook 3 more minutes. Mix Velveeta cheese into white sauce. Drain carrot mixture. Combine all ingredients. Bake at 350° in greased casserole approximately 20 minutes until hot and bubbly.

Marty Janowiak

Corn Hints

A dampened papter towel or terry cloth brushed downward on a cob of corn will remove ever strand of corn silk.

An easy way to remove the kernels of sweet corn from the cob is to use a shoe horn. It's built just right for sheering off those kernels in a jiffy.

Whenever cooking corn on the cob, add a half-cup of milk and one teaspoon of sugar for sweeter corn.

 New! *Baked Corn*

1 can whole kernel corn (water and all)
1 can cream style corn
8 oz. sour cream

2 beaten eggs
1 pkg. corn muffin mix (Jiffy)
1 stick melted margarine

Mix both corns, sour cream and eggs. Fold in muffin mix and melted butter. Pour in buttered casserole and bake at 350° for 1¼ hours. Will appear soft in center, like custard, but will set in a few minutes after removing from oven.

Diana Hanna

Corn Casserole

1 can cream style corn
2 eggs
¼ c. milk
¼ tsp. salt

8 crushed Crackers
2 Tbsp. melted butter
1 Tbsp. chopped green pepper
1 Tbsp. chopped pimento

Mix all ingredients and bake 1 hour and 15 minutes at 400°.

Jodi Steciak

Corn Casserole

2 (12 oz.) cans Niblets corn, drained
1 medium onion, chopped
1 green pepper, chopped
1 stick margarine
2 c. cooked rice

1 can mushroom soup
1 small jar pimento, chopped
2 Tbsp. Worcestershire sauce
1 c. grated cheese

Saute onion and pepper in margarine. Add all other ingredients, except cheese and mix well. Pour in greased casserole dish and cover with grated cheese. Bake in 375° oven until cheese melts.

Try this with fresh Nowakowski corn, cut from the cob!

Judy Seikel

🐦 **New!** *Hominy Casserole*

1 16 oz. can yellow hominy, drained   *¾ c. sour cream*
1 16 oz. can white hominy, drained   *1 4 oz. can of diced, green chilies*
½ lb. grated Monterrey Jack cheese

Mix all ingredients, except the cheese together. Put in 9"x13" inch pan. Put grated cheese on top. Bake 45 minutes at 350°, or until golden brown.

This recipe was handed down to my daughter, Regina, by her later mother-in-law, Mrs. B. L. (Dorothy) Newton.

Pauline Piotrowicz

Salt of the earth...

"The traditional food basket brought for blessing on Holy Saturday included ham, smoked link sausage, beets, sweet rolls and a jar of salt. My mother, Mrs. Felix (Pauline) Mayer, used the salt to make a cross on the ground and prayed for the safety of her family and field crops when storm clouds approached. Inside, palms were burned in the wood stove and blessed candles were lighted.

On February 2, Candlemar Day, candles for church and home use are blessed."

Katie Mayer Magott

🐦 *New! Fazolove' Lusky na Paprice*

(Austrian Green Beans Paprika)

2 qts. water	¾ c. finely-chopped onions
1 tsp. salt	1 Tbsp. sweet Hungarian paprika
1 lb. green beans (about 3 c.), cut into 1" pieces	2 Tbsp. flour
4 Tbsp. butter	1 c. sour cream
	½ tsp. salt

In a 3-quart saucepan, bring the 2 quarts of water and the salt to a boil over high heat. Drop in the beans and bring the water to a boil again. Reduce the heat to medium and cook the beans uncovered for 10-15 minutes, or until just tender. Drain beans in a colander.

Melt the butter in a 10"-skillet. When the foam subsides, add the onions and cook for 4-5 minutes, or until they are translucent. Remove from heat and stir in the paprika and stir until the onions are well coated.

Use a wire whisk to beat the flour into the sour cream in a small bowl. Add the mixture to the skillet, stirring well. Add the salt. Simmer on low for 4-5 minutes, or until the sauce is smooth and creamy. Gently stir in the beans; and simmer about for more minutes until heated through.

The Cookbook Committee

🐦 *New! Polish Mushrooms*

¾ c. diced onion	4 Tbsp. butter
1 ½ lb. sliced mushrooms	Pinch of salt
¼ tsp. peppers	1 c. sour cream
1 tsp. paprika	

Cook onions in 2 tablespoons of butter 10 minutes on low heat.

Remove onions and set aside. Add remaining 2 tablespoons of butter and mushrooms. Cook over low heat 10 minutes. Return onions to pan, add salt, pepper and paprika. Cook 5 minutes and then stir in sour cream right before serving.

Judy Seikel

🐦 New! Red Cabbage with Green Apples

2 Tbsp. margarine or butter
3 med. Granny Smith apples,
  peeled and chopped (about 3 cups)
1 med. head red cabbage, sliced
  (about 8 cups)

2 sm. onions, chopped (about ¾ c.)
1 ½ c. hot water
¾ c. cider vinegar
2 Tbsp. sugar
2 tsp. salt

Melt the margarine in a large pan over medium heat. Cook the apples in the margarine 5 minutes, stirring occasionally.

Stir in remaining ingredients. Heat to boiling; reduce heat. Cover and simmer about 40 minutes, stirring occasionally, until cabbage is tender.

Judy Seikel

🐦 New! Spinach Casserole

1 10-oz. pkg. frozen chopped
  spinach
1 c. sour cream

½ c. chopped walnuts
3 Tbsp. parmesan cheese
1 Tbsp. dehydrated onion soup

Thaw the spinach and drain well. Add the remaining ingredients to spinach and mix. Place in an 8"-square baking dish and bake, uncovered, at 350° for 20 minutes.

Judy Seikel

🐦 Squash Casserole

6 yellow squash
1 box Jiffy corn bread mix
1 Tbsp. sugar

1 medium onion
1 c. milk
1 c. cream of mushroom soup

Bake corn bread according to package directions. Cook squash and medium onion. Crumble corn bread. Dribble milk over corn bread. Add soup. Dot with butter. Toss all ingredients. Bake in casserole at 325° for 30 minutes.

Ina Wiedemann

Squash Casserole

1 pkg. herb seasoned stuffing
2 sticks oleo (1 c.)
2 lb. yellow squash
2 medium onions
1 tsp. salt
1 can cream of chicken soup

1 can chopped water chestnut
1 small can chopped pimento
1(8 oz.) ctn. sour cream
½ lb. grated sharp Cheddar cheese
Water

Melt butter. Mix with stuffing. Place ½ of this in 3 quart casserole. Slice squash and onions. Put in pot. Add salt and water to cover. Cook until just tender. Drain and add soup, chestnuts, pimentos and sour cream. Pour into casserole. Spread cheese on top, then remainder of stuffing. Bake about 30 minutes at 350°. Serves 12.

LouAnn Spaeth

Zucchini Casserole

1 lb. hamburger
Onions
Cut up zucchini
Cut corn off cob

Salt
Pepper
Tomatoes or Ragu sauce

Brown hamburger with onions. Drain. Add zucchini, corn, salt, pepper and tomatoes or Ragu. Cook slow or bake at 350° until flavor is throughout and vegetables are well done.

Frances Rychlec

Sauerkraut

1 qt. or 2 cans sauerkraut
  (homemade or Meeter's kraut
  drained), drained and rinsed if you
  want

2-4 Tbsp. brown sugar
2 Tbsp. bacon drippings
Juice to cover

Combine ingredients. Cook slowly for 15-30 minutes.
Kielbasa can be added or cooked with for more flavor.

Frances Rychlec

 ## Cole Slaw

1 small head cabbage
4 carrots
1 bell pepper
2 Tbsp. salt
5 Tbsp. cooking oil

1 small onion
1 small head cauliflower
2 Tbsp. sugar
5 Tbsp. red wine vinegar

Shred cabbage, slice carrots, onion and cauliflower. Dice pepper. Mix all together. Add sugar, salt vinegar and oil. Cover and chill.

Lucille Keelings

Creamy Cole Slaw

3 lbs. cabbage, shredded
4 ½ oz., or 1 green pepper, chopped

1 medium onion, chopped
2 oz. pimento, chopped

Dressing:

2 ½ oz. sugar
1 ¼ c. mayonnaise

½ c. vinegar
¾ tsp. salt

Beat dressing with whip or spoon until creamy and add to cabbage mixture. This dressing is also good for fruit salad.

Fern Koelsch

Nine-Day Slaw

3 lb. head cabbage
1 green pepper
2 medium onions
2 c. sugar

1 c. salad oil
2 Tbsp. celery salt
2 Tbsp salt
2 Tbsp. sugar

Shred cabbage, green pepper and onions. Blend with sugar. Blend remaining ingredients and bring to a full boil, stirring over a full heat. Pour immediately over cabbage mixture. Let cool. Cover and store in refrigerator. Keeps well for many days.

LouAnn Spaeth

Wyskup Cole Slaw

1 large head green cabbage
1 small head red cabbage
5-6 carrots
Red onions

Salt
Pepper
Dash of wine vinegar
Bottled Italian dressing

Grind cabbage and carrots. Chop onions. Mix and add salt, pepper, vinegar and dressing to taste.

Cora Rudek

White Salad

1 qt. shaved cabbage
1 small can pineapple

½ c. blanched almonds
2 c. marshmallows

Dressing:

4 egg whites
½ c. sugar
1 scant tsp. flour
Juice of 3 lemons

4 Tbsp. white vinegar
Pinch of salt
Whipping cream

Make the dressing by beating the whites of 4 eggs until they begin to froth. Add sugar, flour, lemon juice, vinegar and salt. Cook until it thickens and then thin with whipped cream. Toss with salad ingredients. Chill.

Mrs. A. J. Murphy

Sauerkraut Salad

1 large can sauerkraut, drained
¾ c. sugar
Onion (optional)
1 c. diced celery

½ c. pimento
1 green pepper, chopped
¼ c. vinegar or lemon juice

Make syrup of sugar and vinegar. Bring to boil and let boil a few minutes. Cool slightly. Mix kraut, onion, pimento, celery and pepper. Pour cooled syrup over kraut mixture. Let stand several hours or overnight.

Betty A. Miller, CDA State Regent

Sauerkraut Salad

2 c. sauerkraut (1 lb. can)
½ c. sugar
½ c. thinly-sliced celery

½ c. thin strips of green bell pepper
½ c. shredded carrots
¼ c. finely-chopped onion

Combine sauerkraut and sugar. Let set 20 minutes. Add remaining and chill.

Christiane Sauls

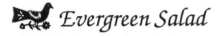

Evergreen Salad

⅔ c. salad oil
⅓ c. wine vinegar
¼ c. crumbled Bleu cheese
1 tsp. sugar
½ tsp. salt

⅛ tsp. pepper
8 c. torn lettuce, chilled
1 c. diced red skinned apple
1 c. diagonally-sliced celery
Chopped pecans

Combine first 6 ingredients in jar. Cover; shake vigorously. Chill to blend flavors. Shake again before tossing with lettuce, apple and celery. Makes 8 servings (about 8 cups).

Josephine Russell

Fresh Spinach Salad

1 clove garlic
½ tsp. lemon pepper
½ c. olive oil
1 lb. fresh spinach

2 to 4 Tbsp. vinegar
½ c. shredded Cheddar cheese
½ c. crisp bacon bits
1 c. cheese and garlic croutons

Mash garlic with lemon pepper and oil in bowl. Let stand at room temperature 2-3 hours. Wash and drain spinach and dry with paper towels. Break into bite-size pieces and chill. Just before serving, drain garlic from oil. Pour over spinach and toss, coating each leaf. Sprinkle vinegar over salad and toss again lightly. Add cheese, bacon bits and croutons. Toss again. Makes approximately 6 servings.

Barbara Witte

Bishop Francis C. Kelly Salad

1 hard-boiled egg yolk per serving
Oil

1 tsp. Worcestershire sauce
1 clove garlic

Dressing:

1 Tbsp. vinegar or lemon juice
1 salad spoon of mashed potatoes
½ tsp. anchovy paste
1 Tbsp. Roquefort cheese

Salt to taste
Paprika to color
1 Tbsp. chopped onion
½ head lettuce per serving

One hard-boiled egg per person, 1 salad spoon oil per person. 1 tsp. Worcestershire sauce. Rub dish first with 1 clove garlic.

Mix 1 tablespoon vinegar or lemon juice, 1 salad spoon of mashed potatoes, ½ tsp. anchovy paste, paprika to color, 1 tablespoon chopped onion, real fine, for dressing.

Use ½ head of lettuce for each person. Pour dressing over lettuce and mix well. Must be served and eaten at once. Made at the table.

Bishop Francis C. Kelly
Oklahoma Diocese Bishop
1924 to 1948

New! Wilted Lettuce

Leaf lettuce or fresh spinach
5 green onions, chopped, or one
*   slice of red onion*
5 slices bacon, uncooked and

*   chopped*
¼ c. vinegar (or less)
⅛ c. sugar
Option: radishes

Tear mixing bowl full of leaf lettuce and/or fresh spinach. Add chopped onions. Green onions and red onion can be combined, if desired. Dice 5 slices of uncooked bacon. Brown bacon and cool slightly.

Mix vinegar (less than ¼ c. may be used, depending on taste preference) and sugar and let sugar dissolve. Pour into bacon and grease. Bring to a boil. Pour over lettuce and onions.

Stir and serve immediately.

Becky Spaeth

Grandma Keck's Dandelion Greens Salad

Dandelion leaves
1 onion

1 boiled egg, diced

Dressing:

1 Tbsp. cornstarch
½ c. sugar
½ c. vinegar

½ c. milk
½ tsp. salt
1 raw egg

Pick young dandelion leaves. Cut them off right at the ground. Wash and cut up leaves. Chop 1 onion. Add 1 diced, boiled egg. Toss. Dressing: Mix together cornstarch, sugar and salt. Add vinegar and milk. Mix together. Mix in 1 raw egg. Cook over low heat stirring constantly until thickened. Let cook. Pour over salad and toss.

Doyle Miller

Five Ingredient Salad

1 large ripe avocado
1 head cauliflower
4 tomatoes

1 can black olives
3 green onions

Dressing:

Oil
Wine vinegar

Salt and pepper

Cut up all ingredients, using only flower tops on cauliflower. Season with oil, wine vinegar, salt and pepper.

Elfriede Raught

Fruity Tips

Scalding tomatoes, peaches, or pears in boiling water before peeling makes it easier on you and the fruit — skins slip right off.

Ripen green fruits by placing in a perforated plastic bag. The holes allow air movement, yet retain the odorless gas which fruits produce to promote ripening.

 Broccoli Salad

1 large head broccoli, finely
   chopped
10 slices bacon, cooked and
   crumbled
5 green onions, slice

½ c. golden raisins
1 c. Hellmann's light mayonnaise
2 Tbsp. vinegar
3 pkgs. Equal sugar substitute

Toss everything together. Refrigerate at least 2 hours before serving.

Pat Hopcus

Cauliflower Salad

1 head cauliflower, broken in pieces
1 jar salad olives

Salad dressing (mayonnaise)

Break cauliflower into small pieces. Mix in olives and mayonnaise to taste. Chill. Ready to serve.

Mary Jo Jorski

Nagging youngsters...

"Moma could handle that hoe out in the garden at age 95. We'd come home and she'd be hard at work and we'd say: 'Moma you don't need to do this or that.' But one day she said: 'I want to tell you kids something... I'm going to do this as long as I can because this is "mine" enjoyment.' She said it in English, and she usually talked to us in Polish. She was still the boss.'

"She had gallblader surgery at age 100 and her doctor said it was a medical miracle."

   — Agnes Czerczyk, talking about her mother, Selena Kusek, one of the original settlers in Harrah, who died at age 105 in 1994.

New! Cucumber Salad

1 peeled and sliced cucumber
Salt
1 sliced onion
1 Tbsp. vinegar

1 Tbsp. water
1 Tbsp. sugar
3 Tbsp. Half and Half

Salt cucumber well and drain in colander 20-30 minutes. Add onion and other ingredients. Adjust spices to taste.

Sour cream can be used instead of Half and Half.

Martha Hopcus

Shoe Peg Corn Salad

5 ribs celery
½ green bell pepper
1 c. drained shoe peg corn
1 small onion, chopped
2 Tbsp. pimento

½ c. salad oil
2 Tbsp. vinegar
1 tsp. dry mustard
1 tsp. sugar
Salt and pepper to taste

Mix celery, green pepper, corn, onion and pimento. Set aside. Mix oil, vinegar, mustard, sugar, salt and pepper. Pour over vegetables. Refrigerate 6 hours or overnight.

Rosalie Marino

Marinated Salad

1 c. vinegar
1 c. sugar
½ c. salad oil
1 (16 oz.) can green beans, drained
2 carrots, sliced
1 can sweet peas, drained

1 green pepper, chopped
1 red onion, sliced
1 (2 oz.) jar pimento, drained
1 cucumber, sliced
2 stalks celery, sliced

Bring vinegar to a boil in saucepan. Stir in sugar and oil. Cool slightly. Combine remaining ingredients. Add vinegar mixture. Cover and refrigerate overnight. Serves 12-15.

Fern Koelsch

🐦 Vegetable Salad

10 potatoes
2 cans green peas, drained
2 cans carrots, drained
1 medium jar sweet pickles, diced
12 eggs, boiled and chopped

1 onion, diced
Salt to taste
Pepper to taste
3 Tbsp. mustard
1½ c. mayonnaise

Cook potatoes in jackets. Cool and dice in a large mixing bowl, put diced potatoes and add peas, carrots, drained and diced sweet pickles, chopped egg, onion, salt, pepper, mustard and mayonnaise. Toss together until mixed well.

Irena Pryk

🐦 Vegetable Salad

½ c. vinegar
1 tsp. salt
½ c. cooking oil
¾ c. sugar
1 tsp. pepper
Small jar chopped pimentos

1 c. chopped green pepper
1 bunch chopped green onions
1 (10 oz.) LeSueur white corn
1 small can peas
1 small can chopped green beans

Mix first 5 ingredients together and bring to a boil. Let cool while preparing vegetable. Add vegetable and mix well, then refrigerate at least 3 hours (overnight is good). Keeps well.

Barbara Liebl

🐦 German Potato Salad

1 c. vinegar
1 c. water
1 c. sugar
½ lb. bacon, diced and ½ drippings

4 Tbsp. cornstarch
1 medium onion, diced
1½ to 2 qt. sliced potatoes (still warm)

Brown bacon and onions. Drain ½ of drippings. Dissolve cornstarch in water. Add to bacon and onions, then add vinegar and sugar. Cook till thick. Pour over warm potatoes. Heat through and serve.

Kay Brown

German Style Potato Salad

6 medium potatoes, peeled and cut
   into ¼-inch slices
6 slices bacon, cooked and
   crumbled
1 medium onion, chopped
½ c. vinegar

½ c. water
½ c. sugar
1 Tbsp. cornstarch
¼ tsp. salt
¼ tsp. pepper

Cook potatoes in boiling water for 15-20 minutes or until tender. Drain well. Combine remaining ingredients in saucepan. Cook for 20 minutes, stirring frequently. Pour vinegar mixture over potatoes. Serve immediately. Yields 6 servings.

Mary Winters

German Potato Salad

6 medium potatoes
1 to 2 bouillon cubes dissolved in
   about 1 c. hot water
1 small chopped onion or
   equivalent chives

1 finely-sliced, peeled cucumber
Vinegar to taste
Cooking oil to taste
Salt and pepper to taste
Crumbled bacon bits

Boil potatoes in jackets. Peel while hot and dice. Pour on some dissolved bouillon, then add all other ingredients. Add as much of the remaining broth to receive the desired consistency. Sprinkle with crumbled bacon.

Elfriede Raught

Sandy's Corn Bread Salad

1 pkg. corn bread mix	1 bunch chopped green onions
1 pkg. Mexican corn bread mix	1 can drained Mexican corn
2 chopped tomatoes	1 can drained kidney beans
2 chopped bell peppers	2 c. mayonnaise

Cook corn bread according to directions. After corn bread has cooled, crumble and add rest of ingredients. Mix and chill at least 8 hours before serving.

Glena Jorski

Cheese Salad

8 oz. sharp Cheddar cheese, shredded	1 or 2 small pkgs. slivered almonds
3 or 4 green onions, chopped	2 Tbsp. Miracle Whip (or add to taste)
4 strips bacon, well cooked and crumbled	Bacon grease (for flavor)

Combine all ingredients and mix well. May be eaten right away, but the flavor improves if it sets overnight in refrigerator.

Beverly Fortelney Winstead

New! Ser i Cebula

(Cottage Cheese and Onion)

1 c. creamed cottage cheese	Salt
1 sweet chopped onion	Fresh ground black pepper

Note: Dry cottage cheese can be used with drained plain yogurt. Drain one large container of low-fat yogurt 48 hours in a coffee filter lined colander over a bowl in the refrigerator. Drained yogurt makes an excellent substitute for sour cream.

Martha Magott Hopcus
in memory of grandmother, Mary Kupczynski

New! Hot Chicken Salad

4 c. cooked, diced chicken
½ c. grated cheddar cheese
1 tsp. Accent (optional)
1 tsp. salt
½ c. mayonnaise

1 c. chicken soup, undiluted
1 c. thinly-sliced celery
½ c. thinly-sliced green peppers
⅔ c. walnuts or almonds
1 Tbsp. chopped onion

Topping:

1 c. prepared seasoned stuffing mix
  or crushed potato chips

½ c. grated cheese
4 Tbsp. melted butter

Spray a 9"x13" glass pan with Pam or other cooking oil spray.
Mix ingredients together and spread in the pan.
For topping, mix ingredients together and spread on top of chicken mixture.
Bake at 350° for 20 minutes or until the top is brown. Cut in squares or
serve by spoonsful.

Fern Koelsch

Chicken Salad

Large chicken, baked or boiled,
  boned and chopped
2 c. chopped celery
1 large onion, chopped
1 large can peas, drained

1 jar mushrooms, chopped
1 pkg. sliced almonds
1 c. mayonnaise
1 c. sour cream
2 Tbsp. lemon juice

Mix chicken, celery, onion, peas and mushrooms and almonds together. In
another bowl, mix mayonnaise, sour cream and lemon juice. Pour over
chicken mixture. Add salt to taste and chill before serving.

Gerry Lamer

🐦 Mexican Salad

1½ to 2 lbs. hamburger
1 pkg. enchilada sauce mix
2 cans drained kidney beans
1 head shredded lettuce
4 diced tomatoes
1 diced onions
1 can drained pitted olives

1 lb. shredded cheese
1 pkg. crushed tortilla chips
1 bottle French dressing or other
   dressing of your choice (I use
   Catalina).
Avocado

Heat hamburger, enchilada sauce and kidney beans. Toss lettuce, tomatoes, onion, olives, cheese chips and dressing. Add hamburger mixture to salad mixture. Garnish with avocado. Serves at least 8-10.

Carol Brookes

🐦 Rice & Artichoke Salad

1 pkg. chicken flavor Rice-A-Roni
2 jars marinated artichoke hearts,
   chopped
4 green onions, chopped

6 sliced olives
½ c. mayonnaise
¼ tsp. curry powder
¼ c. dill pickle juice

Cook Rice-A-Roni according to directions. Combine Rice-A-Roni, artichokes, onions and olives in a bowl. Combine mayonnaise, curry powder and dill pickle juice to a make a dressing. Add to Rice-A-Roni mixture and blend well. Chill.

Joyce Nowakowski

Polish saying:

"Łaknącemu wszystko smaczne." A good appetite needs no sauce.

submitted by Dora Kusek

🐦 Frozen Apple Salad

1 (8 oz.) can crushed pineapple
2 beaten eggs
½ c. sugar
Dash of salt
3 Tbsp. lemon juice

2 c. finely-diced, unpared apple
½ c. finely-diced celery
1 small ctn. Cool Whip
Chopped pecans (optional)

Drain the pineapple and reserve syrup. Add water to syrup to make ½ cup. Combine eggs, sugar, salt, lemon juice and syrup mixture. Cook over low heat, stirring constantly, until thick. Cool. Fold in pineapple, apple, celery and Cool Whip. Spoon mixture evenly into ring mold, Bundt pan or individual serving size molds. Freeze.

To remove, dip container in warm water and invert on a cookie sheet. Return to freezer until serving time. Whipped cream can be substituted for Cool Whip.

I use my food processor to thinly slice celery and chop apples, fast!

Judy Seikel

🐦 Fresh Apple Salad

1 c. sugar
2 Tbsp. all-purpose flour
½ c. milk
1 Tbsp. water
1 beaten egg

1 Tbsp. vinegar
½ tsp. vanilla
4 or 5 large tart apples
½ c. chopped walnuts

Mix sugar, flour, milk, water, egg and vinegar. Boil gently until thick. Add vanilla. Cool. A couple of drops of yellow food color adds color if desired. Pour cooled, cooked mixture over chopped apples and nuts. Mix. Chill until serving time. For elegant serving, put in individual dishes and top each with prepare whipped topping and a long-stemmed cherry.

Carolyn Rudek

Cranberry Salad - Cranberry Fluff

¾ lb. cranberries
¼ c. pineapple, crushed
¼ lb. small marshmallows
1 c. low fat plain yogurt

2 to 5 packets Sweet'N Low or
   NutraSweet
½ c. chopped pecans

Mix cranberries, marshmallows and pineapple and let stand for several hours, then add remaining ingredients and chill until ready to serve.

Pauline Haynes

Cranberry Salad

1 qt. cranberries (whole)
2 c. water
2 boxes cherry Jell-O
2 c. sugar

2 c. pineapple
2 c. diced apple
1 c. chopped celery
1 c. nuts

Combine cranberries and water. Cook for 10 minutes. Add Jell-O and sugar. Let cook, then add remaining ingredients. Chill overnight.

Minnie Nowakowski

Cranberry Salad

1 c. ground raw cranberries
1 c. sugar
1 pkg. lemon Jell-O
1 c. hot water
1 c. pineapple juice

1 c. crushed pineapple, well
   drained and reserved
½ c. nuts (pecans or walnuts)
1 c. chopped celery

Combine cranberries and sugar. Dissolve Jell-O in hot water. Add juice, drained from crushed pineapple. Whip until partially set. Add cranberry mixture, pineapple, celery and nuts. Chill. Serve with or without dressing.

Polly Lane

New! *Pudding Fruit Salad*

1 #303 can sliced, drained peaches.
1 #303 can chunk pineapple
4 bananas, sliced

1 small pkg. vanilla instant pudding
½ 6 oz. can frozen orange juice
Maraschino cherries, sliced

Slice bananas in chunk pineapple and juice. This will make bananas covered with juice. Drain the peaches and add them to the bananas and pineapple. Stir in orange juice concentrate. Add instant pudding. Add sliced cherries. Refrigerate until ready to serve.

Algerd Dilis

Sour Cream *Fruit With Pecans*

1 c. mandarin oranges
1 c. miniature marshmallows
1 c. coconut

1 c. pineapple chunks
½ c. pecans
1 c. sour cream

Mix all ingredients together. Let set overnight in refrigerator.

Pat Hopcus

Fresh Fruit Salad

4 chilled oranges
3 chilled bananas
1 chilled apple

1 pkg. colored marshmallows
½ c. nuts
½ pt. whipped cream

Cut up oranges. Slice bananas. Chop apple. Combine with marshmallows and nuts. Pour whipped cream over the mixture.

Virginia A. Morton

Fruit Salad

2 sliced bananas
¾ c. diced oranges
½ c. seedless grapes
¼ c. chopped dates (optional)
3 Tbsp. lemon juice
½ c. sugar
1 tsp. all-purpose flour

1 egg yolk
2½ tsp. lemon juice
½ c. unsweetened pineapple juice
1 c. whipping cream
¼ c. grated coconut
Nuts

Mix fruit and sprinkle with 3 tablespoons lemon juice. Chill. Combine sugar, flour and egg yolk. Stir in fruit juice. Cook in double boiler until thick. Cool. Whip cream and fold into cooked mixture. Serve on lettuce leaf and garnish with coconut and nuts if desired.

Carolyn Rudek

Daddy's Fruit Salad

3 apples, cut into tiny pieces
3 oranges, cut up
5 bananas, thinly sliced
1 c. raisins
½ c. sunflower seeds

1 c. shredded coconut
2 c. marshmallows
1 or 2 containers any fruit flavored
  yogurt

Blend all ingredients. Chill and enjoy. (Amounts are approximate.)

Amado Rodriguez

New! Fruit Salad Dressing

2½ oz. sugar
1¼ c. mayonnaise

½ c. vinegar
¾ tsp. salt

Beat dressing with whip or spoon until creamy.

Fern Koelsch

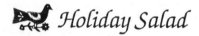 New! *Christmas Wreath Salad*

1 lg. size can crushed pineapple
2 cans mandarin oranges
1 medium jar of maraschino
   cherries
3 bananas

½ c. sugar
2 boxes of Cool Whip or 2 pts.
   whipping cream
½ c. coconut
1 tsp. milk, tinted green

Drain the pineapple, oranges and maraschino cherries. Save several maraschino cherries to quarter for garnish. Mix fruit and chill for one hour. Add sliced bananas. Stir in ½ c. sugar to Cool Whip.

Add green food coloring to the milk. Pour into coconut and stir to tint. Use the green coconut to make a wreath on top of the mixture in bowl. Add quartered cherries for holly.

Rose Throckmorton

Holiday Salad

2 c. raw cranberries
2 apples
1 c. sugar
1 pkg. cherry Jell-O

10 marshmallows, quartered
1 c. cream, whipped or 8 oz. ctn.
   Cool Whip
¼ c. chopped nuts

Wash cranberries and put through food chopper. Add diced apples and sugar. Let stand about 20 minutes. Prepare gelatin according to directions on package. When partially set, fold in all ingredients. Serves 10.

Ina Wiedemann

White Christmas Salad

1 lb. little marshmallows
1 c. milk
1 c. whipping cream

1 c. crushed pineapple
1 small bottle maraschino cherries
Graham cracker crumbs

Mix marshmallows and milk together. Let cool. Add whipping cream. Combine pineapple and cherries. Fold into mixture. Line pan with graham cracker crumbs. Fill pan. Cover and refrigerate.

Sharon Neal

 Extra Good Salad

1 pkg. lemon Jell-O
No. 2 can crushed pineapple
¼ tsp. salt
½ c. sugar

1 pt. cream, whipped or 8 oz. Cool
 Whip
1 c. carrots, grated
1 tsp. lemon juice

Drain pineapple and add enough liquid to make 1½ cups liquid. Bring to boil. Add Jell-O, sugar, salt and lemon juice. Let set until it starts to thicken. Add carrots, pineapple and whipped cream. Let stand overnight.

Ina Wiedemann

New! Lemon & Orange Jell-O Salad

3 oz. orange Jell-O
1 16 oz. can crushed pineapple
3 Tbsp. lemon juice

½ tsp. salt
3 c. grated carrots
2 c. boiling water

Add salt and lemon juice to boiling water and add Jell-O to dissolve. Drain pineapple and add enough water to make 1½ cups liquid. Chill. When it starts to jell, add pineapple and carrots.

Fern Koelsch

Lime Jell-O Salad

6 oz. lime Jell-O
2 c. hot water
6 oz. can crushed pineapple

1 oz. pimento chopped
4 oz. celery, chopped

Dissolve Jell-O in hot water. Cool and add pineapple, pimento and celery. Can be put in bowl or mold.

Fern Koelsch

New! *Grated Cheese Salad*

1 box orange Jell-O
1 c. boiling water
1 c. crushed pineapple and juice
½ c. sugar

1 c. whipped cream
1 c. nuts
1 c. grated Longhorn cheese

Combine Jell-O, boiling water, pineapple with juice and sugar. Chill until almost set. Fold in whipped cream, nuts and grated cheese.

Grace Clark

Glorified Minute Rice

⅔ c. Minute rice
⅔ c. water
½ tsp. salt
¾ c. drained, crushed pineapple

½ c. miniature marshmallows
⅓ c. chopped pecans
6 diced maraschino cherries
2 c. sweetened whipped cream

Combine rice, water, pineapple juice and salt in saucepan. Mix just to moisten rice. Bring quickly to a boil over high heat. Cover and simmer 5 minutes. Remove from heat. Let stand 5 minutes. Add marshmallows, cherries, pineapple and nuts. Cool to room temperature. Fold in whipped cream. Chill 1 hour before serving.

Christiane Sauls

Pineapple Salad

No. 2 can crushed pineapple
1 (3 oz.) pkg. lime Jell-O
3 oz. pkg. Philadelphia cream cheese

1 c. chopped celery
1 c. chopped pecans or walnuts
1 c. whipping cream, whipped

Heat pineapple and Jell-O and cool slightly. Add cream cheese. Dissolve cheese into mixture and let set slightly. Add celery and pecans. Fold in whipping cream. Place in desired dish and refrigerate. (If desired, you may heat ½ package lime Jell-O and when cool, pour over top.) This is very good.

Aline Honea

Strawberry Jell-O Salad

2 family size pkg. strawberry Jell-O
4 c. hot water
2 small cans crushed pineapple

2 (10 oz.) boxes frozen strawberries
2 mashed bananas
1 c. pecans

Filling:

1 (16 oz.) pkg. cream cheese

2 c. sour cream

Make Jell-O as directed on package. Pour about ⅓ of Jell-O into bundt cake pan. Let this set up in refrigerator. Spoon filling over jelled layer. Set. Pour pineapple, strawberries, bananas and pecans into remaining Jell-O and spoon on top set filling. Refrigerate until well set. Unmold. Using Pam on pan helps it to unmold easily.

Joyce Nowakowski

Cherry Stuff Salad

1(8 oz.) Cool Whip
1 can Eagle Brand
1 large can crushed pineapple
1 c. coconut

1 c. mini marshmallows
1 can cherry pie filling
½ c. chopped pecans

Mix all ingredients in bowl. Chill and serve.

Suzanne Visnieski

Cherry Salad

1 large pkg. cherry Jell-O
1 c. boiling water
1 can crushed pineapple and juice

1 can cherry pie filling
1 c. pecans

Dissolve Jell-O in boiling water. Add remaining ingredients and mix. Chill before serving.

Elenora Lipinski

🐦 Cardinal Salad

1 pkg. lemon Jell-O
1 c. boiling water
¾ c. beet juice
3 Tbsp.vinegar
½ tsp. salt

2 tsp. onion juice or grated onion
1 Tbsp. horseradish
¾ c. celery, diced
1 c. cooked beets, diced

Dissolve Jell-O in boiling water. Add beet juice, vinegar, salt, onion juice and horseradish. When slightly thickened, add celery and beets.

Mrs. A. J. Murphy
Mrs. A. J. Murphy is Father James' mother.

🐦 Overnight Salad

1 (29 oz.) can fruit cocktail
1 (20 oz.) can crushed pineapple
1 (11 oz.) can mandarin oranges
4 Tbsp. sugar
4 Tbsp. vinegar or lemon juice

2 beaten eggs
1 c. whipped cream
1 (10 oz.) pkg. miniature
   marshmallows

Drain fruit well and set aside. Over low heat, cook sugar, vinegar and eggs until thick, watching carefully. Set aside to cool. Whip cream and fold into cooled dressing mixture. Fold dressing into fruit and marshmallows. Cover and refrigerate overnight.

Carolyn Rudek

🐦 Watergate Salad

1 large tub Cool Whip
1 box instant pistachio pudding
1 can crushed pineapple

2 c. small marshmallows
1 c. chopped pecans

Mix pudding and Cool Whip. Blend well. Add remaining ingredients and chill.

Martha Greenlee

🐦 Pasta Salad

1 (12 oz.) pkg. of any type of
  (squiggly) pasta noodles
1 bunch fresh broccoli
1 head cauliflower
3 tomatoes
4 carrots

1 c. raisins and 1 c. mushrooms
  (optional)
12 oz. bottle salad dressing (with oil
  in it)
1 pkg. dry Zesty Italian salad
  dressing (other kinds work, too)

Cook pasta noodles according to directions. Chop vegetable into bite-size pieces. Add entire bottle of dressing and package of dry dressing. (Do not add more wet ingredients than that.) Chill and serve.

This recipe introduced me to "ugh" vegetables which I now enjoy a lot.

Jo-Jo Laws

🐦 Pasta Vegetable Salad

1 (12 oz.) pkg. rainbow pasta twirls,
  cooked and drained
3 chicken breasts, boiled boned and
  cut in bite-size pieces
5 to 6 carrots, sliced and cooked

1 bunch broccoli, cut in bite-size
  pieces and cooked
¼ to ½ c. grated parmesan cheese
Seasoned salt
Red Wine vinegar and oil

Combine pasta, chicken, broccoli, carrots and cheese. Season to taste with the seasoned salt, vinegar and oil. I use about ¼ to ⅓ cup oil and probably 15 to 20 shakes of vinegar.

Debbie Raught

Unmolding Gelatin

If you wet the dish on which the gelatin is to be unmolded, it can be moved around until centered.

Vegetable Pasta

¼ c. vegetable oil
1 medium sliced squash
1 medium diced onion
1 c. sliced mushrooms
4 oz. Chicken pea pods
1 large clove garlic

9 oz. vermicelli
2 large chopped tomatoes
4 oz. sliced ham
1½ tsp. salt
Dash of pepper
¼ c. Parmesan cheese

Heat oil. Add squash, onion, mushrooms, pea pods and garlic. Cook 5 minutes until crisp tender. Add tomatoes, ham, salt basil and pepper. Cook 2 minutes until heated through. Cook and drain pasta. Add to vegetables along with ¼ cup Parmesan. Mix well.

Diane Hanna

Stir-Fry Salad

1 (10 oz.) pkg. Bird's Eye Japanese
   style stir-fry veggies
1 Tbsp. wine vinegar

2 tsp. soy sauce
2 c. watercress or shredded lettuce
2 tsp. toasted sesame seed

Cook stir-fry vegetable as directed on package, adding vinegar and soy sauce with the seasoning and water. Arrange watercress on serving platter; spoon on hot vegetables. Sprinkle with sesame seed and serve at once. Makes 4 servings. Contains 100 calories each.

Carol Brookes

Taco Salad

1 lb. ground meat
1 can Ranch Style beans
½ head shredded lettuce
2 or 3 tomatoes, chopped

1 bottle Catalina salad dressing
1 medium size bag Fritos
2 c. grated Cheddar cheese

Brown meat. Season with salt and pepper. Drain off all fat and juices. Layer ingredients in large salad bowl in order given. When serving go to bottom of bowl so part of all ingredients are served.

Darline Ruyle

 Taco Salad

1 lb. hamburger meat
1 head lettuce
1 large tomato
Longhorn cheese
1 bunch green onions

1 small can chopped black olives
1 small can chopped green chilies
3 ripe avocados
1 can Mexican style beans
Picante sauce

Fry meat, season with salt, pepper and garlic salt. Drain and let cool. Dice up lettuce, tomatoes, onions and avocados. Put in large bowl. Add grated cheese, olives, green chilies and drained beans. Add meat and mix all together. Add picante sauce to taste. Serve with tortilla chips or use in taco shells. Very fast and good. Serves 6.

Cindy Garrett

Taco Salad

½ head lettuce, chopped
1 tomato, chopped
Onion to taste
½ bag Doritos, crushed
¾ bottle Catalina salad dressing

½ c. chili bean
1 lb. hamburger meat, cooked
1 c. cheese, shredded
Salt and pepper to taste

Brown meat and drain well. Let cool. Combine lettuce, tomato, onion, beans and meat. Add lightly crushed Doritos, cheese, salt and pepper. Pour dressing over salad and toss. Serve.

Beverly Fortelney Winstead

Polish saying:

"Kto Nie Dhuzny Ten Bogaty." — *He is rich who owes nothing.*

Submitted by Dora Lee Kusek

Taco Salad

1 large onion	*Longhorn cheese*
1 bag corn chips or Doritos, mashed	*Green Goddess dressing or creamy*
1 large tomato	*cucumber*
Lettuce	*Ranch Style beans*

Layer these, one layer at a time: Can beans (drained), layer lettuce, onion, tomatoes, chips, dressing and layer cheese. Let set 1 hour before serving. Use deep salad bowl, 8 inches and 3 inches deep. Serves 8. This can be made into as many servings as you like.

Donna Wyskup

Salad Dressing

1 c. vinegar	*1 tsp. celery seed*
1 c. sugar	*1 tsp. black pepper*
1 Tbsp. garlic powder	*2 c. oil*

Mix vinegar, sugar, garlic powder and celery seed. Boil about 5 minutes. Cool. Add pepper and oil. Mix together well.

Cora Rudek

Salad Dressing

1 c. mayonnaise	*1 pkg. Hidden Valley Ranch*
1 c. plain yogurt	*Dressing*
1 c. sour cream	

Mix all ingredients together well.

Glena Jorski

Salad Dressing

1 c. oil
½ c. sugar
¼ c. vinegar

⅓ c. catsup
2 Tbsp. Worcestershire sauce
1 Tbsp. minced onion

Put ingredients in container with tight fitting lid and shake well. Store in refrigerator.

Karen Kuhns

Diet Tomato Dressing

15 oz. can tomato juice
7 oz. Wesson oil
1 stick celery
½ medium onion

½ medium pepper
¼ tsp. chili salt
¼ tsp. garlic powder

Put all ingredients in a blender and blend until everything is well blended. Chill.

Pat Hopcus

Tomato Soup Salad Dressing

1 c. salad oil
1 c. vinegar
1 c. tomato soup
1 Tbsp. Worcestershire sauce
1 Tbsp. sugar

1 tsp. salt
1 tsp. dry mustard
1 tsp. paprika
1 clove garlic, minced
1 small onion, finely chopped

Mix all ingredients well. Makes 4 cups.

Glena Jorski

New! Beet Barszcz

2 qts. vegetable or meat stock
2 bunches fresh beets with greens
¼ Tbsp. lemon juice

1 Tbsp. sugar
1 Tbsp. flour
⅛ c. sour cream

Wash the beets and greens. Cut into small cubes and add to boiling vegetable or meat stock. Cook 10 minutes. Add sugar, blend the flour with the sour cream and then add 2 Tbsp. of the hot stock and mix. Stir the mixture into the soup and allow it to heat to the boiling point.

Katie Magott

Broccoli Cheese Soup

1 can cream of chicken soup
1 pkg. frozen chopped broccoli,
  cooked and drained

1 soup can of milk
5 thick slices Velveeta cheese
Salt and pepper to taste

In pot blend soup, broccoli and milk. Simmer. Add cheese, salt and pepper. Bring to boil.

Becky Spaeth

Broccoli Cheese Soup

6 Tbsp. butter
1 Tbsp. onion
5 Tbsp. flour
1 c. chicken broth
1 c. milk

¾ tsp. salt
Dash of pepper
1 pkg. frozen broccoli
1 to 1½ c. grated cheese

On stove top in pan, melt butter. Brown the onion and then blend in the flour. Add broth, milk salt and pepper. Let thicken. Add chopped broccoli. Add cheese. Stir until cheese is melted.

Joyce Nowakowski

Broccoli-Cheese Soup

⅓ c. chopped onion
6 c. water
2 Tbsp. chicken bouillon (2 cubes)
6 c. half & half

2 boxes frozen chopped broccoli
1 lb. Velveeta cheese, cubed
Salt and pepper to taste
2 Tbsp. butter or margarine

Saute onion in butter or margarine. Mix water, bouillon, salt, pepper and onion in large pot and bring to boil. Add half & half and bring back to boil. (Careful it doesn't scorch.) Add broccoli and Velveeta. Stir until melted. Simmer for awhile. Freeze well, cheese and all.

Greg Winters

🐦 New! Clam Chowder

7 diced potatoes
1 grated carrot
2 celery stalks, chopped
½ chopped onion
3 cans (10 oz. total) minced clams,
  drained

Juice from clams
2 Tbsp. cornstarch
¼ c. margarine (½ stick)
Salt pepper
Milk

Boil potatoes with carrot, celery and onion until tender. Drain most of the water. Barely leave some. (About one hour for total preparation.)

Add the minced clams, drained (save juice). Mix juice with two heaping tablespoons of cornstarch. Add to mixture. Add ½ stick margarine, salt and pepper. Cover with milk. Cook on low until thickened — about 4-6 hours.

Option: little bit of diced ham.

Becky Spaeth

🐦 Czarnina - Chocolate Duck Soup

1 duck or goose
¾ c. blood* from duck
2 to 3 Tbsp. vinegar
1 Tbsp. salt or to taste
1 tsp. allspice
2 bay leaves
½ large onion, diced
1 Tbsp. vinegar

½ c. raisins
2 c. prunes
2 small apples (optional)
¼ to ½ c. sugar (optional)
Water
3 Tbsp. vinegar
2 c. water
¾ c. flour

To kill duck, pluck feathers from the base of the head. Leave a hole with sharp knife, drain blood in container, about ½ to ¾ cup of blood. Mix ½ to ¾ cup of blood with 2 to 3 tablespoons vinegar. Mix well and chill. Dress duck and cut up in pieces. Cook in large deep pot or kettle. When duck is ½ done, add 1 tablespoon salt or to taste, 1 tsp. allspice, the bay leaves, ½ of good size onion, chunked, 1 tablespoon vinegar, the raisins, the prunes, the apples, quartered and the sugar if desired. Let cook until duck is good and done. Add water to fill kettle. Remove duck, then add duck blood mixture of the blood and vinegar already mixed, plus adding 3 tablespoon vinegar, 2 cups water and ¾ cup flour. Mix well. Add the blood sauce to the water, stirring big and fast. Let boil 5 to 10 minutes. To heat meat, add to soup just before serving then remove and serve separately.

*Chocolate syrup with the vinegar added can be substituted for the blood mixture.

Minnie Nowakowski

Cream Of Jalapeno Soup

3 Tbsp. butter
3 Tbsp. flour
2 c. whipping cream
3 c. chicken broth
5 Tbsp. butter or margarine
1 large onion, minced
1 large carrot, peeled and diced

1 large green pepper, chopped
3 jalapeno peppers, seeded and
   diced
1 c. grated Swiss cheese (3 oz.)
1 c. grated Cheddar cheese
Salt to taste

Mix butter in large heavy skillet or saucepan over low heat. Add flour and stir 3 minutes. Mix in broth and cream. Increase heat and bring to boil, stirring constantly. Reduce heat and simmer until thickened, stirring occasionally, about 10 minutes.

Meanwhile, melt about 1 tablespoon butter in heavy small skillet over low heat. Add onion, carrot and green peppers. Cook until soft, stirring occasionally about 8 minutes. Mix in chilies. Add both cheese to cream mixture and stir until melted. Mix in vegetables. Season with salt and serve with tortilla chips.

For a spicier soup, add more chilies. This is not very hot.

Mary Keller

Italian Bean Soup

1 pkg. pinto beans
1 large onion, chopped
1 large clove garlic, chopped
3 potatoes, cut up in small chunks

1 small pkg. spaghetti cut in ½
2 tsp. butter or oil
Hunk of salt pork or meat

Soak pinto beans overnight. Wash them out after soaking. Cook in salted water or add salt pork or meat. When beans are almost done, remove meat. Add onions, garlic, potatoes and oil. Be sure you have enough liquid in your pan. If not, add water. When potatoes are tender and tasty, add your broken spaghetti pieces. Cook till done and if you cooked your meat with your beans, you have your meat and soup to enjoy.

Orsola Wheeler
Mary Mahan

Italian Holiday Soup

2 small whole chickens
2 onions, cut up
3 diced celery stalks
3 diced carrots
3 diced potatoes
1 lb. hamburger

4 eggs
1 (10 oz.) pkg. frozen turnip greens
   or kale, diced
Salt
Pepper
Celery Salt

Make chicken broth with chickens, onion, celery, carrots, potatoes and spices. After cooking take chicken out of broth and dice as much as you can. Put diced chicken back into broth. While broth is cooking, make small meat balls, brown and let drain. Whip up the 4 eggs. Pour into broth. Let cook 10 minutes. Stir like egg drop soup. Put in diced greens and tiny meatballs. Mix all together and pray you have a nice holiday soup.

Nancy Montalvo

Minestrone Soup

3 cans Campbell's minestrone soup
1 can whole tomatoes, chopped
1 can red Ro-Tel, chopped

2 cans pinto beans
1 lb. ground chuck or chili meat
Worcestershire sauce

Brown meat in skillet with worcestershire sauce. Drain meat and add all other ingredients. Cook in a crock pot for 1 hour on HIGH or 4 hours on LOW.

Mary K. Hornbeck

Potato-Celery Soup

4 c. peeled and cubed potatoes
1 c. diced celery
½ c. chopped onion
2 c. water
3 chicken bouillon cubes

2½ c. milk
5 Tbsp. butter
Salt and pepper to taste
Chopped parsley for garnish

Combine potatoes, celery, onion, water, bouillon cubes and pepper in saucepan. Cook over moderate heat until vegetables are tender about 15 minutes. Most of water will be absorbed. Chill and store in refrigerator in covered container until ready to use. To prepare soup, add ½ cup milk and 2 tablespoons butter for each cup of vegetable mixture used. Add salt and pepper to taste. Heat and serve. (Do not boil).

Another method may be a brown roux may be made into a thick gravy that was made with hot water instead of the milk. This was learned from my mother, Frances Magott.

Mrs. Bill Hopcus

New! Potato Cheese Soup

2 Tbsp. butter or margarine
6 large potatoes, peeled and diced
2 medium onions, chopped
3 stalks celery, chopped
½ tsp. salt

Pepper, to taste
2 c. chicken broth
1 c. half-and-half
2 c. cheese, shredded

Melt the butter in a medium saucepan. Add the potatoes, onions, celery, salt and pepper and saute about 5 minutes. Stir frequently. Add the chicken broth. Cover the soup and simmer until the vegetables are tender.

Pour the soup into a blender or food processor and blend until smooth. Return to saucepan and heat. Stir in the half-and-half and mix. Add cheese such as American or Colby. Heat until the cheese is melted. Serves about four.

Judy Seikel

New! Dynia Zupa

(Pumpkin Soup)

2 c. mashed fresh-cooked pumpkin
2 c. of sweet cream
Homogenized milk

¼ c. sugar, more or less
Salt to taste

Combine all items above with enough milk to make consistency of soup. Bring to a boil. Serve immediately with cooked egg noodles or cooked navy beans.

Soup will thicken, dilute with more milk as needed to reheat.

Elizabeth Drew Magott
in memory of Mary Chwalinski Magott

San Antonio Stew

2 lb. stew meat
2 Tbsp. vegetable oil
1 (10 ½ oz.) can condensed beef broth
1 c. hot water
1 (8 oz.) jar picante sauce
1 medium onion, cut in ½-inch wedges
¼ c. chopped parsley
1 tsp. salt

1 tsp. ground cumin
2 cloves garlic, minced
1 (16 oz.) can tomatoes
3 medium carrots, sliced
2 ears fresh or frozen corn, cut into 1-inch pieces
2 medium zucchini, cut into 1-inch pieces
½ c. cold water
2 Tbsp. flour

Brown meat, half at a time, in hot oil. Put meat in Dutch oven. Add broth, hot water, picante sauce, onion, parsley, salt, cumin and garlic. Bring to a boil. Reduce heat. Cover and let simmer 1 hour or until tender. Drain and coarsely chop the tomatoes, reserving juice. Add tomatoes, juice, carrots, corn and zucchini to Dutch oven. Cover and simmer 25 minutes. Gradually add cold water to flour, mixing until smooth. Gradually stir this into stew. Heat to boiling, stirring constantly, until thickened.

Cora Rudek

 Bigos

1 to 2 jars sauerkraut, rinsed and
    drained
1 onion, chopped
10 black peppercorns
2 bay leaves

Salt to taste
Pepper to taste
Roast pork
Tomato paste (optional)

Cut the roast pork in bite-size pieces and brown in skillet. Saute onion. Add pork, peppercorns, bay leaves, salt, pepper and sauerkraut to skillet with onion. Cook until done (slowly), about 1 hour. Add water or vegetable stock as needed. If a tart taste is desired, 1 can of tomato paste can be added toward the end of cooking.

Irena Pryk

Sauerkraut Soup

1½ pork spareribs, cut into 2 ribs
    each
1½ qt. water
1½ tsp. salt
1½ tsp. pepper

½ qt. sauerkraut, drained
2 eggs
½ c. cold water
¼ c. flour

In a large pot, bring ribs, 1½ quarts water, salt and pepper to a boil. Reduce heat. Cover and cook about 2 hours. Add ½ quart sauerkraut, drained. Beat 2 eggs. Add ½ cup cold water and ¼ cup flour. Add this to meat-kraut mixture. Bring to a boil and cook 2-3 minutes longer.

Father Augustine Horne, O.S.B.

An After Christmas tradition

On the second day of Christmas, a Hunter's Stew — Bigos — is traditionally prepared from sausage and leftover meats.

Steak Soup

5 c. water
2 small onions, chopped
10 oz. mixed vegetables
3 stalks celery, chopped
2 carrots
1 tsp. pepper

1 Tbsp. monosodium glutamate
 (MSG)
1 lb. chopped steak, browned
6 bouillon cubes
½ c. butter
½ c. flour

   Mix all ingredients but the ½ cup of butter and the ½ cup of flour. Cook on stove top on low or in crock pot. One hour before serving, melt butter and mix in flour and pour the mixture in the soup.

Joyce Nowakowski

New! Sweet-Sour Soup

2 lbs. cooked ham
Sugar to taste
Vinegar to taste

6 c. water
12 prunes
2 Tbsp. cornstarch

   To two pounds of cooked ham, add sugar and vinegar to 6 cups water, to suit your taste. My family liked it sweet and sour. Cook 12 prunes until tender. Thicken them with two tablespoons of cornstarch. Serve over Sad Dumplings.

Pauline Piotrowicz

De-Fatting foods

   A small amount of baking soda added to gravy will eliminate excess grease.

   Drop a lettuce leaf into a pot of homemade soup to absorb excess grease from the top.

   If time allows, the best method of removing fat is refrigeration until the fat hardens. If you put a piece of wax paper over the top of the soup, etc. It can be peeled right off, along with the hardened fat.

   Ice cubes will also eliminate the fat from soup and stew. Just drop a few into the pot and stir. The fat will cling to the cubes. Discard the cubes before they melt. Or, wrap ice cubes in paper towel or cheesecloth and skim over the top.

Oven Stew

2 lb. chuck roast, cut in small pieces
5 carrots, cut in 2-inch lengths
5 celery stalks, cut in 2-inch lengths
2 large potatoes, cut in 8 pieces
1 (6 oz.) can tomato juice

2 Tbsp. cooking tapioca
2 Tbsp. brown sugar
2 Tbsp. white sugar
Dash of pepper
Garlic powder

Place roast, carrots, celery, potatoes and onions in 9"x13" baking dish. Cover with remaining ingredients. Bake 4 hours at 250°. Be sure to cover pan tightly with aluminum foil. No need to check during baking. If carrots are thick, cut in half lengthwise. Rinse container from tomato mixture with ½ cup water and add to mixture.

Elenora Lipinski

Polish Fresh Mushroom Soup

½ lb. mushrooms (can use dried)
3 Tbsp. butter
¼ tsp. caraway seed
½ tsp. paprika
1 Tbsp. flour

4 c. chicken stock
1 egg yolk
2 Tbsp. fresh chopped dill
1 c. sour cream

Wash and dry mushrooms, cutting off tough stems. Slice and saute in the butter with caraway seed and paprika for 1 minutes or little longer. Sprinkle with flour. Blend well. Add chicken stock a little at a time. Simmer slowly, covered, for 30 minutes. Meanwhile, whip the egg yolk with a fork until creamy. Add your cream and dill, mixing well. Put this into a soup tureen and pour the hot soup over it slowly, stirring with a whisk to mix thoroughly. Serves 6.

Irene Miller
From my mother-in-law,
Frances Visnieski

New! Wash Day Soup

1 lb. ground round steak	2 Tbsp. chopped parsley
2 eggs	Pepper to taste
½ c. cracker crumbs	Salt to taste
1 tsp. grated onion	

Topping:

Grated cheese

Combine all ingredients for meat balls and mix thoroughly. Shape into balls, drop into 3 pints boiling water, lightly salted. Reduce heat, simmer 20 minutes.

Serve with toast and grated cheese.

Rose Throckmorton

Polish saying:

"Jak sobie kto posicile, tak sie wyspi." — As one makes his bed, so he must lie in it.

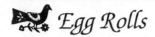 # Egg Rolls

1 lb. hamburger	4 chopped carrots
½ onion, chopped	1 can drained bean sprouts
1 tsp. salt	Soy sauce
½ head cabbage, chopped	Egg roll wrappers
Oil	Water

Brown hamburger, onion and salt. Drain. Saute cabbage in a little oil. When cabbage begins to soften, add carrots and pinch of water. When almost done, add bean sprouts and a little soy sauce. Drain in colander until cool. Add hamburger to colander. Wrap in egg roll wrappers (like a diaper). Seal with a few drops water on each fold. Fry in oil that has been heated 10 minutes.

Becky Spaeth

 # Egg Rolls

2 lb. hamburger	1 tsp. sugar
3 cans bean sprouts	1 tsp. salt
2 cans bamboo shoots	1 tsp. Accent
2 cans water chestnuts	1 tsp. ginger powder
6 stalks celery	6 Tbsp. soy sauce
1 small box fresh mushrooms	4 Tbsp. oil
1 medium onion	2 pkg. egg roll wrappers

Brown hamburger meat and drain, then add sugar, salt, Accent, ginger powder, oil and soy sauce. Heat approximately 5 minutes on simmer. In food processor chop rest of ingredients. Add all to hamburger meat mixture. Heat on simmer for 5 more minutes. Dump mixture in a strainer. Stuff the egg roll wrappers, then deep fry until golden brown.

Terry Fortelney

🐦 Golabki - Cabbage Rolls

1 head cabbage
1 lb. ground beef
½ lb. ground pork or veal
½ c. rice
1 egg

1 onion, chopped
2 Tbsp. butter
Salt to taste
Pepper to taste

Remove the core from a head of cabbage with a sharp knife. Scald the cabbage in boiling water. Remove large outer leaves as they wilt. Cool before using. Wash rice in cold water and stir into 2 quarts of boiling, salted water. Boil 10 minutes and strain. Run cold water through rice in strainer. This rice is only ½ cooked now.

Saute onion in butter until it becomes transparent. Do not let it turn yellow. Combine with meat, egg, rice and seasonings and mix well. Spread each leaf with meat, about ½-inch thick. Fold the 2 opposite sides and roll, starting with 1 of the open ends. Fasten with a toothpick.

To cook, place the cabbage rolls in a baking dish. Cover with 5 slices of bacon and roast, uncovered, for 2 hours at 300°. Baste from time to time. Or brown the golabki in frying pan. Add a cup of water or tomato puree and simmer slowly for 2 hours. Watch closely and add more water if necessary. Golabki may be served with mushroom sauce, tomato sauce, or sour cream.

When reheated the next day, they are even better.

Irena Pryk
Victoria B. Miller

🐦 Golabki - Cabbage Rolls

1 lb. ground beef
½ lb. ground pork sausage
4 c. rice, cooked
1 large onion, chopped fine

2 Tbsp. butter
Salt and pepper
1 can sauerkraut

Remove core from whole head of cabbage. Scald the cabbage in boiling water. Remove a few leaves at a time (as they wilt). Cool. Cook rice to make 4 cups. Add butter, onion, salt and pepper. Add meat (raw) and mix thoroughly. Spread a large spoonful of rice-meat mixture on leaves, one at a time. Roll leaves up and place in baking dish. Spread raw sauerkraut on top of each layer of cabbage rolls. Pour sauerkraut juice over the top of rolls and bake slowly for 1 hour at 300°.

Dora Lee Kusek

Stuffed Cabbage Rolls - Golabki

1 small head cabbage
1 lb. lean ground beef
½ lb. lean ground pork or sausage
   (optional)
1 tsp. salt

¼ tsp. pepper
1½ c. cooked rice
2 Tbsp. fresh or frozen chopped
   dill or ½ tsp. dried dill weed
1 c. beef broth

Cut core from cabbage. Immerse cabbage head in boiling water about 3 minutes. Pull off and save about 12 outer leaves. Cut out center vein of cabbage leaves, keeping each leaf in 1 piece. Chop remaining cabbage. Cook chopped cabbage, uncovered, in boiling water for 2-3 minutes. Drain and set aside. Cook ground beef and pork and onions until meat is browned and onions tender. Drain off excess fat. Add salt and pepper. Stir in rice and dill. (I like my rice about half cooked for this.) Remove from heat.

Place about ¼ cup of meat mixture on each cabbage leaf; fold in sides. Starting at unfolded edge, roll up each leaf, making sure folded sides are included in roll. Place half of the chopped cabbage in the bottom of a 13"x9"x2" baking dish. Arrange cabbage rolls, seam side down, atop chopped cabbage. Cover with remaining chopped cabbage. Pour broth over all. Cover and bake in 350° oven for 1 hour. Serves 6.

Rosie L. Klimkowski

To Eliminate Odors

Add a cup of water to the bottom portion of the broiling pan before sliding into the oven, to absorb smoke and grease.

A few teaspoons of sugar and cinnamon slowly burned on top of the stove will hide unpleasant cooking odors and make your family think you've been baking all day. Be careful not to scorch or burn the sugar cinnamon mixture. Just a short time will do.

A lump of butter or a few teaspoons of cooking oil added to water when boiling rice, noodles, or spaghetti will prevent boiling over.

Rubbing the inside of the cooking vessel with vegetable oil will also prevent noodles, spaghetti and similar starches from boiling over.

A few drops of lemon juice added to simmering rice will keep the grains separate.

Stuffed Cabbage Rolls - Golabki

1 whole head cabbage (about 4 lb.)
Boiling salted water
1 chopped onion
2 Tbsp. oil or bacon drippings
1½ lb. ground beef
¼ to ½ lb. ground fresh pork
    sausage

1½ c. cooked rice
1 tsp. salt
¼ tsp. pepper
1 can tomatoes or 2 cans
    condensed tomato soup
2½ c. water
1 qt. sauerkraut

Remove core from cabbage. Place whole head in a large kettle of boiling salted water. Cover and cook 3 minutes or until softened enough to pull off individual leaves. Repeat to remove all large leaves (about 30). Cut thick center stem from each leaf. Chop remaining cabbage. Saute onion in oil or bacon drippings. Add meat, rice, salt and pepper. Mix thoroughly. Place heaping tablespoon of meat mixture on each cabbage leaf. Tuck sides over filling while rolling leaf around filling. Secure with wooden toothpick. Place ½ the chopped cabbage and kraut on bottom of a large Dutch oven. Fill with layers of the cabbage rolls. Cover with remaining chopped cabbage and sauerkraut. Mix tomato soup with water until smooth and pour over rolls or pour can of tomatoes over rolls, if using tomatoes. Cover and bring to boil. Reduce heat and simmer 1½ hours. Serve with the sauce.

Frances Rychlec

Mom's Cabbage Rolls

1 lb. ground beef
1 tsp. salt
¼ tsp. pepper
2 Tbsp. chopped onion
1 c. cooked rice

1 egg
8 large cabbage leaves
1 can tomato wedges
1 can sauerkraut
½ c. water

Boil water and pour over cabbage leaves. Let stand 5 minutes. Add seasoning to meat. Mix in onion, rice and egg. Roll a portion of filling into each leaf, fastening ends with toothpicks. Place cabbage rolls in skillet. Pour the can of tomatoes over the rolls and then the can of sauerkraut. Cook slowly over low heat for 1 hour.

Judy Seikel

Stuffed Cabbage - Golabki

1 head cabbage	¼ tsp. pepper
1 lb. ground beef	1 large onion, sliced
1 onion, chopped	2 Tbsp. chicken fat or other oil
1 clove garlic, chopped	¾ large can of tomato juice
1 c. rice (uncooked)	1 c. sauerkraut with juice
1½ tsp. salt	1 c. water

Core cabbage head and put in a pot of boiling water. Remove from heat and let stand for 15 minutes. Separate whole leaves.

For filling, mix thoroughly the ground beef, onion, garlic, uncooked rice, salt and pepper. Make 18 cabbage rolls, placing a spoonful of meat mixture on the leaf near the base and rolling the cabbage loosely.

In Dutch oven, fry 1 large onion, sliced in rings in the fat until onions are golden. Add tomato juice and sauerkraut with juice. Arrange cabbage rolls in the Dutch oven with tomato mixture. Pour a cup of water over the rolls and tomato mixture. Cover and simmer over low heat for 1½-2 hours or until rice is soft. Serves 6.

Rosie L. Klimkowski

Cabbage Rolls

12 lg. cabbage leaves	⅛ tsp. pepper
1 lb. ground beef	2 Tbsp. fat
1 c. cooked rice	2 Tbsp. brown sugar
1 tsp. parsley, finely chopped	1 can tomato soup plus ½ can of
1 egg	water
⅔ c. milk	1 bay leaf
¼ c. onion, finely chipped	4 cloves
1 tsp. salt	

Remove outer leaves of a large head of cabbage. Drop 1 at a time into boiling, salted water and parboil for 5 minutes or until soft. Drain and trim out the thick center vein. Combine ground meat, rice parsley, egg, milk, ½ of the chopped onion, salt, and pepper. Place a spoonful on each cabbage leaf. Roll it up and fasten it with a toothpick. Melt the fat in a heavy skillet; brown the cabbage rolls, turning to brown evenly. sprinkle with sugar and cover with soup and water. Add remaining onion, bay leaf and cloves. Cover and simmer about 1½ hours. Add more water as needed. Cabbage rolls can also be baked, uncovered, at about 325° for about 1½ hours. Remove bay leaf.

Joyce Nowakowski

Cabbage Rolls

1 head cabbage	¼ tsp. poultry seasoning
1 lb. ground beef	½ c. rice, partially cooked
½ lb. ground pork	1 egg
1 onion, chopped fine	3 Tbsp. butter
2 Tbsp. vinegar	Salt and pepper
1 tsp. salt	1 c. hot water

Wilt cabbage leaves by scalding in boiling water, to which 2 tablespoons vinegar and 1 tsp. salt have been added. Drain; cool in cold water and pat dry. Cut out heavy ribs. Saute onion in butter until transparent. Combine meat, egg, rice and seasoning. Spread each leaf with 2 tablespoons of mixture. Fold the 2 opposite sides and roll, starting with one of the open ends. Place in pan. Add butter and 1 cup hot water. Simmer slowly for 2 hours. May be served with mushroom sauce, tomato sauce or sour cream. Delicious reheated the next day.

From Polish Heirloom Recipes.
Helen Brown

Polish Pierogi

½ bag or l lb. ctn. dry cottage cheese	1 egg
2 egg yolks	⅔ c. water
Lots of salt and pepper	1 to 2 tsp. salt
3½ c. flour	1 pt. half & half
	½ stick butter or margarine

Stir together cottage cheese, egg yolks, salt and pepper and set aside for the filling.

Mix flour, 1 egg, ⅔ cup water and salt for dough. Work together and roll out on floured board to the consistency of pie crust. Cut into about 4-inch squares. Fill middle of each square with the cottage cheese filling and fold dough over, sealing the edges of dough and pressing together to seal. Drop into boiling water until it floats good (about 5 minutes). Remove with slotted spoon and put in baking dish. Pour 1 pint of Half & Half and ½ stick of melted butter over the bowl of boiled and drained pierogi, then cover and bake in 300° oven for about 15-20 minutes.

Lena Martin

Polish Pierogi

Dough:

4 c. flour
2 eggs

1 Tbsp. cooking oil
1½ c. milk

Filling:

10 medium potatoes, cooked and
    drained
1 large can sauerkraut, cooked
4 slices American cheese

2 medium onions, browned in butter
Salt and pepper to taste
Boiling water

Topping:

1 onion, chopped
1 c. boiling water
Salt and pepper

½ pt. sour cream
¼ c. water

Combine flour, eggs and oil into pie dough consistency. Slowly add 1½ cups milk. Knead it until blended and set aside for 20 minutes in a covered bowl. Roll out dough as thin as possible and cut into 4-inch circles.

Mash filling ingredients together. Fill ½ of circle, then fold and carefully seal all edges of dough and let stand at least 10 minutes. Drop pierogi into boiling water a few at a time for 10 minutes or until all pierogi rise to the top of the boiling water. Serve with topping made by browning onion in 1 cup boiling water. Add salt and pepper. After cooling for 10 minutes add ½ pint sour cream, ¼ up water and mix.

Rosalie Jorski

Pierogi

Dough:

2½ c. flour
½ c. water

3 eggs
1 tsp. salt

Filling:

1 large can sauerkraut
1 large onion

2 Tbsp. margarine

Coating:

½ c. margarine
1 onion

Boiling, salted water

Mix dough ingredients together and form a ball. Knead until satiny. Let stand 10 minutes.

In a saucepan, bring the sauerkraut to a boil. Drain off juice. Cover with water and bring to a boil a second time. Drain and squeeze excess water out of sauerkraut.

Chop onion and fry in about 2 tablespoons of margarine. Add sauerkraut and simmer for 10 minutes, stirring so it does not burn. Add salt and pepper to taste. Let cool 1 hour.

Roll out dough on a floured surface. Cut into 3-4 inch squares. Place 1½-2 tablespoons of sauerkraut filling on square. Fold corner over to make a triangle and pinch sides together to seal.

Drop into boiling, salted water and let boil for 10 minutes. Remove from water carefully with a wooden spoon.

Have ready a skillet with ½ cup of margarine melted and a chopped onion, fried until brown. Place cooked pierogi in skillet and coat with mixture. Place them on a platter. Makes about 2 dozen.

Helen Lukaszek

Quick Pierogi

2 c. all-purpose flour
2 eggs

½ tsp. salt
⅓ c. water

Sausage Filling:

10 oz. Polish sausage, skinned and chopped
¼ c. dry bread crumbs

½ c. grated cheese or chopped mushrooms
1 egg

Mound flour on a bread board and make a well in center. Drop eggs and salt into well. Add water and working from the center to the outside of the flour mound, mix flour into liquid in center with 1 hand. Knead until dough is firm and well mixed. Cover with a warm bowl. Let rest 10 minutes.

Filling: Combine sausage, cheese, bread crumbs and egg thoroughly. Make about 2 cups.

Divide dough into halves. On floured surface, using half of the dough at a time, roll dough as thin as possible. Cut out 3-inch rounds with large biscuit cutter or glass. Place small spoonful of filling a little to one side on each round. Moisten edge with water. Fold over and press edges together to seal.

Drop the pierogi in boiling salted water. Cook gently 3-5 minutes or until pierogi float. Lift out using slotted spoon.

Minnie Nowakowski

The Host with the most...

"When I was a young girl, at Christmas time around the dinner table, we would pass a host (communion wafer) around and each person would break off a tiny piece to eat and we would wish each other happiness and good luck.

After I was married, we began the tradition in my home and still do this today."

Vernie (Rychlec) Visnieski

🐦 Pierogi

2 eggs	*2 c. flour*
½ c. water	*½ tsp. salt*

Filling:

1 c. cottage cheese	*3 Tbsp. sugar*
1 tsp. butter, melted	*3 Tbsp. currants*
1 egg, beaten	*¼ tsp. cinnamon*

Mound flour on a kneading board and make a well in the center. Break eggs into hole and cut into flour with a knife. Add salt and water and knead until firm. Let rest for 10 minutes in a warm, covered bowl. Divide dough in half and roll thin. Using a large biscuit cutter or glass, cut circles. Place a small spoonful of filling a little to one side on each circle of dough. Moisten the edge of the circle of dough with water. Fold over and press edges together firmly. The edges must be sealed well to prevent the filling from running out. Drop the pierogi into boiling, salted water and cook for 3-5 minutes. Use a slotted spoon to carefully lift out cooked pierogi.

The dough has a tendency to dry out as you work. If the dough is too dry, it will not seal completely. A quick method of assembly to reduce the chance of drying too fast is to roll out the dough and place the spoonfuls of filling on the rolled out dough far enough apart to allow for cutting. Remove excess dough and quickly fold over and seal the pierogi.

After they are cooked, put melted butter over them, then they won't stick together. If you stack them unbuttered, they may stick together.

Cottage Cheese Filling: Cream cottage cheese with melted butter. Add remaining ingredients and mix well. Serve with melted butter and sour cream.

Angela Zayonc

Christmas Manger

As a child, our family always spent Christmas Eve in the home of my grandparents, Stach and Anna Skropka. Straw was put under the tablecloth to symbolize Christ's birth in the stable. Cooked wheat, pierogi and kolache were my favorite foods. After dinner, we sat at the table and sang Christmas carols.

Instead of having a Christmas tree, Grandpa built a manger in the corner of the living room. One gift was hidden in the straw for each child. We took turns finding our gift and opening it. After relaxing for a while, the horses were harnessed and hitched to the wagon and we were off to Midnight Mass, singing carols all the way. Oh, what fond memories!

Barbara (Goeders) Dull

 Pierogi Dough

2 c. sifted flour
1 egg
½ c. lukewarm water

1 tsp. salt
2 Tbsp. melted butter

Mix all ingredients together lightly and knead in bowl. Rest for ½ hour, covered. Knead dough on floured board and roll out to ⅛" thickness. Cut out circles with a cup, glass or doughnut cutter. Remove center cutter if using doughnut cutter.

Fill with favorite filling, pressing edges well together like a turnover. Bring water to boil and add salt as for noodles. Drop the pierogi gently into the boiling water. When the pierogi float to the top, turn heat down to a slow boil. A full rolling boil will make the pierogi fall apart. Boil for approximately 10 minutes. Take out with slotted spoon. Rinse lightly. Pour slightly browned butter over the pierogi.

Katie Magott

Pierogi

4 eggs
1 Tbsp. melted butter
1 tsp. salt
1 pkg. active dry yeast
¼ c. warm water

1 c. sour cream
1 Tbsp. sugar
1½ tsp. grated lemon peel (optional)
4 c. all-purpose flour

Beat eggs with melted butter and salt until thick and fluffy. Dissolve yeast in warm water in a large bowl. Let stand 10 minutes. Add egg mixture to yeast. Beat in sour cream, sugar and if desired, lemon peel. Stir in flour, 1 cup at a time, until dough is firm, but not stiff.

Turn dough on floured surface. Knead 3 times. Place dough in a greased bowl. Cover with plastic wrap. Let rise in a warm place until doubled, about 1 hour.

Roll out dough to ⅜" thickness on floured surface. Cut into 3-inch rounds. Place a spoonful of filling a little to one side of each round. Moisten edges. Fold over and seal. Place on greased baking sheet. Bake at 350° for 20-35 minutes or until golden brown.

Minnie Nowakowski

Pierogi - (Stuffed Tiny Pies)

1¾ c. unbleached flour
½ tsp. salt
2 eggs, slightly beaten
⅓ c. water

1 recipe of filling
Sour cream
Butter or margarine, melted

Potato-Cottage Cheese Filling:

⅓ c. chopped onion
1 Tbsp. butter
¼ tsp. salt
1½ c. mashed, cooked potatoes

1 tsp. fresh or frozen dill or ½ tsp.
    dried dill weed
⅔ c. dry curd cottage cheese

Farmer's Cheese Filling:

2 c. shredded Farmer's cheese (12
    oz.)
2 eggs

2 egg yolks
1 tsp. lemon juice
½ tsp. salt

Sauerkraut Filling:

2 Tbsp. cooking oil
1 c. chopped onion
1 c. fresh mushrooms, finely
    chopped
¼ tsp. salt

1 (14 oz.) can sauerkraut, rinsed,
    drained and snipped
¼ tsp. pepper
2 Tbsp. sour cream

In mixing bowl, combine flour and salt. Beat eggs well. Blend in water. Add to flour mixture, stirring till combined. (Dough should be pliable, but not sticky.) On floured surface, knead gently 15-20 strokes. Cover; let stand 10 minutes.

Divide dough in half. On floured surface, roll half the dough at a time to a 12-inch circle, about ⅛-inch thick. With a 3-inch round cookie cutter, cut out circles of dough. Place 1 heaping tsp. of filling on half of each circle. Fold other half of circle over, making a half moon shape. Pinch edges together well to seal. If necessary, crimp with fingertips again to ensure a good seal. Place on kitchen towel or floured surface; cover while making remaining pierogi.

In large saucepan, gently slide some of the pierogi into boiling water, stirring with a spoon to keep them from sticking together. Do not crowd. Boil gently, uncovered, 4-5 minutes or until pierogi float. Remove to a colander; rinse quickly under hot running water, shaking gently. Turn into shallow oven-proof bowl. Gently stir in a little melted butter or margarine to keep pierogi from sticking together. Keep it warm in oven while cooking remaining pierogi.

To serve, top with a little sour cream or additional melted butter. Sprinkle with fresh or frozen snipped dill if desired. Makes about 30.

Potato-Cottage Cheese Filling: Cook onion in butter or margarine until tender. Combine with potatoes, dill, salt and a dash of pepper. (Do not add milk or seasoning when you mash the potatoes.) Stir in cottage cheese. Makes 2 cups.

Farmer's Cheese Filling: The cheese used for filling is white, semi-dry and crumbly like Feta cheese. Beat eggs and egg yolks. Add cheese along with lemon juice and salt. Mix well. Makes 2 cups.

Sauerkraut Filling: Heat oil in skillet and add onions and mushrooms. Cook until tender, but not brown. Stir in sauerkraut, salt and pepper. Cook 8-10 minutes, stirring occasionally. Remove from heat. Stir in sour cream. Cool slightly. Makes 2 cups.

Rosie L. Klimkowski

 *Pirozhki*

Pastry:

9 oz. cream cheese
1½ c. flour

¼ c. butter (not margarine; I use an extra 1-2 Tbsp. butter)

Filling:

3 Tbsp. butter
1 large onion, chopped fine
¼ tsp. thyme
½ tsp. salt

½ tsp. pepper
1 (8 oz.) can mushrooms, chopped
¼ c. sour cream
2 Tbsp. flour

Combine cream cheese and butter. Add flour. Shape into 2 balls. Wrap in plastic wrap and refrigerate. Saute onion in butter. Add mushrooms and seasonings. Add flour and simmer for a couple minutes, then add sour cream. Roll dough; cut in thin 3-inch circles. Place about 1 tsp. of mushroom mixture on each circle. Fold in half and press edges together. Bake at 450° for 15 minutes on ungreased cookie sheet. (May be frozen before baking.)

Dorothy Janowiak Zurbriggen

 Pierogi Cheese & Potato Filling

1 c. mashed potatoes
1 c. dry cheese
1 egg

Cook potato and mash. Add dry cheese and 1 egg. Mash all together. Salt and pepper to taste. May add more or less cheese to taste or use potato filling only. Fill pierogi.

Katie Magott

Pierogi Prune Filling

1 c. cooked prunes
1 tsp. lemon juice
1 tsp. sugar

Place prunes in a bowl. Cover with water and soak overnight. Cook with sugar and lemon juice. Cool. Remove any pits. Fill pierogi. Serve with bread crumbs browned in melted butter.

Angela Zayonc
Katie Magott

Pierogi Mushroom Filling

1 c. chopped mushrooms
1 onion, chopped fine
Salt and pepper
2 egg yolks
Butter

Saute onion in butter. Add mushrooms. Season. Remove from stove and add egg yolks. Stir well. Cool before filling pierogi. Serve with chopped onion browned in butter.

Angela Zayonc
Victoria B. Miller

Mushrooms & Meat Pierogi Filling

½ c. beef, cooked
½ c. mushrooms, chopped
1 medium onion, diced

Butter
Salt and pepper
2 Tbsp. sour cream

Use meat grinder or food processor to grind meat into small pieces. Saute onion in butter. Add mushrooms and meat. Salt and pepper to taste. Add sour cream. Cool before using.

Angela Zayonc
Victoria B. Miller

Plum Pierogi Filling

Ripe plums
Sugar
Cinnamon

Egg white
Whipped cream

Peel and pit plums. Fill cavity of plum with sugar and cinnamon. Roll plum in sugar. Cover with the dough and seal the edges, using egg white. Serve with whipped cream.

Angela Zayonc
Victoria B. Miller

Cabbage & Mushroom Filling

1 small head cabbage
2 c. mushrooms
2 Tbsp. sour cream

1 small onion, chopped fine
Butter
Salt and pepper

Cut cabbage into quarters and cook in salted water for about 15 minutes. Drain, cool and chop fine. Saute chopped onion in butter. Add mushrooms and continue to cook for 5 more minutes. Add cabbage and cook until flavors are blended. Add sour cream and cool.

Variation: Two cups of sauerkraut, rinsed and chopped may be substituted for cabbage.

Angela Zayonc

Cottage Cheese Filling

1 c. dry cottage cheese
Dash of salt
1 tsp. lemon juice

1 Tbsp. sugar
1 egg
1 egg yolk

Force cottage cheese through sieve. Mix with other ingredients thoroughly.

Angela Zayonc
Victoria B. Miller

New! Bierock (German)

½ lbs. hamburger
1 onion, chopped
4 Tbsp. water
1 medium head cabbage, chopped

Salt and pepper to taste
Small jar pimentos
4 cans biscuits

Cook hamburger, onion, salt and pepper in skillet until brown. Drain. Mix in cabbage and pimento, add water. Cover and steam 20 minutes, stirring frequently. Cool. Roll out 2 biscuits for each square. Place 2 tbsp. meat mixture in center of each dough square, then gather 4 corners of each square to center and pinch dough sealed. Place square folded side down on greased baking sheet. Bake 15-20 minutes until golden brown in 350° oven.

Optional: You can use frozen dinner rolls or 2 loaves of frozen bread dough in place of the biscuits.

Kristi Kretchmar

Tree trimmings...

"Mama always decorated the Olander tree in the house with bits and pieces for a Christmas tree. Popcorn strings, bits of ribbon, construction paper ring chains were some of the things we made for the tree. It was something we enjoyed and looked forward to doing each year."

Rosie L. Klimkowski

Easy Bierocks

1 medium head cabbage, chopped	Pillsbury hot roll mix
1 small onion, minced	2 c. Monterey Jack cheese
1 to 2 lb. hamburger	(optional, added to filling mixture)
Salt to taste	

Simmer cabbage and onion together in pot until tender. Fry hamburger in skillet. Drain cabbage and onion mixture well and stir into hamburger. Cool. Make hot roll mix as directed on package and allow to rise until double in size. After it has risen, divide dough into 2 or 3 parts. Roll dough out thin on a floured surface. Cut into 4 or 5 inch squares. Put a mound of the filling in the center of square. Fold each corner to center and pinch together with floured fingers. Turn pinched side down on a greased cookie sheet. Allow them to rise until dough is about double. Bake at 350° for about 25 minutes or until lightly browned.

Judy Seikel

Polish Holidays

These are the national holidays currently observed in Poland:

January 1	New Year's Day
April 17	Easter Monday
May 1	Labor Day
May 3	Constitution Day
Late May or early June	Corpus Christi
August 15	Assumption
November 1	All Saints' Day
November 11	Independence Day
December 25 & 26	Christmas

One Saturday per month is by custom considered a working Saturday, but there is no consistency among institutions or exact observance as such.

🐦 Chinese Pepper Steak

1 lb. beef tip round steak (¾-inch
   thick)
1 Tbsp. cornstarch
½ tsp. sugar
¼ tsp. ginger
¼ c. light soy sauce

3 medium green peppers
2 small tomatoes
2 Tbsp. cooking oil
1 clove minced garlic
¼ c. water

Partially freeze steak to firm and slice diagonally across the grain into very thin strips. Combine cornstarch, sugar and ginger and stir in soy sauce. Pour mixture over meat and stir. Cut green peppers into 1-inch squares and cut tomatoes into wedges. Quickly brown beef strips (⅓ at a time) in hot oil and remove from pan. Reduce heat; add green pepper, garlic and water in pan and cook until green pepper is tender-crisp, about 5-6 minutes. Stir in meat and tomatoes. Heat through. Makes 4 servings, 283 calories per serving.

Linda Beam
Carol Brookes

🐦 Broccoli & Green Pepper Steak

1 lb. beef chuck or round, fat
   trimmed
¼ c. soy sauce
1 clove garlic
1 ½ tsp. grated fresh ginger or ½
   tsp. ground ginger
¼ c. salad oil

1 c. green onion, thinly sliced
1 c. red or green peppers, cut into
1-inch squares
1 c. broccoli
2 stalks celery, thinly sliced
1 Tbsp. corn starch
1 c. water

With a very sharp knife cut beef across grain into thin strips. Combine soy sauce, garlic and ginger. Add beef. Toss and set aside while preparing vegetables. Heat oil in large frying pan or wok. Add beef and toss over high heat till browned. If not tender, cover and simmer for 30-40 minutes over low heat. Turn heat up and add vegetables. Toss until vegetables are tender and crisp, about 10 minutes. Mix corn starch with water. Add, stir and cook until thickened. This can be prepared ahead.

Barbara Witte

Beef Bourguignonne

1-inch thick round steak	*1 to 2 Tbsp. butter*
6 slices bacon	*Salt*
1 large onion, sliced	*Pepper*
2 Tbsp. flour	*½ tsp. garlic powder*
2 c. burgundy wine	*Egg noodles*
1 c. beef bouillon	*1 to 2 Tbsp. butter*
8 large mushrooms or more	*1 to 2 Tbsp. flour*

Cut beef into serving size portions. Flour beef lightly and brown in butter in large Dutch oven. Set beef aside. Cook bacon in Dutch oven. Drain all fat but 1-2 tablespoons. Add onions and garlic powder and cook until onions are tender. Cut bacon into small pieces. Add meat, bacon, salt and pepper to onions.

Cover with wine and bouillon and cook on medium heat on top of stove for 1 hour or until meat is tender. About 10 minutes before the hour is up, saute the mushrooms in 1-2 tablespoons of butter. Add mushrooms to beef, reserving butter. To the reserved butter, add 1-2 tablespoons of flour and mix well. Add to beef mixture to thicken. Cook egg noodles according to package directions. Serve Beef Bourguignonne over noodles. Sirloin can be used.

Joyce Nowakowski

Beef & Green Peppers

½ lb. beef (lean), sliced in thin
   strips

3 Tbsp. oil for frying

Marinade:

1½ Tbsp. soy sauce
2 tsp. corn starch
1 Tbsp. wine
1 Tbsp. sesame seeds

1 tsp. ginger
¼ tsp. Accent
Dash of black pepper

Vegetables:

1 large green pepper, seeded and
   cut in 1-inch strips
¼ tsp. salt
¼ tsp. Accent

1 can water chestnuts, sliced
1 medium onion, quartered and
   separated

Glaze:

1 tsp. corn starch
2 Tbsp. soy sauce

½ c. water

    Soak beef in marinade for 4 hours or longer. Saute vegetables in oil.
Sprinkle on salt and Accent. Fry 2-3 minutes. Remove to platter. Heat oil in
same pan. Add meat and marinade. Fry 3-4 minutes. Add vegetables and
mix.

    Glaze: Mix and pour over meat and vegetables. Stir until thick. Add more
water if needed. Serve over rice.

Carolyn Werchan

Zronzy

Meat Roll

Veal or round steak
Salt to taste
Pepper to taste

1 onion, sliced thin
1 cucumber, sliced thin
½ lb. mushrooms, sliced thin

Pound veal or round steak very flat and thin. Salt and pepper to taste. Mix the onion, cucumber and mushrooms. Place over meat and roll up. Tie. Brown in skillet on all sides. Fry very slowly, about 1½ hours, adding small amounts of water when needed.

Irena Pryk

Swiss Steaks In Tomato Sauce

2 tsp. olive or vegetable oil
½ c. diced onion
½ c. diced celery
2 tsp. all-purpose flour
¾ c. water
1 c. canned whole tomatoes, chopped
½ c. tomato puree

2 packets instant beef broth and seasoning mix
1 c. green bell pepper strips (3"x½")
4 beef top or bottom round steaks (5 oz. each), broiled until rare
2 Tbsp. chopped fresh Italian (flat leaf) parsley

Preheat oven to 350°. Heat oil in 10-inch, non-stick skillet. Add onion and celery and saute until onion is translucent. Sprinkle flour over vegetables and cook, stirring constantly for 1 minute. Gradually stir in water. Stir in tomatoes, puree and broth mix. Stir constantly. Bring to boil. Remove from heat and stir in pepper strips. Arrange steaks in a 2-quart casserole and top with vegetable mixture. Cover and bake until steaks are tender, about 45 minutes. Serve sprinkled with parsley.

Carol Brookes

Beef-Green Beans In Tomato Sauce

1½ lb. stew beef
1 large can tomatoes
1 large can tomato sauce
¼ tsp. garlic powder

¼ tsp. ground allspice
1 can green beans
Salt and pepper to taste

Brown beef in pan. Salt and pepper to taste. Add tomatoes, tomato sauce, garlic and allspice to meat. Simmer. Add green beans to mixture and simmer until meat is done. Good over rice or mashed potatoes. Cooking time is according to size of cut up beef.

Jean Maddox

Burgundy Beef

2 lb. stew meat (or beef), cut into
    small cubes
1 pkg. dry onion soup mix
1 can cream of mushroom soup

1 (4 oz.) can mushrooms
½ c. red wine or burgundy
Rice

Cook all ingredients, except rice, in crock pot on LOW for 8 hours or HIGH for 5 hours. Serve over rice.

Muriel Lachance

Barley Hot Dish

¾ c. onion
1 c. barley
1 Tbsp. butter
4 c. water
1 tsp. paprika
½ c. bread crumbs
1 tsp. sesame seed
2 Tbsp. shortening

2 lb. round steak, cut into cubes or
    fingers
1 can mushroom soup
½ tsp. salt
1 tsp. Worcestershire sauce
1 small can mushrooms (stems and
    pieces)

Mix all ingredients. Bake at 350° for 2 hours. Serves 5-6.

Bonita (Konop) Yox
Esther Konop

🐦 Barbecued Steak

1 c. ketchup
½ c. water
¼ c. vinegar
¼ c. chopped green pepper
¼ c. chopped onion
1½ Tbsp. Worcestershire sauce

1 Tbsp. prepared mustard
2 Tbsp. brown sugar
½ tsp. salt
¼ tsp. pepper
4 lb. round steak, cut ½-inch thick

Combine all ingredients, except round steak, in a saucepan. Bring to a boil, then simmer gently for about 5 minutes over low heat. Keep barbecue sauce hot. Pound round steak to break connective tissue down. Cut into serving size portions. Place pieces in a large roasting pan. Pour hot sauce over meat. Cover tightly and bake in moderate 350° oven for 1½-2 hours.

Anita Craiger

🐦 Sirloin Marinade

½ c. chopped onion
½ c. oil
½ tsp. celery salt
½ tsp. pepper
½ tsp. thyme
½ tsp. rosemary

½ c. lemon juice
½ tsp. salt
½ tsp. oregano
1 clove garlic
Sirloin steak

Combine all ingredients, except meat and mix well. Marinate the steak 4-5 hours, turning 2-3 times. Use marinade to baste steak while grilling.

Joyce Nowakowski

🐦 Saturday Night Special

1 lb. ground beef
1 (28 oz.) can pork and beans
1 (No. 2) can tomatoes
1 tsp. salt

1 finely-chopped onion
¼ c. brown sugar
Bacon

Brown meat in hot, dry skillet (no fat). Add beans, tomatoes and salt. Pour ½ of mixture into baking dish. Cover with strips of bacon and onion. Sprinkle with brown sugar. Bake at 350° for 1 hour.

Rosie Skropka

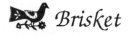 Chinese Hamburger

1 lb. ground beef	2 tsp. soy sauce
1 can cream of chicken soup	1 c. sliced mushrooms
1 can cream of mushroom soup	2 medium onions, chopped
1 can water	½ c. uncooked rice
1 c. sliced cele:y	1 can Chinese noodles

Brown meat in skillet, then add all ingredients, except noodles. Pour into a 2-quart casserole. Bake at 350° for 30 minutes, covered. Uncover and bake for 30 minutes more. Sprinkle the top with noodles and bake 15 minutes.
Serve with green salad.

Helen C. Nixon

Brisket

6 to 7 lb. Beef Brisket	Onion salt
Garlic salt	½ bottle liquid smoke
Celery salt	½ bottle Worcestershire sauce

Line baking pan with enough aluminum foil to cover and seal the brisket. Put fat side down and sprinkle liberally with garlic salt, onion salt and celery salt all over the brisket. Add liquid smoke. Cover with foil and refrigerate overnight. Next morning, add Worcestershire sauce. Bake at 275° for 5-6 hours. With brisket still wrapped in foil, let cool slightly before serving.

Elenora Lipinski

Baked Brisket

4 to 6 lb. brisket	½ tsp. garlic powder
2 onions, sliced	¼ c. soy sauce
Lemon pepper to season	10 oz. bottle Pepsi-Cola

Place onions in the bottom of a roasting pan. Season brisket and place fat side up on top of onions. Brown, uncovered in a 450° oven for ½ hour. Remove from oven. Pour Pepsi over the brisket and reduce oven temperature to 325°. Cover and bake, basting with more Pepsi about 3½ hours or until tender.

Mary Keller

New! Brisket

4-5 lb. brisket
½ c. brown sugar
⅓ c. vinegar

¼ c. ketchup
4 dashes Worcestershire sauce
6 dashes soy sauce

Line broiler pan with foil. Place beef in pan. Salt and pepper well. Wrap foil around brisket. Bake at 350° for 1 hour. Reduce heat to 300° and bake 2 hours. Combine above ingredients. Drain grease from brisket. Pour ¾ of the sauce on brisket. Wrap foil loosely around meat. Cook for 1 hour, adding remaining sauce during the last 20 minutes of cooking. To serve, pour sauce over sliced brisket.

Kristi Kretchmar

New! Oven Dried Jerky

1½ to 2 lbs. lean, boneless meat,
    partially frozen
¼ c. soy sauce
1 Tbsp. Worcestershire sauce

¼ Tbsp. pepper
¼ Tbsp. garlic powder
½ Tbsp. onion powder
1 Tbsp. hickory smoke-flavored salt

Trim and discard all fat from meat — it becomes rancid quickly. Cut meat into ⅛- or ¼-inch slices with the grain, or across grain, as you wish. If necessary, cut large slices to make strips about 1½ inches wide and as long as possible. In a bowl combine all other ingredients. Stir until seasonings are dissolved. Add meat strips and mix to thoroughly coat all surfaces. (The meat will absorb most of the liquid.)

Let set for 1 hour or cover and refrigerate all night. Shake off any excess liquid. Arrange strips of meat close together, but not overlapping. Set in shallow-rimmed baking pans directly on oven rack or on cake racks. Bake until done in 250° oven 4-6 hours.

Rosie L. Klimkowski

New! *Stillwater, Okla. Beef Jerky*

4-5 flank steaks, about 3 lbs.
1 c. Worcestershire sauce
1 c. soy sauce
½ tsp. garlic powder

½ tsp. red pepper
2 tsp. seasoned salt
2 tsp. Cavender's Greek seasoning

Partially freeze so meat will be easy to slice. Slice across the grain into ¼ inch slices. Make sauce from Worcestershire sauce, soy sauce, garlic powder, red pepper, seasoned salt and Greek seasoning. Cover meat in sauce and marinate for 24 hours. Cook in smoker about 2½ to 3 hours.

Soak chips in water before placing in smoker.

I like mine in oven at 250° for 5-6 hours.

Rosie L. Klimkowski

Choctaw Pot Roast

4 to 5 lb. chuck or rump roast
3 Tbsp. cooking oil
2 tsp. salt
¼ tsp. pepper
½ c. water
1 (8 oz.) can tomato sauce
3 medium onions, thinly sliced
2 cloves garlic, minced

2 Tbsp. brown sugar
½ tsp. dry mustard
¼ c. lemon juice
¼ c. vinegar
¼ c. ketchup
1 Tbsp. Worcestershire sauce
6 Tbsp. flour
½ c. water

Brown roast on all sides in hot oil in Dutch oven. Add salt, pepper, ½ cup water, tomato sauce, onion and garlic. Bring to boil. Reduce heat. Cover and simmer 1½ hours. Combine brown sugar, mustard, lemon juice, vinegar, ketchup and Worcestershire sauce. Pour over meat. Cover and simmer 1½ hours or until tender. Remove meat to warm platter. Skim off most of the fat. Measure broth. Add enough water to broth to make 3 cups. Return liquid to Dutch oven. Mix flour with ½ cup water in a small bowl. To make a smooth paste, stir into broth. Cook, stirring constantly until mixture comes to a boil. Boil 1 minute. Slice roast and serve with gravy. Makes 8-10 servings.

Mary Winters

Strufato

Chuck roast
½ c. white wine
1 medium can tomato wedges
½ tsp. garlic salt
1 medium onion, sliced
½ tsp. parsley flakes

1 bay leaf
1 tsp. salt
½ tsp. pepper
½ tsp. basil
¼ tsp. thyme

Brown the roast. Pour in wine. Add tomatoes, onion and seasonings. Bake 4 hour at 300°, turning once. Serve with rice.

Judy Seikel

Hungry Boy Casserole

1½ lb. ground beef, browned
1 c. sliced celery
½ c. chopped onion
½ c. chopped green pepper
1 clove garlic, minced
¾ c. (6 oz) can tomato paste

¾ c. water
1 tsp. salt
1 tsp. paprika
1 lb. can pork and beans
1 lb. peas

Biscuit:

1½ c. flour
2 tsp. baking powder
½ tsp. salt

¼ c. butter
½ c. milk

Saute in skillet the beef, celery, onion, green pepper and garlic until vegetables are tender. Drain. Add water, tomato paste, salt and paprika. Reserve 1 cup for biscuit. Add beans and peas simmer and prepare biscuits.

Sift flour with baking powder and salt. Cut in butter until fine. Add milk to flour mixture. Stir until moist. Knead on floured surface 12 times. Roll to a 12"x9" rectangle. Spread reserved meat over dough. Roll up and cut in 1-inch pieces. Place meat mixture in 12"x8" baking dish and top with biscuits. Bake at 425° for 25-30 minutes.

Anita Craiger

Jack Pot Casserole

1 lb. hamburger
¼ c. chopped onion
1 clove garlic
1 can tomato soup
1 can cream corn
Salt and pepper to taste

¼ c. chopped stuffed olives
1½ c. water
2 Tbsp. Worcestershire sauce
½ pkg. noodles
1 c. grated cheese

Brown beef. Add garlic, onion, soup, water and cooked noodles. Cook until tender. Add corn and olives. Put in greased casserole dish. Sprinkle with grated cheese. Bake at 350° for 45 minutes.

Maudie Kubiak

Chinese Dinner

1 lb. lean ground chuck
1 Tbsp. oil
2 chopped onions
1½ c. chopped celery
1 can cream of mushroom soup

1½ c. hot water
¼ c. soy sauce
½ c. uncooked rice
1 (3 oz.) can Chinese noodles
½ c. cashew nuts

Brown beef in oil with onions and celery. Add soup, water and soy sauce to rice and combine with meat. Cover and bake 30 minutes at 350°. Uncover and top with noodles and nuts. Bake additional 30 minutes.

Patricia Furchak

Frying Hints

When pan frying, always heat the pan before adding the butter or oil.

A little salt sprinkled into the frying pan will prevent splattering.

When browning any piece of meat, the job will be done more quickly and effectively if the meat is very dry and the fat is very hot.

After flouring chicken, chill for one hour. The coating adheres better during frying.

Macaroni & Beef Casserole

1 lb. lean ground beef
½ c. chopped onion
½ c. chopped celery
2 (8 oz.) cans tomato sauce

½ tsp. salt
¼ tsp. pepper
1 (7 oz.) pkg. macaroni
1 c. grated Cheddar cheese

Cook macaroni in boiling salted water for 6-8 minutes. Brown meat, onion and celery. Drain off excess fat. Stir in tomato sauce, salt and pepper. Pour all ingredients into a 2-quart casserole and top with cheese. Bake at 350° for 25 minutes.

Pat Bacon

Skillet Macaroni & Beef

1 lb. ground beef
1 c. uncooked small elbow
   macaroni
½ c. minced onion
½ c. chopped green pepper

1 tsp. salt
⅛ tsp. pepper
1 c. water
2 or 3 tsp. Worcestershire sauce

Cook beef in large skillet. Drain fat. Stir in macaroni, onion, green pepper, salt and pepper. Cook, stirring until macaroni is transparent. Add tomato sauce, water and Worcestershire sauce. Cover and simmer 20 minutes. Stir and let stand 5 minutes.
Very good.

Elenora Lipinski

🐦 One-Dish Meal

1 lb. hamburger
1 onion, chopped
1 can tomato soup

½ soup can water (cold)
1 can peas
4 or 5 potatoes, sliced

Fry hamburger until browned. Add remaining ingredients and stir gently. Cover; cook slowly over low heat for 20-30 minutes. stirring occasionally. Yields 4-5 servings.

Linda Beam

🐦 Christmas Eve Casserole

2 lb. lean ground beef
2 (No. 2) cans tomatoes
2 (No. 2) cans cream style corn
1 large onion, chopped
1 large green pepper, chopped
1 tsp. salt
½ tsp. pepper
1 c. sliced stuffed olives

2 tsp. Worcestershire sauce
½ c. slivered almonds
1 (4 oz.) can sliced mushrooms
1 (14 oz.) pkg. egg noodles
½ c. butter or margarine
1 can water chestnuts, sliced
1 lb. sharp cheese, grated

Brown meat in large pan. Add tomatoes, corn, onion, green pepper, salt and pepper. Cook over medium heat for 15 minutes, stirring often. Add olives, chestnuts, mushrooms, almonds and Worcestershire sauce. Reduce heat and simmer until blended. Cook noodles per package directions to al dente stage. Add butter and stir till coated. Add to meat mixture and ½ of cheese. Mix well.

Pour into greased baking dish. Cover with foil and bake 45 minutes in 325° oven. Top with remaining cheese and bake 15 minutes uncovered. To freeze, divide into serving portions after 45 minutes baking time and wrap well.

Carolyn Werchan

One Dish Meal

1 lb. hamburger
1 lb. sausage
1½ c. rice
1 slightly beaten egg

1 lb. (or 2 c.) sauerkraut
1 onion, chopped
1 (8 oz.) ctn. sour cream
Salt to taste

Pan fry hamburger and onion. Salt to taste. Cook the rice according to package directions. Drain rice and stir in the slightly beaten egg. Drain sauerkraut. Mix rice mixture with hamburger. Add the kraut. Pour into casserole dish, cover, and bake at 350° for about 45 minutes. Spread sour cream across the top of the casserole to serve. If desired, sour cream can be added to individual portions at the table.

Dorothy Wyskup

More

2 minced onions
1½ lb. ground meat
½ lb. sausage
1 lb. cooked broken spaghetti
1 can sweet peas and liquid

1 can drained ripe olives
1 can cream style corn
1 small jar pimento
1 large can tomatoes
½ lb. cheese

Brown onion, ground meat and sausage. Add spaghetti. Add all vegetables. Season with salt and pepper. Put in large pan. Grate cheese over top. Bake 1 hour at 350°.

Suzanne Visnieski

New! Margaret's Spanish Rice

Hamburger	Chili, taco or burrito seasoning
Salt	packet
Pepper	2 Tbsp. butter
Garlic seasoned salt	One can mushrooms, drained
Onion, chopped	1 c. instant rice
Bell pepper, chopped	Cheese slices, to taste or shredded
2 small cans tomato sauce	cheese
One tomato can of water	

Brown hamburger with salt and pepper, garlic seasoned salt, onion and bell pepper. Drain.

Add two small cans of tomato sauce and approximately one can of water. Add a little bit of chili, taco or burrito seasoning packet. Add two tablespoons of butter. Add drained mushrooms. Simmer until it begins to thicken (but not too thick).

Add 1 cup uncooked rice and stir. Put lid on and remove from heat. Let stand five minutes. Fluff and add cheese slices or shredded cheese. Replace lid. When cheese melts, it's ready. This can be microwaved to rush cheese process. Serve with picante sauce.

Becky Spaeth

Doritos Casserole

1 pkg. Doritos taco chips	1 c. cheese, grated
1 lb. hamburger or 2 c. bite-size	1 c. Ro-Tel tomatoes
cooked chicken	1 c. refried beans
1 onion, chopped	½ c. sliced ripe olives (optional)
2 cans cream of mushroom soup	

Bring the soup and tomatoes to a boil. Heat beans, adding a little water if needed. Cook hamburger with onion and drain, (if using chicken, slightly saute onion and add cooked chicken just to heat.) Put a layer of slightly crushed Doritos taco chips in bottom of casserole dish. Put layer of meat, then half of soup mixture, pour beans on top, then start over with Doritos, remaining meat and soup. On top of last layer, sprinkle ripe olives, adding cheese on top. Heat in 350° oven until cheese melts.

Sue Nickel

Beef & Nacho Casserole

1½ lb. ground beef
½ lb. bulk pork sausage
1¼ c. chopped onion
¼ tsp. garlic powder
1 c. sour cream

1 (8 oz.) can tomato sauce
1 (7 oz.) can chopped green chilies
1 (6 oz.) can tomato paste
1 (3.2 oz.) can medium pitted ripe
  olives (reserve ¼ c.)

Saute beef and sausage until no longer pink. Add onions and garlic. Continue cooking until onions are almost tender and meat browns. Pour off drippings. Reduce heat to medium. Stir sour cream, tomato sauce, chilies, tomato paste and olives into meat mixture. Heat through; do not boil. Remove from heat. Layer in baking dish ⅔ of chips, all of meat mixture and remaining chips. Put cheese on top. Bake, uncovered in 375° oven for 20-30 minutes or until heated through. Garnish with chopped green onions and olives.

Darline Ruyle

Grandma Rodriguez' Enchiladas

18 corn tortillas (6 extras for
  mistakes)
1 lb. lean ground beef
Chili powder
1 large onion, chopped

1 lb. Cheddar cheese, grated
1 lb. Mozzarella Cheese, grated
Toothpicks (optional)
Salt and pepper to taste

Brown beef. Drain fat. Salt and pepper to taste. Blend in large tablespoon of chili powder. Remove from skillet and set aside. Place into skillet 1½ cups of water with 1 tablespoon of chili powder and simmer over low heat. Drop a tortilla into mixture and soak until pliable. Remove tortilla and place on cookie sheet. Add a little beef, cheese and onion and roll. Secure with toothpick if necessary. Continue until all enchiladas are made. Extra ingredients, especially cheese, can be sprinkled on top of tortillas before baking in oven at 400° until cheese is melted.

This recipe has been in my family forever.

Amado Rodriguez

🐦 Enchilada Casserole

1½ lb. ground meat or ground
  meat and sausage
1 large onion
Chopped green pepper (optional)
½ c. sour cream (optional)
1 pkg. tortillas (12 in pkg.)

1 can cream of mushroom soup
1 can cream of chicken soup
1 can enchilada sauce (hot or mild)
1 c. milk
1 lb. American cheese, grated

Saute meat and onion, browning meat until onion is transparent. Add 1 can cream of mushroom soup, 1 can cream of chicken soup, 1 can enchilada sauce (hot or mild) and 1 cup of milk. Mix all together. (Sometimes I put a little chopped green pepper and ½ cup of sour cream also. But you do not have to.) Line pan with 6 tortillas. Pour ½ of mixture over tortillas. Sprinkle ½ of cheese over meat mixture. Repeat layers. Bake in 325° oven for 30 minutes.

Irene L. Miller

🐦 New! Mexican Lasagna

1 pkg. flour or corn tortillas
1 lb. ground beef
1 c. salsa
1 15 oz. can tomato sauce
1 pkg. taco seasoning mix

1 16 oz. carton cottage cheese
2 eggs
1 tsp. oregano
1½ c. shredded cheddar and
  Monterrey Jack cheese, mixed

Heat oven to 375°. Brown meat and drain. Stir in salsa, tomato sauce and taco seasoning. Simmer, stirring frequently for 5 minutes.

In separate bowl, combine cottage cheese, eggs and oregano. Line bottom of lightly-greased 9"x13" baking dish with half of the tortillas, overlapping edges. Top with half the meat mixture. Spoon cottage cheese mixture over meat. Arrange remaining tortillas over cheese mixture. Spread remaining meat mixture over all and top with shredded cheese.

Bake for 30-35 minutes or until bubbly. Let stand 10 minutes before serving.

The Cookbook Committee

Baked Lasagna

1 lb. lean ground beef
2 (6 oz.) cans tomato paste
1 can water
1 finely chopped clove garlic
¼ c. finely chopped onions
1 bay leaf

1 (8 oz.) pkg. lasagna noodles
1 (8 oz.) pkg. Mozzarella cheese,
  cut into strips
2 c. low fat cottage cheese
Parmesan cheese

Brown meat and drain. Add tomato paste, water, garlic, onions and bay leaf. Bring to boil, reduce heat and simmer for 20 minutes. Preheat oven to 350°. Prepare lasagna according to package directions. When meat mixture is cooked, remove bay leaf. Grease a 9½"x13" baking dish and layer ½ of each, the noodles, meat, cottage cheese and Mozzarella. Layer remaining ingredients in same manner. Sprinkle generously with Parmesan. Cover with aluminum foil and bake 30 minutes or until heated through. Makes 4-6 generous servings.

Carol Brookes

Aunt Betty's Lasagna

1 box wide lasagna noodles
2 cloves fresh garlic, sliced
1 (4 oz.) can mushrooms
1 lb. ground beef
Oregano to taste
2 tsp. lemon juice with pinch of
  sugar added

1 c. tomato sauce
1 can Campbell's beef consomme
  soup
½ pt. sour cream
Parmesan cheese to taste
Pinch of pepper
1 lb. Mozzarella cheese, shredded

Brown hamburger and drain well. Add garlic slivers, salt, spices, mushrooms, consomme, tomato sauce and mix. Simmer (not bubble) over medium heat. Remove from heat. Add sour cream. Oil bottom of casserole dish. Layer noodles, mixture and Mozzarella. Top with Mozzarella. Bake, uncovered at 350° for 45 minutes. (Allow an additional 10-15 minutes if it has been made ahead and refrigerated.) Let stand about 15 minutes after removing from oven.

Judy Seikel

Kraut & Frankfurter Mashed Potato Pie

1 Tbsp. butter or margarine,
  softened
3 c. mashed potatoes
3 Tbsp. minced onion

Salt and pepper to taste
1 (16 oz.) pkg. frankfurters
2 c. drained sauerkraut (16 oz.)
Parsley for garnish

Grease bottom and sides of a 2-quart casserole with butter. Combine potatoes, cheese, onion, salt and pepper. Spread potato mixture on the bottom and sides of the casserole dish. Slice each frankfurter lengthwise in quarters, then each quarter in half. Place ½ of the frankfurters over potatoes. Spoon on all of the kraut. Top with remaining frankfurters, in spoke fashion. Bake, uncovered, in a 350° oven for 30 minutes. Garnish with parsley. Serves 6.

Pauline Haynes

Spaghetti Pie

6 oz. spaghetti
2 Tbsp. butter or margarine
⅓ c. grated Parmesan cheese
2 well beaten eggs
1 c. (8 oz.) cottage cheese
1 lb. ground beef or bulk pork
  sausage
½ c. chopped onion

¼ c. chopped green pepper
8 oz. can cut up tomato
6 oz. can tomato paste
1 tsp. sugar
1 tsp. crushed, dried oregano
½ tsp. garlic salt
½ c. shredded Mozzarella (2 oz.)

Cook spaghetti according to package directions. Drain (should have about 3 cups). Stir butter or margarine into hot spaghetti. Stir in Parmesan cheese and eggs. Form spaghetti mixture into a "crust" in a buttered 10-inch pie plate. Spread cottage cheese over bottom of spaghetti crust. In skillet, cook ground beef or sausage, onion and pepper until vegetables are tender and meat is browned. Drain off excess fat. Stir in undrained tomatoes, tomato paste, sugar, oregano and garlic salt. Heat through. Turn meat mixture into spaghetti crust. Bake, uncovered, in 350° oven for 20 minutes. Sprinkle the Mozzarella cheese atop. Bake 5 minutes longer or until cheese melts. Makes 6 servings.

Carol Brookes

Chili Cheese Burgers

1 c. sour cream
1 tsp. chili powder
3 tsp. salt
2 lb. ground chuck
1 (4 oz.) can green chilies drained,
  seeded and chopped

2 c. (8 oz.) shredded Monterey Jack
  or Cheddar cheese
½ tsp. cumin seed, crushed
¼ tsp. pepper
4 buns

Combine sour cream, chili powder and 1 tsp. salt. Set aside. Mix beef, chilies, cheese, 2 tsp. salt, cumin and pepper. Shape into 8 patties. Grill on a gas grill. Set on medium and cook to desired degree of doneness, about 8 minutes each side. Top each patty with 2 tablespoon of sour cream mixture and serve open face on half of bun. Makes 8 servings.

Carolyn Rudek

Fiesta Beans & Burgers

1 lb. ground beef
¾ c. cracker crumbs
1 egg
¼ c. chili sauce or picante sauce
¼ c. chopped onion
¼ tsp. salt

Dash of pepper
1 (10½ oz.) can tomato soup
1 (15½ oz.) can pinto beans,
  drained
⅓ c. chopped green pepper
½ c. grated Cheddar cheese

Combine ground beef with cracker crumbs, egg, onion, picante sauce, salt and pepper. Shape into 4 patties. In large skillet, brown patties on both sides. Pour soup over each patty. Top with beans and green pepper. Cover and cook over low heat for 20 minutes. Sprinkle with cheese. Cover and cook 5 minutes longer.

Diana Hanna

Getting Catsup Out of Bottle
    Catsup will flow out of the bottle evenly if you will first insert a drinking straw, push it to the bottom of the bottle, and remove.

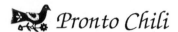 New! Hollywood Hamburgers

Ground beef　　　　　　　　　　**Sliced tomatoes**
Sliced onion　　　　　　　　　　　**Cheese**

Make large hamburger patty - press out on wax paper, not too thick. Put sliced onion, tomato and cheese on patty. Cover with another patty and seal together well. Cook slowly on grill or griddle.

I've learned that making these in the morning and leaving in the refrigerator (covered) for several hours, seals the filling in better than cooking right away.

Barbara Dull

 Pronto Chili

½ lb. ground beef　　　　　　　**1 (15½ oz.) can Campbell's**
1 small onion, chopped　　　　　　**Ranchero beans in a zesty sauce**
¼ c. chopped green pepper　　　**Hot, cooked rice**
1 small clove garlic, minced

In 1½ quart saucepan over medium heat, cook ground beef, onion, peppers and garlic until beef is browned and vegetables are tender, stirring to separate meat. Add beans. Heat to boil. (Do not drain beans.) Reduce heat to low. Simmer 5 minutes, stirring occasionally. Serve over hot, cooked rice. Makes 2½ cups or 4 servings.

Linda Beam

Chili Pie

1 (15 oz.) can chili　　　　　　**1 large chopped onion**
2½ c. corn chips　　　　　　　　**1 c. grated American cheese**

Empty chili into saucepan. Over medium heat, bring to boil, Preheat oven to 350°. Spread 1¼ cups of the corn chips in bottom of 1½ quart baking dish. Sprinkle with chopped onions and ½ of the grated cheese. Cover with the hot chili. Top with remaining chips, then sprinkle with remaining cheese. Bake 10 minutes. Yields 4 servings.

Carolyn Rudek

 Chili Pie

4 c. corn chips
1½ c. shredded Cheddar or Colby
   cheese

⅔ c. onions, chopped
1 (19 oz.) can Wolf brand chili
   without beans

Optional toppings:

Sour Cream

Sliced ripe olives

Layer 2½ cups of the corn chips in a 1½ quart casserole along with the chopped onion, ¾ cup of cheese and chili. Top with remaining corn chips. Bake at 375° for about 25 minutes. Sprinkle on remaining cheese and bake for 5 minutes more or until cheese is melted. Can be topped with sour cream and ripe olives.

Cora Rudek

New! Spaghetti Pizza

1 lb. spaghetti, cooked and drained
1 small jar mushrooms
2 eggs
1 c. milk

1 qt. spaghetti sauce (like Ragu)
4-8 oz. sliced pepperoni
2 c. shredded mozzarella cheese

In a large bowl, beat eggs and milk. Toss spaghetti in egg mixture. Layer in greased jelly roll pan:

1. spaghetti; 2. mushrooms; 3. sauce; 4. pepperoni; 5. cheese;
Bake at 325° for 25 minutes.

Diana Hanna

Beef In Tomato Rice Ring

For the beef treat:

½ c. chopped celery
½ c. chopped onion
1 lb. ground beef
2 Tbsp. shortening
1 tsp. salt
¼ tsp. pepper

2 tsp. prepared mustard
1 tsp. Worcestershire sauce
2 c. cooked peas (reserve liquid)
1 can (1¼ c.) tomato juice
½ c. liquid from peas

For the tomato-rice ring:

2 cans (2½ c.) tomato soup
4 c. water
¼ c. grated onion

2 c. uncooked rice or broken thin
    spaghetti

Lightly brown celery, onion and meat in melted shortening. Stir occasionally. Add remaining ingredients. Heat thoroughly. Fill center of tomato rice ring.

Rice ring: Heat to boiling, soup, water and onion. Add rice. Cook, covered, over low heat for 20 minutes. Stir occasionally. Remove from heat. Uncover and allow to set about 10 minutes or until rice absorbs remaining moisture. Pack in greased 1½ quart ring mold. Set in hot water until ready to serve. Unmold on platter, fill center. Makes 6 servings.

Sandra (Wyskup) McClure

Still counting ...

"For the longest time, I was the baby and I was always under Mama's feet. One day when I was about five, she was making dumplings. She had this cream of tomato soup to put them in. I wanted to help, so she told me to count the dumplings. I was sitting up on a wooden chair and I was counting the dumplings when Papa came in. He put his hands on his hips and told me to get down out of Mama's way. Mama turned and said: 'I gave this baby permission to count these dumplings.' He threw up his hands and said: "You're just spoiling this kid to pieces.' That night at dinner, he was at the head of the table and I was clear at the other end. He asked me: 'Baby, exactly how many dumplings did you really count?' I ran all the way around the table to his end and put my hands on my hips and told him just exactly how many. He said: 'Well baby, maybe that's why they taste so good.' Seventy years later, I'm still counting the dumplings. It's just something I do."

— Agnes Czerzcyk

Fifteen-Minute Smoked Sausage Jambalaya

1 c. instant rice
1 lb. Hillshire Farms smoked
   sausage or polska kielbasa, cut
   into 2-inch pieces.
1 chopped medium onion
½ c. chopped green pepper

½ c. sliced celery
1 (8 oz.) can tomatoes
4 drops hot pepper sauce
¼ tsp. pepper
Butter Pam cooking spray

Cook rice according to package directions. While rice is cooking, coat inside of large skillet with butter Pam cooking spray according to directions; heat skillet over medium heat. Add sausage, onion, green pepper and celery and saute until vegetables are tender. Add tomatoes, hot pepper sauce and pepper. Drain cooked rice and stir into sausage mixture. Cook over low heat, stirring frequently, until thoroughly heated. Makes 4-6 servings.

Carol Brookes

Sausage & Corn Bread Dressing

1 recipe of Aunt Jemima or Quaker
   corn bread
1 lb. pork sausage
2 c. celery, sliced
1 c. chopped onion
6 c. soft bread crumbs
¼ c. margarine, melted

½ to 1 tsp. sage
1 (10 oz.) can condensed chicken
   broth
¾ c. water
2 eggs beaten
Turkey

Brown sausage with celery and onion. Drain. In a large bowl, mix sausage mixture, corn bread (crumbled), bread crumbs, melted margarine and sage. Mix well. Add broth, water and eggs. Toss until bread is thoroughly moistened. You may add more water if needed. Stuff turkey and bake. Extra dressing can be baked in a casserole dish, covered during the last 35-40 minutes of roasting time. Makes about 12 cups.

Cora Rudek

🕊 Kartofle Zapiekane Ze Smietana

(Potatoes With Eggs & Cream)

3 c. diced cooked potatoes
1 Tbsp. butter
Salt and pepper

2 eggs, beaten
1 c. sour cream
1 Tbsp. chopped chives

Melt butter in frying pan and saute potatoes until heated. Salt and pepper to taste. Add sour cream, eggs and chives. Bake, covered, in 350° oven for 1 hour.

Dora Lee Kusek

🕊 New! Potato Dumplings & Sauerkraut

3 med. potatoes
⅓ c. water
¼ tsp. salt

Flour
Butter
Sauerkraut

Grate 3 medium size potatoes. Put in a skillet on low fire and stir until it turns to paste. Add ⅓ c. water; put in a bowl; add about ¼ tsp. of salt. Add flour until you make a thick dough. Drop by spoonfuls in boiling water like other dumplings. Drain; add butter. Cook your kraut; season it first; add dumplings.

Receipt originated from Poland. My Grandma taught me how to make these dumplings when I was about 12 years old.

Veronica Kupczynski

Blessed are they...

"When entering another person's home, a blessing was given in Polish, then the recipient answered with a response."

Mrs. Bill (Martha) Hopcus

🐦 *New!* Cottage Cheese Dumplings

1 lb. dry cottage cheese
1 egg yolk

½ chopped onion (optional)

If onion is used, saute onion in butter. Combine with cottage cheese and egg yolk.

Dough:

flour
egg
water

Optional:

sour cream
melted butter

Make a dough of flour, egg and water. Roll thin on floured board. Place spoonfuls of cheese mixture down the middle of rolled dough. Fold over the dough. Cut each mound with inverted tumbler dipped in flour. Press edges together.

Boil a few at a time in salt water for seven minutes.

Serve with sour cream or melted butter.

Lillian Le Lievre

🐦 *New!* Sad Dumplings & Kraut

Dumplings:

3 c. flour
2 tsp. salt

1 c. water

Kraut:

1 qt. kraut
1 tsp. dill seed

1 tsp. black pepper
4 Tbsp. bacon drippings

Mix dough as for noodles; let rest 10 minutes. Roll out as for pie crust. Cut into strips 2-3 inches wide. Stack strips with flour between layers. Cut into ¼ inch strips. Have boiling water ready and drop in noodles. Stir to separate. Boil about 20 minutes. Put in colander and rinse well with cold water. Add to kraut that has been heated well, with dill seed, black pepper, and bacon drippings. Mix well. Put in casserole dish and bake 25 min. at 325°.

Pauline Piotrowicz

🐦 Sauerkraut, Spareribs & Dumplings

From Grandmother Schmeider

1 large side spareribs	*4 tsp. baking powder*
2 cans sauerkraut (not Bavarian	*1 tsp. salt*
style)	*1 c. milk*
Salt to taste	*1 Tbsp. salad oil*
Pepper to taste	*Water*
2 c. sifted flour	

Rinse ribs. Cut into fourths. Place in large kettle. Cover ribs with water to exceed 1 inch above meat. Salt and pepper to taste. Bring to boil. Cover and simmer 1½ hours. Add sauerkraut. Return to boil. Meanwhile, combine milk with oil. Sift flour, baking powder and 1tsp. salt together. Add liquid all at once. Stir. Cover and simmer 45 minutes. Return to boil. Add liquid-dumpling mixture in to the hot bubbling mixture by tablespoon. Cover and simmer 20 minutes. Do not lift lid for 20 minutes or dumplings will fall. Cut ribs into smaller sections when serving. Makes 8 large servings.

Good with mashed potatoes.

Joan Taulbee

🐦 New! Polish Reuben Casserole

2 10-oz. cans cream of mushroom	*1 8-oz. pkg. medium noodles,*
soup	*uncooked*
1⅓ c. milk	*1½ lb. Polish sausage*
1 Tbsp. prepared mustard	*2 c. shredded Swiss cheese*
½ c. chopped onions	*¾ c. fine dry bread crumbs*
2 16-oz. cans sauerkraut	*2 Tbsp. melted butter*

Rinse and drain sauerkraut. Spoon into greased 9"x13" casserole. Top with uncooked noodles.

Mix soup, milk, mustard and onions. Spoon soup mixture over noodles.

Cut sausage into ½" pieces and spread over casserole. Add cheese.

In a small bowl, stir bread crumbs with butter. Sprinkle over cheese layer.

Cover tightly with aluminum foil and bake in a 350° oven for 1 hour or until noodles are tender. Makes 8 servings.

Rosalie Jorski

Polynesian Dutch

2 lb. pork steak	1 lb. small shrimp
2 large onions	1 tsp. Sidjo Ardjo Kroepeok
1½ c. rice	1 tsp. Sambal Oelek
3 c. water	1 tsp. red pepper
2 tsp. Chinese salt or garlic powder	3 eggs
3 tsp. paprika	1 tsp. Trassi

Cook rice in water and drain. Cut pork steak in small pieces and brown in oleo or butter. Cut onions thin and place over meat and brown. Sprinkle Chinese salt, Trassi, paprika, red pepper and stir real well. Add rice and beaten eggs. Stir good and let simmer at low flame for 30 minutes. Add shrimp and simmer 15 minutes more. Add Sambal Oelek and Sidjo Ardjo Kroepoek.

These seasonings can be found in oriental food stores. Very good.

Helen C. Nixon

Schweineschnitzel

(Pork Cutlets Breaded)

4 pork chops, cut ½-inch thick and boned	1 c. crumbs, grated from hard rolls or French bread
2 eggs, beaten	6 Tbsp. shortening or 3 Tbsp. each butter and vegetable shortening
2 Tbsp. water	
½ tsp. salt	

Pound the boned pork chops with a metal or wooden mallet until ⅛-inch thick. Blend eggs, water and salt. Dip meat in egg, then coat with crumbs. Fry in shortening until crisply browned on each side. Makes 4 servings. Serve with lemon wedges. Sprinkle lemon juice over schnitzel at table. Garnish with parsley sprigs.

Anneliese Lancaster

Gourmet Pork Chops

4 pork chops
Flour
Salt and pepper
Paprika
1 small bay leaf

¼ c. vinegar
¼ c. water
1 Tbsp. brown sugar
1 clove garlic

Flour pork chops and brown in a little hot fat in skillet. Sprinkle both sides with salt, pepper and paprika. Combine vinegar and water. Add brown sugar and blend well. Pour around chops. Add bay leaf and garlic. Cover skillet and simmer chops slowly until tender about 1-1½ hours. Add more water if liquid cooks away. Remove garlic and bay leaf. Serve chops with liquid spooned over them.

Good with rice.

Elenora Jarvis

Pork Chop Dinner

6 medium size pork chops
1 small onion
6 large potatoes

1 can cream of mushroom soup
¾ c. milk

Brown chops on each side. Slice potatoes and onions. In large (9"x13") baking dish, put 1 layer of potatoes, then 1 layer of onions. Place 3 chops over onions and repeat with another layer of potatoes and onions. Place remaining 3 pork chops on top of onions. Use rest of potatoes for top. Mix milk and mushroom soup and pour over all. Bake 2 hours at 300° or 325°.

Barbara Liebl

🕊️ Polish Sausage - Kielbasa

1½ lb. pork loin or butt
½ lb. veal
Salt to taste
Pepper to taste

1 clove garlic
1 tsp. whole mustard seeds
3 Tbsp. water
Casings

Remove bones from meat. Cut meat into small pieces and run through a food grinder. Add 3 tablespoons of water, the garlic, crushed, the mustard seed, salt and pepper. Mix thoroughly and stuff casing. The sausage is ready for smoking. The sausage can also be baked. Place the sausage in a baking dish. Cover with cold water and bake at 350° until the water is absorbed.

Victoria B. Miller

🕊️ **New!** Salami

2 lbs. ground beef
2 tsp. liquid smoke
⅛ tsp. garlic powder
½ tsp. coarse ground pepper

½ tsp. mustard seed
3 Tbsp. "Morton's Tender-Quick
   Curing Salt"
½ c. water

Mix ingredients and seal in a plastic container and refrigerate. Take out and mix 3 mornings in a row. On the fourth morning, mix and shape in small cans such as soup or vegetable cans. Turn upside down on broiler rack and bake at 150° for 8 hours. Cure in refrigerator for two days.

Al Dilis

Late night snack...

"Mama always took food to church at Easter time to have it blessed during the Vigil Mass. Ham, colored eggs, kielbasa, cheese, butter, a sweet bread, and honey were things she included. We kids started eating from the basket on the way home from church."

Rosie L. Klimkowski

 Homemade Salami

2 lb. ground lean hamburger meat
2 Tbsp. Morton's Tender-quick
  curing salt
¼ tsp. onion powder

¼ tsp. garlic powder
Pinch of ground sage
1⅓ tsp. liquid smoke
1 c. water

Crumble all together and form in 2 rolls. Cover tightly with Saran Wrap. Let cure for 24 hours in icebox. Bake for 1 hour at 300°, unwrapped and let drain in pan while cooking in oven.

Terry Fortelney

Salami

2 lb. ground beef
2 tsp. liquid smoke
⅛ tsp. garlic powder or clove of
  garlic, mashed
½ tsp. mustard seed

½ tsp. coarse ground black pepper
  or mashed peppercorns
2½ to 3 Tbsp. Tend er-Quick
  curing salt (Morton's)
½ c. water

Mix all ingredients well. Cover and put in refrigerator. Mix again the second night and the third night. Fourth night, mix and shape into rolls. Wrap in cheesecloth and bake 8 hours at 150° in broiler pan or pan where grease can drain. Remove cheesecloth and wrap in foil. Refrigerate 2 days to cure.

Gerry Lamer

Holiday treat ...

"Moma always made Polish Sausage every Christmas and Easter. There was a special way to prepare them. The heat had to be from hickory wood, and the coals had to be just right. Moma would take a clove of garlic and rub the sausage just enough to give it just a hint of garlic. The garlic never left her hand. Everything she did was from scratch."

— Agnes Czerzyck

New! *German Sauerkraut & Pork*

2½ lbs. pork
1 qt. salted water
1 can sauerkraut
1 medium onion
1 bay leaf

3 cloves
1 medium potato
salt, to taste
white pepper, to taste
pinch of sugar, or to taste

Wash pork under cold water and cook pork 1½ hours.

Add sauerkraut, but pull apart before adding to the meat. (Kraut can be washed in cold water to remove some salt.)

Boil one more hour. Peel potato and chop very fine. Add to sauerkraut and meat and boil a little more. (The potato will blend your kraut like the flour in gravy.)

Irene Burke

Smoked Sausage Pizza

1 pkg. hot roll mix
1 lb. sausage
Liquid smoke to taste
¼ c. chopped onion
1 clove garlic
1 Tbsp. olive oil

1 (8 oz.) can tomato sauce
¼ tsp. oregano
¼ tsp. rosemary
½ c. sliced olives
3 c. grated cheese (preferably
    Longhorn or sharp Cheddar)

Follow directions on hot roll mix. Cook onions, sausage and garlic in olive oil. Stir in tomato sauce. Crumble herbs into mixture. Roll dough thin and pull into shape for shallow pan.

Spread pizza mix evenly. Sprinkle olives on it and top with cheese. Let rise 10 minutes. Bake in 400° oven for 20 minutes.

Minnie Nowakowski

Baked Better Potatoes With Ham

4 Idaho potatoes
2 c. shredded Cheddar cheese
1½ c. ham, cubed*
½ pt. sour cream

¼ c. butter or margarine, melted
¼ c. green onions, sliced
½ tsp. salt
¼ c. ripe olives, sliced

Bake potatoes and allow to cool. Quarter potatoes; cut potatoes in halves lengthwise and then cut each half in half lengthwise to make potato quarters. Using a knife, scoop out potato meat, leaving potato peels with about ¼-inch of potato. Lightly spray or oil a 9"x12" baking dish with vegetable oil. Line the potato peels in the baking dish, meat side up. Lightly brush peels with part of the melted butter. Set aside.

Put potato scoopings into a large bowl and use knife to cube into small bite-size pieces. Add the remaining melted butter and the salt to cubed potatoes and toss. Reserve 1 tablespoon of the shredded cheese and the green onions for garnish. Add the remainder to potatoes. Add the cubed ham. Toss. Stir in sour cream and coat mixture entirely. Pour potato, ham and cheese mixture and shredded cheese over top of mixture to garnish. Add ripe olives to garnish. Bake, uncovered, in a 400° oven for 20-25 minutes or until the cheese is melted. Or, microwave on HIGH for 12-15 minutes or until cheese is melted. Serving suggestion: Serve with tossed green salad and mixed fruit bowl. Serves 6 to 8.

Turkey or chicken, cooked and cubed, or hamburger, cooked and well drained, can be substituted for variety.

Judy Seikel

Ham & Rice Casserole

1 c. cooked rice
3 c. white sauce (thin)
1 can celery soup

2 c. diced ham
2 c. grated cheese
Salt to taste

Preheat oven to 350°. Mix ingredients. Bake in casserole for 1 hour.

Frances Rychlec

Ribbon Meat Loaf

3 slices soft bread, cubed
1 c. milk
1 lb. ground beef
1 egg yolk
¼ c. minced onion

1¼ tsp. salt
¼ tsp. each pepper, dry mustard,
   sage, celery salt and garlic salt
1 Tbsp. Worcestershire sauce

Cheese Filling:

1 egg white, slightly beaten
1 Tbsp. water

2 slices soft bread, cubed
4 oz. shredded Cheddar cheese

Mix all the meat loaf ingredients and pat ½ of the mixture into a loaf pan. Combine the filling ingredients and pat onto the meat loaf. Cover the filling with the remaining meat loaf mixture. Bake at 350° for 1½ hours.

Gay Turner

Meat Loaf

1½ lb. ground beef
⅔ c. bread crumbs
1 c. milk
2 beaten eggs
¼ c. grated onion
1 tsp. salt

1 tsp. sage
½ tsp. pepper
6 Tbsp. brown sugar
½ c. catsup
½ tsp. nutmeg
2 tsp. dry mustard

Soak bread crumbs in milk. Add eggs, onion, salt, sage and pepper. Form into loaf and put in baking pan or dish. Mix brown sugar, catsup, nutmeg and mustard and spread this over top of meat loaf and bake 1 hour at 350° or until done.

Mary Winters

Microwave Pizza-Style Meat Loaf

¼ c. diced green bell pepper
1 Tbsp. instant chopped onion
8 oz. can tomato sauce, divided
1 lb. ground beef
1 large egg, lightly beaten
½ c. Italian seasoned dry bread
  crumbs

1 tsp. Italian seasoning
1 tsp. seasoned salt
¼ tsp. garlic powder
¼ tsp. pepper
2 Tbsp. shredded Mozzarella cheese
3 pimento stuffed green olives,
  sliced

Place green pepper and onion in a 2 quart glass bowl. Microwave on HIGH 1½ minutes. Reserve ¼ cup tomato sauce and add remaining sauce to onion mix. Add ground beef, egg, bread crumbs, Italian seasoning, seasoned salt, garlic powder and pepper. Mix well and shape into loaf. Place on a microwave safe meat or bacon rack. Cover with wax paper. Microwave on MEDIUM HIGH for 10 minutes. Pour reserved tomato sauce over loaf. Sprinkle with cheese and decorate with olives. Do not cover. Microwave on 70% for 2 minutes. Let stand 10 minutes before slicing. Makes 4-5 servings.

Carol Brookes

Texas Chili Meat Loaf

1 (15 oz.) can dark red kidney beans
1 c. 3-Minute brand oats
½ c. onion, finely chopped
¼ c. green pepper, chopped
1 (7½ oz.) can whole tomatoes, cut
  up
1 egg, slightly beaten

2 Tbsp. chili powder
1½ tsp. garlic salt
½ tsp. Tabasco sauce
1½ lb. hamburger
1 c. shredded Cheddar cheese
½ c. crushed corn chips

Drain beans, reserving liquid. Stir beans, oats, onion, green pepper, tomatoes and egg together. Add chili powder, garlic salt and Tabasco. Mix well. Add hamburger and cheese. Pat into meat loaf pan. Bake at 350° for 1 hour. Remove from oven. Pour reserved liquid over meat loaf. Sprinkle with remaining Cheddar cheese and corn chips. Bake an additional 10 minutes.

Cora Rudek

Mexican Meat Loaf

1½ to 2 lb. ground beef
2 small cans taco sauce
1 can cream of chicken soup
1 can cream of mushroom soup
1 small can green chilies, chopped
1 small can tomato paste

1 small onion, diced
1½ c. cooked rice
Salt and pepper to taste
1 bag Doritos
Grated cheese

Brown beef and onions. Drain. Add remaining ingredients, except chips and cheese. Blend. Bring mixture to a boil. Place ½ mixture into large casserole dish. Place large amount of Doritos over mixture. Add remaining mixture and top with lots of cheese. Heat in 350° oven until cheese is melted.

Suzan Schirf

To Cook Rabbit

Bacon
1 onion

Wine
Rabbit

Line casserole with bacon. Slice a layer of onion in the bottom of casserole. Put in layer of rabbit, then a layer of bacon, layer of onion, rabbit and bacon on top. Pour over 1 cup any good wine and let bake slowly for around 3 hours.

Our Lady's Cathedral Cookbook
Circa 20s or 30s

Gravy Magic

Pale gravy may be browned by adding a bit of instant coffee straight from the jar — no bitter taste, either.

If you will brown the flour well before adding to the liquid when making gravy, you will avoid pale or lumpy gravy.

Lumpless gravy can be your triumph if you add a pinch of salt to the flour before mixing it with water.

A different way of browning flour is to put it in a custard cup placed beside meat in the oven. Once the meat is done, the flour will be nice and brown.

Thin gravy can be thickened by adding a mixture of flour or cornstarch and water, which has been mixed to a smooth paste, added gradually, stirring constantly, while bringing to a boil.

🐦 Hasenpheffer Sour Rabbit

Rabbit
Vinegar
1 tsp. pepper
2 Tbsp. salt

2 medium onions
Garlic
3 Tbsp. flour
Butter

Cut up rabbit; put in stone crock and cover with vinegar to which has been added 1 tsp. pepper, 2 tablespoons salt, 2 medium size onions and button of garlic. Cover with plate and set in cool place for about a week. Take meat out and boil until tender. Brown 3 tablespoons flour mixed with melted butter for gravy. Add to this 2 tablespoons of vinegar in which the rabbit was soaked. Put the meat back into this gravy and let simmer 10 minutes and season to taste.

Our Lady's Cathedral Cookbook
Circa 20s or 30s

🐦 Pork Stuffed Enchiladas

1½ c. cubed cooked pork
1 c. grated Cheddar cheese
½ c. chopped onion
1 can tomato soup

1 can cream of mushroom soup
1 (10 oz.) can mild enchilada sauce
12 corn tortillas

Combine meat and ½ cup of cheese and onion. Set aside. In saucepan, combine soups and enchilada sauce. Heat to boiling. Dip tortilla in sauce. Put in meat mixture and roll up. Place in baking dish. Top with sauce and sprinkle with cheese. Bake at 350° for 25-30 minutes.

Suzanne Visnieski

Good Chicken Enchiladas

4 large chicken breasts, cooked and
   diced (with broth)
¼ c. picante sauce
12 to 14 corn tortillas
6 oz. grated Monterey Jack cheese

6 oz. Cheddar cheese
1 can cream of mushroom soup
4 oz. sour cream
1 tsp. chili powder

Microwave tortillas until soft. If no microwave, soak tortillas in warm chicken broth left from cooking the chicken. Place chicken and picante on tortillas; add cheese. Roll up and place in greased pan. When they are all made and in the pan, top with mixture of mushroom soup, sour cream and chili powder. Grate some cheese over the top. Bake at 350° for 30 minutes.

Good with beer!

Marty Janowiak Casteel

Almond Chicken Breast

6 chicken breasts, skinned and
   boned
3 Tbsp. butter
1 can Campbell's cream of chicken
   or mushroom soup

½ c. milk
1 c. shredded cheese
½ c. slivered almonds
⅓ c. water

Brown chicken breasts in melted butter. Add ⅓ cup water and simmer for 15 minutes. Add can of soup that has been diluted with the ½ cup of milk and mixed with a third of the shredded cheese. Top with the remaining cheese and the slivered almonds. Bake in a 350° oven for 45 minutes.

Victoria Seikel

Chicken Breast Stuffed With Cheese

3 whole chicken breasts
Salt to taste
Pepper to taste
½ c. butter (room temperature)
2 Tbsp. parsley, finely chopped
1 tsp. marjoram
½ tsp. thyme
¼ lb. Mozzarella cheese
½ c. flour
2 eggs, beaten
1 c. bread crumbs (fresh)
White wine (optional)

Skin, bone, halve and flatten chicken breasts to ½-inch thickness. Season breasts and spread with ½ of the butter. Blend remaining butter with parsley, marjoram and thyme and set aside. Cut cheese into 6 sticks. (Fontina or Muenster can be used, too.) Place cheese in center of each breast and roll, being sure to tuck in ends so cheese won't melt and run out. Roll in flour; dip in egg. Roll in bread crumbs. Arrange breasts on well buttered baking dish. Melt butter and herb mixture. Pour evenly over breasts. Place dish in oven and bake 20 minutes at 350°. Add more butter or liquid (white wine is good) if necessary and continue cooking, basting frequently with pan drippings an additional 15 minutes.

Joyce Nowakowski

New! Chicken & Broccoli Au Gratin

¼ c. butter or margarine
¼ c. chopped onion
¼ c. flour
1 tsp. salt
½ tsp. curry powder
Dash pepper
1 can (4 oz.) sliced mushrooms
1 can (12 oz.) evaporated milk
1 bunch broccoli cut up, cooked
    and drained
3 c. chicken, cooked and cut in
    bite-sized pieces
1 c. (4 oz.) shredded Monterrey
    Jack cheese

Melt margarine in skillet. Saute onions until transparent. Remove from heat. Stir in flour, salt, curry powder and pepper. Drain mushrooms,. reserving liquid. Add enough water to the mushroom liquid to make ½ cup. Gradually stir the liquid into flour mixture and return to heat. Blend in evaporated milk until smooth. Add mushrooms. Cook and stir over medium heat until sauce begins to thicken.

Arrange broccoli and chicken on bottom of a 13"x9" baking dish. Pour sauce over. Top with cheese. Bake at 375° for 20 minutes, or until bubbly around edges. Makes 6 servings.

Diana Hanna

🐦 Rolled Chicken Supreme

8 chicken breasts	3 eggs
8 slices Swiss or Mozzarella cheese	3 c. seasoned bread crumbs
8 slices ham	1 stick butter (½ c.)

Debone chicken. Wrap cheese and then ham around each. Secure with toothpicks. Beat eggs and dip each "supreme" in eggs. Roll in bread crumbs. Melt butter in shallow dish and add supremes. Place on low rack of 350° oven. Bake 35 minutes. Turn only once during cooking. Add butter as needed.

Vicki Dimmer

🐦 Chicken Caruso

2 whole chicken breasts, skinned, boned and cut into inch-long strips	2 c. diced celery
Garlic salt	1 tsp. Italian seasoning
Pepper	1 jar spaghetti sauce or 2 c.
2 Tbsp. butter or margarine	homemade

Season chicken with garlic salt and pepper. Saute in butter 2 minutes. Add celery. Cook until tender-crisp. Stir in Italian seasoning and spaghetti sauce. Simmer 15 or 20 minutes. Serve over rice. Sprinkle with Parmesan cheese.

Jean Maddox

Grandmother's faith...

"When Grandmother lived with us, she would put straw under the tablecloth for our Christmas meals. After Christmas was over, the straw was burned in the yard, then we jumped over the ashes to bring about a good year."

Rosie L. Klimkowski

🐦 Polish-Style Chicken

1 chicken, quartered	Salt
2 c. water	1 Tbsp. butter
1 stalk celery	1 Tbsp. flour
1 carrot	½ c. wine
1 sprig parsley	2 egg yolks
½ c. mushrooms, chopped	

Cover chicken with water and bring to boiling point. Add vegetables, mushrooms and salt. Simmer for about 1 hour until tender. Heat butter. Add flour and blend. Add remaining chicken soup stock and stir over heat until thickened. Add the mushrooms and wine. Slowly stir in the egg yolks and add the chicken. Heat thoroughly, but do not boil. Good with mashed potatoes.

Victoria B. Miller

🐦 Crunchy Italian Chicken

2½ to 3 lb. chicken, cut up	½ tsp. garlic powder
½ c. all-purpose flour	¼ tsp. pepper
3 Tbsp. dry bread crumbs	1 egg
2 Tbsp. Parmesan cheese	2 Tbsp. water
1½ tsp. Italian herb seasoning	Oil
1 tsp. salt	

Place flour, bread crumbs, seasoning and cheese in a bag and shake to mix. Shake chicken pieces, a few at a time, to coat. Dip coated chicken in egg, beaten with water. Shake chicken pieces in flour mixture again. Set aside. Use an electric fry pan or heavy skillet. Fill ⅓ full with oil. Heat to 375°. Fry chicken about 11 minutes, skin side down. Turn pieces and fry another 10-15 minutes. Let stand about 7 minutes before serving. Serves 4-6.

Cora Rudek

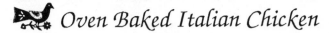 Oven Baked Italian Chicken

2½ to 3 lb. cut up fryer
1 stick melted margarine
1½ tsp. Italian herb seasoning
1 tsp. salt

½ tsp. garlic powder
¼ tsp. pepper
⅔ c. grated Parmesan cheese
Crushed cracker crumbs

Dip chicken in melted margarine. Shake in the next 5 ingredients mixed together. Roll in crushed cracker crumbs. Place in a buttered 11"x14" Pyrex dish. Bake at 375° for 1 hour.

Carol Brookes

Chicken Spaghetti

1 fat fryer
1 bay leaf
2 c. celery, minced
1 c. onion
2 cans cream of celery or
*   mushroom soup*

2 cans cream of chicken soup
Spaghetti noodles
6 or 8 boiled eggs
Green olives
¼ lb. oleo

Boil fryer or hen until tender, reserving liquid. Salt chicken well. Saute bay leaf, celery and onion. Cook slowly in ¼ pound oleo. Add soups and simmer while preparing spaghetti. Remove chicken from broth and add water if needed to cook spaghetti. Cook spaghetti in broth until tender. Remove bone and skin from chicken. Add chicken to soup mixture. Pour over cooked spaghetti and mix well. Add green olives and hard-boiled eggs. Toss gently.

Maudie Kubiak

Chicken Supreme

2 to 2½ lb. frying chicken
2 env. onion soup mix
2 c. rice

2 cans cream of mushroom soup
2 soup cans of water

Cut chicken up as for frying. In a 9"x13" pan, put in the rice. Lay chicken pieces on the rice. Mix the soup mix, soup and water. Pour over the chicken. Bake in 300° oven for 2 hours or until rice is done.

Pauline Piotrowicz

Chicken Supreme

1 whole chicken or 3 chicken
   breasts
3 c. water
4 peppercorns (optional)
Handful of celery tops

2 c. precooked rice
1 can chicken gravy or 2 cans
   cream of chicken soup
½ c. bread stuffing

Combine chicken with water, salt, peppercorns and celery tops. Cook until tender. Strain broth in 4 cup measure. Pour in water if needed to make 2½ cups. Let chicken stand until cool, then remove bones and skin and cut into pieces. Cook rice in 2 cups broth in pan. Mix ½ cup broth with soup. Heat until bubbly. Spoon rice into large baking dish. Top with chicken. Pour soup over this. Melt butter and mix with ½ cup stuffing. Sprinkle on top. Bake at 400° for 20 minutes or until bubbly hot.

Linda Beam

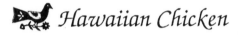 Microwave Chicken Breasts

2 chicken breasts, boned, skinned
  and split
4 oz. (approx.) fresh sliced
mushrooms or 1 small can

  mushrooms
1 can French fried onion rings
4 oz. Monterey Jack cheese, grated

Place chicken in dish; lightly salt and pepper. Cover with plastic wrap, leaving 1 corner open slightly for venting. Microwave on HIGH power 6 minutes. Top with mushrooms then onion rings. Recover with wrap and microwave on HIGH power for 6 minutes. Add cheese. Use more or less to taste. Cover and microwave on HIGH 1 minute.

Tips: Turn after 3 minutes in first and second stages. Recipe can be doubled, but must extend cooking time.

Sue Nickel

Hawaiian Chicken

2 lb. broiler-fryer pieces
Salt
Pepper

  2 Tbsp. honey
1 (8¼ oz.) can sliced pineapple
⅓ c. Heinz 57 sauce

Place chicken in baking dish, 12"x7½"x2". Season with salt and pepper. Bake in 400° oven for 30 minutes. Meanwhile, drain pineapple. Reserve 2 tablespoons liquid. Combine reserved liquid, 57 sauce and honey. Pour over chicken. Bake an additional 25 minutes, basting occasionally. Arrange pineapple over chicken. Bake 10 minutes longer. Drain excess fat from sauce. Spoon sauce over chicken. Makes 4 servings.

Cora Rudek

Sweet 'n Sour Chicken

1 lb. boned and skinned chicken, cut in cubes	1½ c. water
2 Tbsp. oil	1 (8 oz.) can chunk pineapple in juice
1 c. green pepper chunks	½ c. catsup
1 c. carrot slices	3 Tbsp. soy sauce
1 clove minced garlic	1½ c. dry Minute rice

In large skillet, saute chicken in oil until well browned. Add green pepper, carrot and garlic. Saute 1-2 minutes longer. Add water, pineapple with juice, catsup and soy sauce. Bring to a full boil. Stir in rice. Cover; remove from heat and let stand 5 minutes. Stir. Makes 4 servings, 410 calories each with white meat chicken, 430 calories each with dark meat chicken.

To microwave: Omit oil and reduce water to 1¼ cups. Combine chicken, carrots and garlic in 2-quart, nonmetal baking dish. Cover and cook at HIGH power for 3 minutes. Stir in remaining ingredients. Cover and cook 6 minutes longer. Remove from oven and let stand, covered, for 5 minutes. Stir.

Carol Brookes

Chicken In Cream

3 to 4 lb. fryer, cut up	1 onion
Salt to taste	Clove garlic, sliced
Pepper to taste	1 c. water
Flour	1 c. sour cream

Take a large fryer and season with salt and pepper and roll in flour. Brown in skillet in small amount of fat. Put into a pan with a tight cover. Add onion and garlic clove (sliced), water and sour cream. Cook slowly until well done.

Minnie Nowakowski

🐦 New! Smothered Chicken

(Pruzona Kura)

1 fryer chicken	½ green pepper, chopped
1 chopped onion	Salt
1 rib celery, chopped	Black pepper

Cut chicken in pieces and soak them in cold salty water for an hour. Rinse.
Place in dry skillet and top with rest of ingredients. Cover and cook until
tender. Remove lid and continue to cook until all liquid is absorbed and meat
browns.

Martha Magott Hopcus
in memory of mother, Frances Kupczynski Magott

🐦 Smothered, Stuffed Chicken

1 whole chicken	½ c. butter
Salt	

Stuffing:

Chicken liver, chopped	2 Tbsp. butter
1 c. bread crumbs	Salt
1 tsp. dill, finely chopped	Pepper

To make the stuffing, fry the chopped liver in butter. Add dill and bread
crumbs. Rub inside the chicken with salt. Put stuffing in chicken. Place in
casserole. Salt and cover with butter. Cover and cook at 350° until tender.

Victoria B. Miller

Wonderful chicken from the wood stove ...

*In the '30s when we were children, Mother would flour chicken with salt,
pepper and add a chopped onion. Put all into an iron Dutch oven with a little
water and put on the lid. This was left to cook in the wood stove oven with sweet
potatoes. When we returned about three hours later, Mother added 2-3 tablespoons of thick sour cream and made the most delicious gravy to serve with the
potatoes.*

— Martha Magott Hopcus

New! Swiss & Mushroom Chicken

Pam Spray
2 chicken breasts
Swiss cheese slices
1 c. mushroom soup

¼ c. milk
2 c. herbed dressing mix
¼ c. butter, melted

Prepare baking dish by spraying with Pam spray. Place chicken breasts in baking dish and top each breast with a cheese slice.

Mix mushroom soup and milk. Pour mixture over the chicken. Sprinkle herbed bread crumbs dressing mix over the chicken. Drizzle ¼ c. melted butter over all.

Bake at 350° for 45 minutes to one hour, depending on thickness of the chicken.

Cookbook Committee Collection

Cornish Hens With Pecan Stuffing

2 (1 to 1½ lb.) Cornish hens
Salt and pepper

2 tsp. apricot brandy
¼ c. margarine, melted

Pecan Dressing:

⅓ c. unsweetened apple juice
2 Tbsp. apricot brandy
2 Tbsp. margarine

2 Tbsp. chopped pecans
1 c. corn bread stuffing

Thaw hens 2 days. Prepare dressing as directed below.

Remove giblets from hens. Rinse hens with cold water and pat dry. Sprinkle cavity of each with salt and pepper. Secure neck skin to back with toothpick. Lift wing tips up and over back so they are tucked under hen. Lightly stuff cavity of hens with Pecan Dressing. Close cavity and secure with toothpicks. Tie leg ends to tail with string. Brush hens with ½ of butter and sprinkle generously with pepper. Combine remaining butter and brandy. Place hens, breast side up, in a large shallow baking pan. Bake at 350° for 1-1½ hours. Baste every 10 minutes with brandy mixture.

Dressing: Combine apple juice, brandy and butter in large pan. Cook over medium heat, stirring occasionally, until butter melts, or microwave. Add stuffing and pecans and stir.

Becky Spaeth

Cornish Hens

6 Cornish hens	**Beau Monde seasoning to taste**
1 stick butter	**Garlic powder to taste**
1 c. wine	**Onion flakes to taste**
½ c. soy sauce	**Mushrooms (butter or sliced)**
Salt to taste	**3 cans Spanish artichoke hearts**
Pepper to taste	

Season hens with salt, pepper and onion flakes. Put hens in baking pan. Mix melted butter, wine and soy sauce. Pour over hens. Sprinkle with garlic powder and Beau Monde seasoning. Cover pan with foil. Bake hens for 2 hours. For the last hour, add mushrooms and canned Spanish artichoke hearts (3 cans for 12 people). Serve with Hawaiian Rice.

Hawaiian Rice:

¾ stick oleo	**1 large can whole mushrooms plus**
1 c. rice	**juice**
4 green onions, chopped	**1 tsp. oregano**
2 cans beef bouillon	

Brown onions and rice in oleo. Add other ingredients. Bake at 350°, uncovered, in oblong Pyrex dish for 1 hour.

Mary Keller

For Fluffy Rice

When cooking rice, add a spoonful of vinegar or the same amount of lemon juice and it will be light, fluffy and separated.

To Cook Wild Ducks

2 to 6 ducks	*1 tsp. cinnamon*
1 qt. canned tomatoes	*1 tsp. allspice*
6 large white onions	*¼ tsp. pepper*
1 tsp. cloves	

Pick ducks (saving all small feathers and down for pillows). Cut off wings and head; singe well, then put in cold water and rub well. Draw and save livers, gizzards and hearts for your gravy. It is best to dress your ducks a day or so before cooking. Drain them well. Place in an aluminum kettle, breasts up (anywhere from 2-6 ducks). Pour over them 1 quart canned tomatoes, 5 or 6 large white onions (sliced), 1 tsp. cloves, 1 tsp. cinnamon, 1 tsp. allspice and ¼ tsp. pepper. Let simmer on a very slow fire for 1½ hours.

After they have simmered for 1 hour, turn them over being careful not to prick the breast. After simmering the 1½ hours, place in your roasting pan, breasts side up and pour over all the juice (onions, etc.). Let bake in a moderate oven for 1½ hours. The gravy will be rather dark, but very delicious when served over steamed rice.

The Cookbook Committee
Our Lady's Cathedral Cookbook
Circa 20s or 30s

One Pot Chicken Dinner

3 lb. chicken pieces	*1 can cream of celery soup*
3 Tbsp. shortening	*Flour*
5 medium potatoes	*1 soup can water*
4 carrots	

Flour chicken pieces and brown in hot shortening. Remove chicken from pan. Add the soup and 1 can water, stirring to get up brown bits. Add the chicken and simmer for 30 minutes. Add the potatoes and carrots that have been peeled and chopped. Simmer until done, approximately 30 minutes.

Karen Kuhns

Crock Pot Chicken

1 whole or cut up chicken	2 tsp. salt
2 carrots, sliced	½ tsp. coarse black pepper
2 onions, sliced	½ c. water, chicken broth or white
2 celery stalks with leaves, cut in	wine
1-inch pieces	½ Tbsp. sweet basil

Remove skin from chicken and trim fat. Place carrots, onions and celery in bottom of crock pot. Add chicken. Top with salt, pepper and liquid. Sprinkle sweet basil over top. Cover and cook until done on LOW for 7-10 hours or HIGH for 2½-3½ hours, using 1 cup water. Remove chicken and vegetables with spatula.

Joyce Nowakowski

Baked Chicken & Rice

1 c. rice (raw)	¾ tsp. salt
2 c. chicken broth	⅛ tsp. thyme
4 oz. can mushrooms	Several chicken pieces, browned
2 Tbsp. parsley	

Combine the first 6 ingredients and heat to boiling. Pour over browned chicken pieces in casserole. Cover with foil or casserole cover. Bake at 350° for 1 hour.

Ann S. Huffman

Sticky Tips

Meat loaf will not stick if you place a slice of bacon on the bottom of the pan.

Vinegar brought to a boil in a new frying pan will prevent foods from sticking.

Muffins will slide right out of tin pans if the hot pan is first placed on a wet towel.

No sticking to the pan when you're scalding milk if you'll first rinse the pan in cold water.

A dip of the spoon or cup into hot water before measuring shortening or butter will cause the fat to slip out easily without sticking to the spoon.

Before measuring honey or other syrup, oil the cup with cooking oil and rinse in hot water.

Marty's Chicken Casserole

1 fryer, boiled and deboned
  (reserve broth)
1 can mushroom soup
1 can cream of chicken soup
1 can Ro-Tel tomatoes, diced

1 doz. corn tortillas
1 large onion, chopped fine
2 c. grated Cheddar cheese
1 glass red wine

Cook chicken and let cool. Mix soups and tomatoes in a bowl. Debone and cut chicken into small pieces. In a 2½ or 3 quart casserole, place ingredients in layers: Tortillas, chicken, onion, cheese and soup mixture. Repeat. Add a little more cheese on top. I usually pour some chicken broth on top so that it doesn't dry out.

The wine is for the cook!

Marty Janowiak Casteel

Chicken Casserole

½ stick butter
½ c. orange juice
½ c. water
1 can cream of mushroom soup

1 c. Uncle Ben's converted brown
  rice
1 pkg. Lipton onion soup mix
1 cut up chicken

Butter bottom of casserole dish with ½ stick of butter. Spread rice in casserole. Mix juice, water and mushroom soup. Pour mixture over rice and combine well. Sprinkle ½ of onion soup mix over rice mixture. Place chicken pieces on rice. Sprinkle remaining onion soup mix over chicken. Cover with aluminum foil. Bake at 350° for 1½ hours. Remove foil last few minutes to let chicken brown.

Betty Lang

Bread Crumb Shaker
Empty salt cartons with spouts make dandy containers for bread crumbs. A funnel is used to get the crumbs into the carton.

Chicken Casserole

At least 4 pieces chicken
½ c. regular rice
1 small can canned mushrooms

1 can mushroom, celery or cream
of chicken soup

Variation:

½ chicken in pieces
½ cup regular rice
1 small can canned mushrooms

1 can mushroom, celery or cream
of chicken soup

Variation:

1 whole chicken in pieces
1 c. regular rice
2 small cans canned mushrooms

1 can mushroom, celery or cream
of chicken soup

Place chicken pieces in Corning Ware pan. Pour rice over chicken. Drain mushrooms. Pour over rice. Pour soup over all. Bake at 350° for 1 hour. Add salt and pepper if desired. Serve with tossed salad, bread and butter and broccoli — it is a good side dish.

Eugene Marshall, O.S.B.

Chicken Casserole

1 stewed chicken, cut in small
pieces
1 can cream of mushroom soup
1 can cream of chicken soup

1 (16 oz.) bag frozen broccoli
Shredded Cheddar cheese
Bread pieces
Stick of butter, melted

Layer bottom of pan with broccoli. Mix chicken with soups and pour over broccoli. Cover with shredded Cheddar cheese. Top with bread pieces. Pour butter over bread. Bake at 350° for 30 minutes.

Mary Ann Padgett

Broccoli With Rice & Chicken

1 c. rice
½ c. finely chopped celery
1 medium onion, finely chopped
½ c. margarine
1 (10¾ oz.) can cream of chicken
 soup

½ tsp. salt
1 tsp. soy sauce
1 (4 oz.) jar pimento cheese spread
1 (10 oz.) pkg. broccoli spears
2 boiled chicken breasts or 1 small
 can chicken

Cook rice according to package directions and drain. Saute celery and onion in margarine. Stir in remaining ingredients, except rice and broccoli. Set aside 4 tablespoons of the sauce. Add rice to remaining sauce. Pour into buttered baking dish.

Cook broccoli until slightly undercooked and drain. Arrange on rice mixture and spread with reserved sauce. Bake in a 350° oven for 45 minutes. Makes 4-5 servings.

You can use 2 slices of American cheese instead of cheese spread if desired. Ham can be substituted for chicken.

Frances Wyskup

Chicken & Rice

1 chicken
1 can cream of chicken condensed
 soup
1 can cream of mushroom
 condensed soup

½ c. mushrooms (canned)
4 oz. cream cheese
1 c. sour cream
Rice

Mix 2 cans of soup together. Pour over chicken in baking dish and bake at 350° for 2-2½ hours. Debone the chicken. Return chicken to dish. Add mushrooms, cream cheese and sour cream. Mix. Serve over rice which has been prepared according to package directions.

Joyce Nowakowski

Chicken Casserole

2 to 2½ lb. chicken or 4 to 5
   chicken breasts
1 can cream of chicken soup
1 medium chopped onion
1 (16 oz.) can French style green
   beans

1 (2 oz.) jar diced pimentos
1 (8 oz.) can water chestnuts
1 c. mayonnaise
1 pkg. Uncle Ben's wild rice
Paprika
Parmesan cheese

Boil chicken and debone. Prepare wild rice according to package directions. Drain green beans and water chestnuts. Mix all ingredients together. Put in 11"x13" casserole dish. Sprinkle with paprika and Parmesan cheese. Heat about 25 minutes at 350°.

Joyce Nowakowski

Chicken & Rice Casserole

Chicken, cut up
1½ c. uncooked rice
1 can cream of celery soup
1 can cream of chicken soup

½ c. water
1 fryer, cut up
1 can onion soup

Place rice in greased casserole dish. Add celery and chicken soups and water. Place chicken pieces on top. Pour onion soup over this. Bake at 350° for 1½-2 hours.

Patricia Furchak

Fish Tricks

Thaw fish in milk. The milk draws out the frozen taste and provides a fresh-caught flavor.

Chicken Noodle Casserole

1 (12 oz.) pkg. noodles (I use
    spinach noodles.)
3 c. boiled, bite-size pieces chicken
½ c. mayonnaise
½ onion, chopped
1 c. sliced celery

¼ stick margarine
½ tsp. salt
1 can cream of mushroom soup
1 c. milk
1 c. grated cheese

Saute celery and onions in margarine. Add soup, milk, salt and cheese to this mixture and heat until cheese is melted. In large casserole combine cooked noodles, chicken pieces, mayonnaise and the soup mixture. Bake at 425° for 20 minutes.

Diana Hanna

Spinach Noodle Chicken Casserole

2 lb. chicken
1 stick butter
1 c. onions, chopped
1 c. celery, chopped
1 bell pepper, diced
1 lb. grated Velveeta cheese

1 can cream of mushroom soup
1 can mushrooms
1 can sliced water chestnuts
1 pkg. spinach noodles
1 can sliced ripe olives

Boil fryers. Debone and save broth. Saute the onions, celery and pepper in butter. Cook noodles in chicken broth and drain. Mix all ingredients together. Garnish with sliced ripe olives.

Cook in preheated 350° oven for 45 minutes.

Joyce Nowakowski

Great Chicken Casserole

1 pkg. Pepperidge Farm herb
   dressing, divided
1 cube melted oleo (½ c.)
1 stewed chicken, deboned

1½ c. chicken stock
1 can cream of chicken soup
1 c. sour cream

Grease 9"x13" pan. Mix dressing with oleo. Reserve 1 cup of the mixture. Mix remaining mixture with chicken stock. Pour into baking pan and top with chicken. Beat soup and sour cream with wire whisk. "Ice" mixture with the soup and sour cream. Sprinkle the reserved dressing on top. Bake 30 minutes at 350°.

Marty Janowiak Casteel

Microwave Chili Chicken Casserole

2 small cans chicken
1 can cream of chicken soup
½ c. water
1 small onion, chopped

1 small can chopped green chilies,
   drained
3 c. corn chips
4 slices cheese

Place ½ of the chips in a 1½ quart casserole dish. Drain the chicken and spread over the corn chips. Layer the onion, chilies and cheese slices over the chicken. Cover with remaining chips and top with the soup, mixed with the water. Cover and microwave for about 10 minutes. Turn dish halfway at 5 minutes. Serves 4.

Cora Rudek

Quick Tuna Casserole

1 can tuna fish
2 cans cream of mushroom soup

1 can drained peas
2 c. macaroni

Cook macaroni first, then mix all the rest of the ingredients. Put in casserole dish. Bake at 375° for 30 minutes.

Bena Meany

New! *Roast Lamb, Greek Style*

6-7 lbs. leg of lamb
1½ tsp. salt
¼ tsp. pepper
3 cloves garlic

¼ c. butter or margarine
¼ c. lemon juice
1 tsp. dried rosemary leaves
2 tsp. dried oregano leaves

Egg & Lemon Sauce:

2 Tbsp. butter or margarine
2 Tbsp. flour
¾ tsp. salt
1 can (13¾ oz.) chicken broth

3 Tbsp. lemon juice
4 egg yolks
1 lbs. chopped parsley

Preheat oven to 325°.

Wipe lamb with paper towels. Rub surface with salt and pepper.

Peel garlic, cut crosswise into thin slivers. Using paring knife, cut 12-16 small slits, about 1-inch deep in lamb. Insert garlic slivers.

Place lamb in shallow roasting pan without rack. Brush lamb with melted butter. Pour lemon juice over meat. Sprinkle with rosemary and oregano.

Insert meat thermometer in thickest part of meat, away from bone and fat. Roast uncovered and basting occasionally, about 2 hours, or until meat thermometer registers 170° for well done. Remove lamb to heated platter. Let roast stand 20 minutes for easier carving.

Meanwhile, make the Egg and Lemon Sauce. Melt butter in top of double boiler over direct heat. Remove from heat; stir in flour and salt until smooth. Gradually stir in chicken broth and lemon juice. Cook over low heat, stirring constantly, until mixture boils. Place over hot, not boiling water.

In a small bowl, beat egg yolks slightly. Slowly beat in small amount of hot mixture. Slowly add to rest of mixture. Slowly add to rest of mixture in double boiler, stirring constantly.

Cook over hot water, stirring constantly, until thickened. Remove from heat and stir in chopped parsley.

Very good. Try it, you will like it.

Mark Klimkowski

🐦 New! *Quick & Easy Lamb Stew*

1 lb. lean American lamb, cut in ¾
   to 1-inch cubes
Non-stick spray coating
2 med. onions, cut in wedges
1 clove garlic, minced or ½ tsp.
   bottled, minced garlic
1 Tbsp. prepared horseradish
1 Tbsp. prepared or brown mustard
1 tsp. dried thyme, basil, oregano,
   marjoram, or rosemary, crushed

1 (15 oz.) can stewed tomatoes,
   undrained
3 or 4 med. potatoes, peeled and
   cubed
2 carrots, cut in ½" slices
2 stalks celery, cut in ½" slices
1-1½ c. small fresh mushrooms
   (4 oz.)
1 c. frozen peas
1 12 oz. jar brown gravy

Spray a large saucepan or kettle with non-stick spray. Brown lamb cubes and add onion, garlic, horseradish, mustard, and herb; mix well. Stir in tomatoes, cover and simmer 15 minutes.

Add potatoes, carrots, celery and mushrooms. Cover and cook 15-20 minutes, or until meat and vegetables are tender. Stir in peas and gravy; heat through.

Serve with a crisp green salad and warm cornbread.

The Cookbook Committee

Easter tradition...

   "We always had to have pickled herring at Easter time."

Rosie L. Klimkowski

🐦 Tuna Fish Casserole

1 can tuna
1 can cream of mushroom soup
1 pkg. noodles

6 to 8 slices pimento cheese
1 soup can of milk or cream

Cook noodles as directed on package. Drain and add tuna, soup and 1 soup can of milk or cream. Mix in 4 slices of cheese, broken in pieces. Pour in greased casserole dish. Sprinkle remaining cheese pieces over top and bake until cheese has melted and browned. Bake at 350°.

Minnie Nowakowski

🐦 New Orleans Shrimp Salad

½ c. uncooked rice, cooked
1½ lb. cooked shrimp
½ c. chopped green pepper
1 small onion, chopped or 1 bunch
   green onions
1 c. fresh cauliflower, broken into
   small flowerets

1 c. green olives
¼ c. lemon juice
½ c. mayonnaise
½ c. French dressing
Tabasco to taste
Salt and pepper

Cook rice. For shrimp, spice cooking water with chopped lemon, peppercorns and any other desired spices. Combine cooked rice, cooked shrimp and vegetables. Mix lemon juice with mayonnaise and French dressing. Add Tabasco to taste. Add salt and pepper. Toss to coat rice, shrimp and vegetable mixture.

Can substitute a little mayonnaise mixed with a little ketchup and Worcestershire sauce for dressing.

Judy Seikel

 New! *Shrimp Fettucini*

2 med. onions, chopped
3 green onions, chopped
1 med. bell pepper, chopped
2 ribs celery, chopped
1½ stick oleo
1 Tbsp. flour
1 tsp. parsley

2 lbs. peeled shrimp
½ c. jalapeno relish
½ lb. Velveeta cheese
½ pt. half & half
3 cloves garlic
½ lb. fettucini noodles
Parmesan cheese

Saute vegetables in oleo until soft. Add flour, parsley and shrimp. Cook for 15 minutes. Add jalapeno relish, Velveeta, half and half and garlic. Cook 15 minutes. Cook noodles according to package directions. Fold noodles and sauce together and cover with parmesan cheese. Bake in 9"x13" dish for 15 minutes at 350°.

Vicki Ledet
In memory of Mrs. A. C. Ledet

Egg Souffle

7 slices bread
1 stick melted butter
4 oz. El Paso chopped green chilies
6 oz. Cheddar cheese, grated

2 c. half & half (1 pt.)
9 eggs
1 c. chopped ham, bacon or sausage

Cut crust off bread. Dip in melted butter and place in bottom of 9"x13" pan. Pour chilies and meat over bread. Sprinkle cheese on top. Separate eggs. Add half & half to yolks and beat. Beat egg whites and combine with yolks. Pour over cheese and bake at 350° for 45 minutes.

Vicki Dimmer

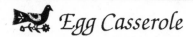 *Egg Casserole*

8 slices white bread
9 to 11 eggs
1½ c. milk
½ tsp. dry mustard

½ tsp. salt
Ham or Canadian bacon
1½ to 2 c. American or Colby
Longhorn cheese

Remove crust from bread. Place slices in a greased 9"x13" pan. Cover bread with meat (ham, Canadian bacon). Cover good with grated American or Colby Longhorn cheese. Beat eggs, milk, mustard and salt together. Pour egg mixture over bread and meat in casserole dish. Cover with foil and refrigerate 24 hours. Bake at 350°, uncovered, for 30 minutes. Let stand before cutting.

Barbara Dull

This is a Graduation Breakfast tradition at St. Teresa's.

Breakfast Casserole

8 slices bread
9 to 11 eggs
1½ c. milk
½ tsp. dry mustard

½ tsp. salt
1 lb. sausage or bacon
8 oz. grated Cheddar cheese

Grease 9"x13" pan. Remove crust from bread and place in casserole pan. Cover bread with 1 pound sausage, crumbled and fried and drained or 1 pound bacon, fried and crumbled. Beat together eggs, milk, mustard and salt. Cover meat with 8 ounces grated Cheddar cheese, then cover with egg mixture. Bake, uncovered, at 350° for 30 minutes.

Carolyn Miles

Hints for Bacon

No "curly" bacon for breakfast when you dip it into cold water before frying.

Keep bacon slices from sticking together: roll the package into a tube shape and secure with rubber bands.

A quick way to separate frozen bacon: heat a spatula over a burner, slide it under each slice to separate it from the others.

Breakfast Casserole

8 oz. Monterrey Jack cheese, grated
8 oz. Mozzarella cheese, grated
8 oz. Cheddar cheese, grated
½ to 1 sm. can green chilies,
    chopped
1 c. chopped ham or cooked and
    crumbled bacon

2 eggs
2 c. milk
1 c. flour
½ tsp. salt

Layer cheeses, green chilies and meat in a greased 9"x13" pan. Combine eggs, milk, flour and salt and pour over cheese mixture. Bake at 350° for 45 minutes. Cut in squares to serve.

Diana Hanna

Green Chili-Rice Bake

1 c. raw rice
8 oz. Monterrey Jack cheese,
    shredded
1 (7 oz.) can chopped green chilies,
    drained

1 c. sour cream
¼ c. butter or margarine, melted
½ tsp. salt
½ c. shredded Cheddar cheese
Paprika

Cook rice according to package directions. Drain if necessary. Cool. Preheat oven to 350°. In large bowl, combine cooked rice, Monterrey Jack cheese, green chilies, sour cream, butter and salt. Pour into a shallow casserole dish. Sprinkle Cheddar cheese and paprika on top. Bake 30 minutes or until heated through and bubbly around edges.

Darline Ruyle

Welsh Rarebit Crepes

Sauce:

2 Tbsp. butter
1 c. beer
2½ c. sharp Cheddar cheese
2 Tbsp. flour

1 egg, beaten
1 tsp. Worcestershire sauce
½ tsp. dry mustard
Dash of cayenne (red) pepper

Crepes:

2 eggs, slightly beaten
⅔ c. milk
½ c. all-purpose flour

½ tsp. salt
1 tsp. butter or margarine

Filling:

2 c. chopped tomatoes
2 c. diced avocado

½ lb. bacon, cooked and crumbled

Sauce: In saucepan, melt butter over low heat. Add flour, mustard and worcestershire sauce. Add beer. When warm, stir in cheese. Stir constantly until cheese is melted. Stir in beaten egg.

Crepes: Beat all ingredients, except butter, in small bowl until smooth. Refrigerate, covered, at least 2 hours. Heat butter in 7-inch skillet or crepe pan until bubbly. Pour about ½ cup batter into skillet. Quickly tilt and rotate skillet to coat bottom evenly with batter. Cook over medium heat until light brown. Turn crepes to brown on other side. Make 12 crepes for baking.

Filling: Fill crepes with about 2 tablespoons each of tomatoes and avocado. Roll crepes and arrange in oven-proof dish. Spoon cheese sauce over crepes and sprinkle with bacon. Bake in preheated 375° oven about 10 minutes.

These are delicious for luncheons or for dinner. This was from a "Danny's Day" program in January, 1977.

Pauline Haynes

Cheesy Tricks

Cheese won't harden if you'll butter the exposed edges before storing.

A cloth dampened with vinegar and wrapped around cheese will also prevent drying out.

 Macaroni & Cheese

1 (7 oz.) pkg. macaroni
3 Tbsp. butter or oleo
3 Tbsp. flour
2 c. cheese, divided

2 c. milk
½ tsp. salt
Pepper
2 c. grated American cheese

Cook macaroni according to directions on package (do not overcook). Melt butter. Blend in flour. Add milk. Cook until thick, stirring constantly. Add seasonings and 1½ cups cheese. Stir until melted. Put macaroni in greased 1½ quart shallow baking dish. Pour sauce over macaroni. Sprinkle with rest of cheese. Bake at 350° for 30 minutes. Sprinkle with paprika.

Jodi Steciak

Spinach Souffle

3 Tbsp. butter
3 Tbsp. flour
Salt
Pepper
1 c. milk

1 (10 oz.) pkg. frozen spinach
½ tsp. chopped onion
3 eggs, separated
½ lb. Cheddar or American cheese

Melt butter; add flour, salt and pepper. Stir in milk. Cook until slightly thick, making a white sauce. Cook spinach and drain thoroughly. Add grated cheese to white sauce. Beat egg yolks and gradually stir into sauce. Add onion and cool. Beat egg whites until stiff. Combine all ingredients and pour into buttered (1 quart) casserole dish. Set in pan of hot water and bake in preheated 350° oven for 50-60 minutes. Serves 4.

Using less spinach than 10 ounces, makes a better souffle. Omit salt if on low sodium diet.

Sister Bernadette Zayonc

Zucchini Crust Pizza

3 zucchini, shredded
1 Tbsp. flour
3 eggs
Mozzarella cheese
Fresh sliced tomatoes

Sliced mushrooms
Sliced onions
Sliced black olives
Basil to taste
Oregano

Toss shredded zucchini with flour. Mix in eggs. Press into pizza pan and bake at 350° for 10 minutes. Top with sliced tomatoes, mushrooms and olives. Sprinkle on seasonings to taste. Top with shredded cheese. Bake 20 minutes at 350°.

Judy Seikel

All-Gone Lasagna - Vegetarian

9 long lasagna noodles, cooked
2 c. cottage cheese
2 lb. cheese (any type), grated
½ c. diced onion

1 large jar spaghetti sauce
Parmesan cheese for topping
½ c. chopped mushrooms (optional)

In 9"x11" pan, lay down 3 noodles side-by-side. Top with ⅓ of all ingredients. Lay down the next 2 layers in the same way until 3 layers are completed and all ingredients are gone. Sprinkle with Parmesan cheese.

Bake 20 minutes, uncovered, at 350° or until sauce bubbles. Cool 10 minutes, if you can wait that long. Our kids never do.

This is a good dish for the kids to make.

Rita Laws

Lenten memory...

"Pete Senkowski, a grocery store owner, took orders each Lent for miniature kegs of salted herring to be served on meatless days of Lent.

Mother washed off excess salt, then soaked the herring 24 hours in fresh water. She would change the water every eight hours.

She would then boil vinegar with a few allspice, black pepper and a touch of sugar. After this mixture was cool, she would blend in some cream. She would serve this with onion slices and the herring."

Mrs. Bill (Martha) Hopcus

 Berry or Cherry Cobbler

1 c. flour
1 c. sugar
Pinch of salt
1 tsp. baking powder
½ c. milk

2 Tbsp. butter
1 pt. berries or cherries (canned,
    frozen or fresh)
1 c. sugar or sweeten to taste

Sift together flour, sugar, salt and baking powder. Cut in butter and milk. Spread on bottom of buttered pan, 11½"x 7½". Sweeten fruit and bring to a boil. Pour boiling fruit over batter. Bake 20-25 minutes at 400° or until golden brown.

Martha Greenlee

Cobbler

1 stick butter, melted
1 c. self-rising flour
1 c. sugar
1 c. milk
2 tsp. baking powder

½ tsp. salt
2 cans pie filling
Approx. ⅓ c. brown sugar
Approx. 2 to 3 tsp. cinnamon
Approx. 2 tsp. sugar

Combine baking powder and salt. Mix with butter, flour, 1 cup sugar and milk in glass casserole or pan. Pour pie filling on top. Combine brown sugar, cinnamon and approximately 2 tsp. sugar. Sprinkle over pie filling. Bake at 375° for 30-50 minutes.

Mary Horn

Fruit Cobbler

1 (No. 2) can cherries
2 c. sugar
1 c. flour

1 tsp. baking powder
2 Tbsp. melted butter or oleo
Stick butter

Combine cherries with 1 cup sugar. Let stand while combining flour, 1 cup sugar, baking powder and butter or oleo. Pour batter into shallow baking dish and smooth gently. Pour fruit and sugar mixture on top. Do not stir. Dot with butter. Bake 45 minutes at 325° in glass casserole.

Other fruits may be substituted for cherries, using 2 or 2½ cups.

Virginia A. Morton

Peach Jiffy Cobbler

1 qt. Peaches (sweetened), or large
   can fruit
1 c. sugar
1 c. flour
1 Tbsp. baking powder

1 c. milk
1 stick oleo
¼ tsp. salt
½ tsp. cinnamon

Melt oleo in baking pan. Mix sugar, flour, baking powder, cinnamon, salt and milk to a soft batter. Pour batter over oleo. Mix ½ tsp. cinnamon into fruit then spoon fruit over batter. Bake at 350° for 45 minutes or until brown. (If peaches are frozen, heat while thawing to prevent darkening.) Use ¼ less sugar if cobbler is to be topped with ice cream.

Mrs. Frank Wyskup

No Sticky Fingers

To measure ½ cup of shortening, fill a 1 cup measuring glass with ½ c. of water. Add shortening until water rises to the top. Shortening will be under water.

No more "Cake Pan" fingers: Use a sandwich bag as a "glove" when greasing cake pans. Takes the mess out of the job!

🐦 Cherry Cheese Pie

1 (8 oz.) pkg. cream cheese,
   softened
1 (14 oz.) can Eagle Brand
   sweetened condensed milk (not
   evaporated milk)
⅓ c. ReaLemon juice

1 tsp. vanilla extract
1 (21 oz.) can cherry pie filling,
   chilled
1 (9-inch) graham cracker crust pie
   shell

In large mixer bowl, beat cheese until fluffy. Gradually beat in Eagle Brand condensed milk until smooth. Stir in lemon juice and vanilla. Pour into prepared crust. Chill 3 hours or until set. Top with desired amount of pie filling before serving. Refrigerate leftovers.

Jeri Schuessler

🐦 Cherry Pudding Pie

4 c. canned cherries (2 cans)
1 c. sugar
4 Tbsp. butter
2 c. flour

2 c. sugar
2 Tbsp. baking powder
¼ tsp. salt
1 c. milk

Heat cherries and sugar. Make a paste of butter, flour, 2 cups sugar, baking powder, salt and milk. Put into greased 9"x13" pan. Pour in cherry mixture. Bake at 350° for 40 minutes.

Mrs. Tom Jorski

🐦 Chocolate Pie

2 eggs
⅓ c. flour
½ c. sugar
2 c. milk

½ c. chocolate chips
1 c. miniature marshmallows
3 Tbsp. butter
Dream Whip or Cool Whip

Mix eggs, flour, sugar and milk in a saucepan and cook until thickened. Stir in butter, chocolate chips and marshmallows and beat until melted. Pour into a prepared pie crust. Top with Dream Whip or Cool Whip.

Adeline ZurSchmiede

Chocolate Cream Pie

½ c. sugar
⅓ c. flour
¼ tsp. salt
2 c. milk
2 eggs, beaten
1 Tbsp. butter

½ c. chocolate chips
1 tsp. vanilla
1 baked pie shell
Dream Whip
Shaved chocolate (optional)

In saucepan, mix sugar, flour and salt. Add 1 cup milk. Mix until smooth. Bring to a boil over medium heat, stirring constantly. Remove from heat. With fork, beat eggs. Add the remaining cup of milk. Gradually stir into hot mixture and cook until thick, stirring constantly. Remove from heat and add butter, vanilla and chocolate chips. Beat well and pour into baked pie shell. Chill, then add Dream Whip as topping. Garnish with shaved chocolate if desired.

Carolyn Miles

Chocolate Icebox Pie

1 c. flour
½ c. margarine
½ c. chopped pecans
1 - 8 oz. pkg. cream cheese
1½ c. powdered sugar
1 large ctn. Cool Whip

5 c. milk
1 large box instant vanilla pudding
1 large box instant chocolate
    pudding
Chopped pecans

Mix flour and margarine until crumbly. Add pecans. Press into bottom of 9"x13" pan. Bake at 350° for 20 minutes. Let cool completely. Beat cream cheese and powdered sugar. Fold into ½ of the Cool Whip. Spread over cooled crust. Stir milk and puddings together. Let set until congealed. Spread over cream cheese mixture. Top with remaining Cool Whip and sprinkle with chopped pecans.

Adeline Jorski

Chocolate Mocha Pie

1 Tbsp. unflavored gelatin
1/4 c. cold water
2 Tbsp. cocoa
3/4 c. sugar
1/8 tsp. salt
1 tsp. instant coffee

1 1/4 c. milk
1 baked pie shell
1 c. heavy whipping cream
1 tsp. vanilla
Nuts (optional)

Combine in a saucepan the gelatin and water. Bring to a boil the cocoa, sugar, salt, instant coffee and milk, stirring constantly. Remove from heat; add softened gelatin. Cool till slightly thickened. Beat cooked mixture until smooth. Whip heavy cream. Add vanilla. Fold into cooked mixture, then pour into pie shell. Chill. Top with nuts if desired.

Anita Craiger

Coconut Cream Pie

3/4 c. sugar
1/4 c. cornstarch
1/8 tsp. salt
3 c. milk
3 egg yolks, beaten
3/4 c. coconut

1 1/2 Tbsp. butter or margarine
1 tsp. vanilla
1 basic pastry shell
3 egg whites
1/4 tsp. plus 1/8 tsp. cream of tartar
1/4 c. plus 2 Tbsp. sugar

Combine first 3 ingredients in a heavy saucepan. Combine milk and egg yolks. Gradually stir into sugar mixture. Cook over medium heat, stirring constantly, until mixture thickens and boils. Boil 1 minute, stirring constantly. Remove from heat; stir in 1/2 cup coconut, butter and vanilla. Pour filling into baked pastry shell. Cover filling with waxed paper. Beat eggs (at room temperature) and cream of tartar at high speed for 1 minute. Gradually add remaining sugar, 1 tablespoon at a time, beating until stiff peaks form and sugar dissolves (2-4 minutes).

Remove wax paper from pie filling; spread meringue over hot filling, sealing to edges of pastry. Sprinkle meringue with 1/4 cup coconut.

Bake at 350° for 12-15 minutes, until golden brown. Cool to room temperature. Yields 1 (9-inch) pie.

Mary Winters

Coconut Macaroon Pie

1½ c. sugar
2 eggs
½ tsp. salt
½ c. soft butter

¼ c. flour
½ c. milk
1½ c. shredded coconut
9 inch unbaked pie shell

Beat eggs, sugar and salt until mixture is lemon colored. Add butter and flour; blend well. Add milk and fold in 1 cup of the coconut. Pour into pie shell. Top with remaining ½ cup of coconut. Bake in slow 325° oven, approximately 1 hour.

Joyce Nowakowski

New! Coconut & Pineapple Pie

3 eggs
1 c. light corn syrup
1 c. crushed pineapple
1 c. coconut

1 c. sugar
2 tsp. flour
½ stick oleo, melted
1 10-inch unbaked pie shell

Combine eggs and corn syrup. Beat until well blended. Stir in remaining ingredients. Mix well. Bake at 350° for 30 minutes, or until crust is brown and filling is firm.

Marjorie Magott

Cottage Cheese Pie

1 c. cottage cheese
2 large eggs
1½ c. milk
1 tsp. vanilla
¾ c. sugar

¼ tsp. salt
⅓ c. whipping cream
2 Tbsp. butter
Prepared pie shell
Nutmeg

Preheat oven to 425°. In large bowl, cream sugar and melted butter and eggs until fluffy. Add salt, vanilla, cottage cheese and whipping cream. Mix well. Add 1¼ cups hot milk. Pour into prepared pie shell and sprinkle with nutmeg. Bake at 425° for 50 minutes.

Bena Meany

Dream Pie

1 can cherries (sour)
1 can crushed pineapple
1½ c. sugar
½ c. flour
1 large pkg. raspberry Jell-O or
   strawberry

½ tsp. red food coloring
5 or 6 bananas, cut up
1½ c. chopped nuts
2 baked pie shells
Whipped topping

Drain cherries and pineapple, reserving the juice. Mix sugar and flour. Add juice from cherries and pineapple and cook until thick. Add cherries and pineapple. Cook a few minutes more; remove from heat. Add Jell-O, food coloring, bananas and nuts. Pour into 2 large baked pie shells after the filling is cooled and top with Cool Whip or Dream Whip or whipped cream, whichever you prefer. Chill. A very rich pie.

You can put a few maraschino cherries on top if you like.

Mary Ellen Fortelney

New! Fluffy Frozen Peanut Butter Pie

3 graham cracker crusts
8 oz. cream cheese
2 cups powdered sugar

1 c. creamy peanut butter
1 c. milk
2 - 9 oz. containers Cool Whip

Whip cheese, beat in sugar and peanut butter. Slowly add milk and blend thoroughly. Fold in Cool Whip. Pour into graham cracker crusts. Freeze. Remove from freezer a few minutes before serving.

Everyone asks for this recipe!

Diana Hanna

To Tint Coconut

To tint coconut, add a small amount of milk or water to coconut and toss. Add a few drops of food coloring. Toss again to color. Drain the liquid from the coconut and spread coconut on paper towels or wax paper to dry.

🐦 Grandma's Rhubarb Pie

Rhubarb	**1 Tbsp. flour**
1 egg	**½ tsp. salt**
½ c. milk	**1 tsp. vanilla**
1 c. sugar	**1 unbaked pie shell**

Cut rhubarb into unbaked pie shell. Mix remaining ingredients. Pour over rhubarb and bake at 325° until rhubarb is done and pie is golden brown.

Kay Brown

🐦 Graham Cracker Pie

4 pt. whipping cream	**Maraschino cherries**
1 (16 oz.) can Hershey's syrup	**Graham crackers**

Beat whipping cream until thickened; stir in the syrup and mix well. Use a 10"x13" dish. Layer graham crackers on bottom of dish, then top with mixture (make 3 layers). Add cherries on top. Cover with lid or aluminum foil. Chill in freezer overnight.

Terry Fortelney

🐦 Grasshopper Pie

1 (8 oz.) pkg. cream cheese, softened	**¼ c. green creme de menthe**
1 can Eagle Brand sweetened condensed milk	**¼ c. white creme de cacao**
	1 (9 oz.) container frozen non-dairy whipped topping
3 Tbsp. lemon juice (fresh or bottled)	**Chocolate curls**
	1 graham cracker crust

Let cream cheese stand at room temperature until softened. In large bowl, beat cream cheese until light and fluffy. Slowly add sweetened condensed milk, beating until smooth. Stir in lemon juice and liqueurs. Fold in whipped topping. Chill slightly. Gently pile into crust. Chill 3 hours or until set. Garnish with chocolate curls.

Minnie Nowakowski

Impossible Pie

4 eggs
2 c. milk
1 c. sugar
1 sick oleo (½ c.)

½ c. flour
1 c. coconut or pineapple
2 tsp. vanilla

Place ingredients in blender and blend. Pour into well-greased 10-inch pie pan. Bake at 350° for 30 minutes or until brown. Makes its own crust.

Betty A. Miller, CDA State Regent

New! Sour Cream Apple Pie

1 c. sour cream
1 c. sugar
2 Tbsp. of flour
¼ tsp. of salt

1 tsp. of vanilla
1 egg
2 c. apples, peeled and thinly-sliced
9-inch pie crust, unbaked

Topping

½ c. brown sugar
⅓ c. flour

¼ butter, chopped

Beat together one cup sour cream, one cup sugar, two tablespoons of flour, ¼ teaspoon of salt, one teaspoon of vanilla, and 1 egg. Add to two cups of peeled and thinly-sliced apples.

Pour into a 9-inch, unbaked pie shell and bake for 30 minutes at 350°.

Remove from oven and sprinkle with ½ c. brown sugar, ⅓ c. flour, and ¼ cup butter that has been mixed well. Return to oven and bake an additional 20 minutes.

Pauline Piotrowicz

Blueberry Pie

2 sticks oleo (1 c.)
2 c. flour
½ c. brown sugar
1 c. chopped pecans
1 (8 oz.) cream cheese

1 c. sugar
1 Tbsp. vanilla
1 env. Dream Whip
1 can blueberry pie filling

To make crust, melt oleo with flour, brown sugar and pecans. Press into bottom and sides of 2 pie pans and bake at 350° for 15 minutes. Cool.

For filling, beat cream cheese, sugar and vanilla. Mix 1 envelope of Dream Whip as directed on package. Mix Dream Whip mixture with cream cheese mixture and pour into crust. Pour blueberry pie filling over top and spread evenly.

Pauline Johnson

Buttermilk Pie

3 eggs
1 c. sugar
3 Tbsp. flour
¼ tsp. salt

2 c. buttermilk
4 Tbsp. melted butter
1 (9-inch) unbaked pie shell

Beat egg yolks, sugar, flour, salt and small amount of the buttermilk until well blended. Add buttermilk and melted butter. Fold in stiffly-beaten egg whites. Pour into unbaked 9-inch pie shell. Bake at 450° for 10 minutes and at 350° for 35-40 minutes or until done.

Helen Hopcus

Lemon Pie

1 graham cracker crust
1 pkg. pink lemonade mix
1 can Eagle Brand milk

1 small ctn. Cool Whip
Nuts (if desired)

Beat milk, lemonade mix and Cool Whip with mixer until well mixed. Put in pie crust and chill. May be frozen.

Gerry Lamer

Lemon Chiffon Pie

1 c. sugar
3 Tbsp. corn starch
1½ c. cold water
1 tsp. grated lemon rind

¼ c. lemon juice
1 Tbsp. Mazola or margarine
3 eggs, separated

In 2-quart saucepan or double boiler heat sugar and corn starch. Add water and egg yolks, stirring constantly until thickened. Cool. Fold in beaten egg whites and pour into baked pie shell.

Anelia Block

Lemon Chiffon Pie

1 c. sugar
3 Tbsp. flour
2 rounded Tbsp. butter
Juice and rind of 1 lemon

2 egg yolks
2 egg whites
1 c. milk
1 unbaked pie shell

Cream together sugar and butter. Add juice and rind of lemon. Mix well. Add egg yolks and cream well. Add milk. Fold in stiffly-beaten egg whites. Bake in unbaked pie shell for 40 minutes at 350° or until done.

Helen Hopcus

Lemon Chiffon Pie

4 egg yolks, beaten
⅔ c. sugar
Pinch of salt

¼ c. lemon juice
4 egg whites
⅓ c. sugar

Beat egg yolks well. Add ⅔ cup sugar and a pinch of salt. Add the lemon juice. Cook in a double boiler until thick, stirring often. Beat the 4 egg whites until they are stiff, gradually adding the ⅓ cup sugar to them. Fold ½ of the egg whites into the egg yolk mixture. Pour mixture into baked pie crust and chill before serving. Use the other ½ to top pie. Or, all of the egg whites can be folded into egg yolk mixture.

Ruby Hornbeck

Mystery Pie

3 egg whites
½ tsp. baking powder
1 c. white sugar

1 tsp. vanilla
20 Ritz crackers
¾ c. pecans, chopped

Topping:

½ c. whipping cream or Dream
   Whip
¼ tsp. nutmeg

2 Tbsp. white sugar
¼ c. chopped pecans

Beat egg whites until stiff. Fold in baking powder, then fold in 2 tablespoons sugar at a time until 1 cup is used. Fold in vanilla and Ritz crackers, then fold in ¾ cup chopped pecans. Put this mixture in an ungreased 9-inch pie pan and bake 30 minutes at 325°. Let cool 30 minutes then top with topping.

Topping: Beat whipping cream until stiff. Fold in nutmeg, sugar and pecans. Spread smoothly over pie and chill at least 4 hours.

Victoria Miller

Pineapple Cream Pie

1 can (medium) crushed pineapple
¾ can water
¼ c. white syrup
1 heaping Tbsp. tapioca
2 Tbsp. flour
Dash of salt
1 Tbsp. sugar
3 eggs, beaten

1 Tbsp. butter
4 to 6 squirts lemon juice
8 oz. cream cheese
½ can Eagle Brand milk
½ tsp. vanilla
Pinch of salt
1 baked pie shell
Cool Whip topping

Cook first 8 ingredients until thick, about 10 minutes. Add 1 tablespoon butter or margarine and 3 or 4 squirts lemon juice. Set aside to cool. Beat 8 ounces cream cheese with ½ can Eagle Brand milk. Add ½ tsp. vanilla, 2 squirts lemon juice and pinch of salt. Put cream cheese layer in baked pie shell, then add pineapple filling. Add your own topping (Cool Whip or Dream Whip).

Carolyn Miles

 *Pecan Pie*

3 eggs
½ c. sugar
2 Tbsp. flour
Pinch of salt

1 c. white Karo syrup
1 c. pecans
1 tsp. vanilla
2 Tbsp. melted oleo

Mix eggs, sugar, flour and salt well (best if you don't use mixer). Add Karo syrup, vanilla and melted oleo. Mix until smooth. Add pecans. Pour into 9-inch unbaked pie shell. Bake in 350° oven for 15-20 minutes. Turn oven back to 325° and cook for 25-30 minutes.

Marilyn Tytanic

Simple Pecan Pie

9 inch pie shell
1 c. pecan halves
3 eggs, beaten
1 c. light corn syrup
1 pinch salt

1 Tbsp. melted butter
½ tsp. vanilla
1 c. sugar
1 Tbsp. flour

Arrange pecan halves in pie shell. Beat eggs and add corn syrup, salt, butter and vanilla. Blend well. Combine sugar and flour. Mix well with egg mixture. Pour over nuts in pie shell. Let stand until nuts rise, so they'll get a nice glaze during baking. Bake at 350° for 45-50 minutes.

Minnie Nowakowski

New! Pumpkin Pie

1 large can Pumpkin
2 c. milk or Milnot
1 c. sugar
1 c. brown sugar

¾ tsp. nutmeg
1 tsp. cinnamon
4 eggs

Mix ingredients well and pour into two 9-inch unbaked pie shells. Bake for 45 minutes at 425°, or until a knife in the center comes out clean.

Marjorie Magott

New! Pecan Pie Squares

3 c. all-purpose flour
¼ c. plus 2 Tbsp. sugar
¾ c. margarine or butter, softened

¾ tsp. salt
Filling (below)

Heat oven to 350°. Grease jelly roll pan (15½" X 10½" X 1"). Beat flour, sugar, margarine and salt in large bowl on medium speed until crumbly (mixture will be dry). Press firmly in pan. Bake until light golden brown, about 20 minutes.

Prepare filling. Pour over hot baked layer; spread evenly. Bake until filling is set, about 25 minutes; cool. Cut into 1½-inch squares. Makes 70 squares.

It takes a little longer to cut these squares, but it is well worth the effort!

Filling:

4 eggs, slightly beaten
1½ c. sugar
1½ c. light or dark corn syrup

3 Tbsp. margarine or butter, melted
1½ tsps. vanilla
2½ c. chopped pecans

Mix all ingredients except pecans until well blended. Stir in pecans.

I haven't made pecan pie since I found this recipe. It has become a family holiday favorite.

Diana Hanna

New! 100 Year Old Recipe for Raisin Pie

2 c. raisins
1 Tbsp. flour
Butter, size of a walnut
Pinch of salt

1 c. sugar
1 Tbsp. vinegar
1½ c. boiling water
Crust, for two-crust pie

Combine raisins, sugar, flour, vinegar, butter, salt in boiling water.

Roll pie dough and spread bottom of crust with butter or Crisco. Add the raisin mixture. Wet edge of crust with water. Place top crust on top of filling and seal edge down good. Bake in hot oven 425° for 15 minutes. Then lower heat to 350° and bake until brown.

Ruby Hornbeck

Sun Maid Lattice Raisin Pie

1 c. seedless raisins
1 c. water
2 eggs
1 c. brown sugar, packed
¼ tsp. salt

1 Tbsp. butter or margarine
1 tsp. vanilla
1 c. chopped walnuts
9 inch crust (double)

Simmer raisins in water 5 minutes. Combine beaten eggs, sugar and salt. Gradually add to hot raisins. Cook, stirring constantly, until thickened. Stir in butter, vanilla and walnuts. Cook slightly. Pour into pastry-lined pie pan. Cover with pastry strips arranged lattice fashion. Bake in very hot 450° oven for 10 minutes. Reduce heat to 350° and bake 20 minutes longer. Makes 1 pie.

Anita Craiger

Pumpkin Ice Cream Pie

with Almond Brittle

1¼ c. whole natural almonds
1 c. graham cracker crumbs
¼ c. sugar
6 Tbsp. margarine or butter, softened
1 (1 lb.) can pumpkin
½ tsp. salt
1 tsp. cinnamon

½ tsp. ginger
¼ tsp. allspice
1 tsp. vanilla
1½ c. whipping cream
1 pt. vanilla ice cream, softened
1 c. sugar
½ c. sugar

Chop ¾ cup of the almonds. Combine with crumbs, ¼ cup sugar and the margarine until crumbly. Press into a 9-inch pie plate, making the edge as high as possible. Place in freezer. Mix pumpkin, salt, spices, vanilla and 1 cup sugar. Whip 1 cup cream. Fold in. Spread ice cream into firm pie shell. Top with pumpkin mixture and freeze. Place remaining ½ cup almonds in warm place so they are warm to the touch. Stir ½ cup sugar in skillet over medium high heat until melted. Add warmed almonds and stir until coated. Turn onto foil. Cool; break up brittle. Whip remaining ½ cup cream. Spread over frozen pie. Top with almond brittle. Cover tightly with plastic wrap and freeze. Remove pie from freezer 15-20 minutes before serving to allow it to soften slightly.

Pauline Haynes

🐦 Sour Cream Raisin Pie

1 c. sour cream	¼ tsp. nutmeg
1 c. sugar	¼ tsp. cinnamon
2 egg yolks	1 c. raisins
1 Tbsp. flour	Unbaked pie crust
Pinch of salt	

Blend all ingredients. Bake in unbaked crust at 350° until done.

Maudie Kubiak

🐦 Fresh Strawberry Pie

½ c. sugar	Dash of salt
3 Tbsp. cornstarch	4 c. strawberries, cut up or halved
4 Tbsp. strawberry Jell-O	Baked pie shell
1½ c. water	

Cut up strawberries or halves. Sugar them like you would for table use. Set aside. In a stew pan, put ½ cup sugar, 3 tablespoons cornstarch, 4 tablespoons strawberry Jell-O, 1½ cups water, dash of salt and few drops of red food coloring. Boil until thick like pudding. Set aside to cool at room temperature. When thick, stir in strawberries. Fill the baked pie shell. Top with whipped cream or Dream Whip.

Hattie Janowiak

🐦 Strawberry Pie

1 (9-inch) baked pie shell	½ c. sugar
Frozen strawberries	1 c. boiling water
1 pkg. strawberry Jell-O	Whipped cream

Have ready 1 (9-inch) baked pie shell. Thaw the frozen strawberries just until they separate. Dissolve the Jell-O and sugar in the boiling water. Cool. Add frozen strawberries and mix until Jell-O begins to set. Pour into pie shell. Serve with whipped cream topping. We enjoy this strawberry pie.

Minnie Nowakowski

Sweet Potato Pie

1¼ c. or 3 medium sweet potatoes,
   mashed
½ to ¾ c. sugar
2 eggs, beaten
⅛ tsp. nutmeg

¼ tsp. cinnamon
½ tsp. salt
1 c. canned milk
3 Tbsp. melted butter

Beat until smooth. Pour into pie tin lined with plain pastry. Bake in hot 425° oven for 20 minutes, after which reduce to slow 300° oven for 30 minutes. Test with knife. Makes 1 (9- inch) pie.

Ruby Webb

White Potato Pie

2 medium potatoes
⅔ c. butter
1 c. sugar
½ tsp. baking powder
⅛ tsp. salt
½ c. whipping cream
½ c. milk

2 tsp. grated lemon rind
2 Tbsp. lemon juice
1 tsp. vanilla
⅛ tsp. ground nutmeg
4 eggs, beaten
Unbaked pie shell (9 inch)

Cook potatoes; peel and mash. Mix potatoes with butter, sugar, baking powder and salt. Gradually add whipping cream and milk. Blend well. Stir in grated lemon rind, lemon juice, vanilla and nutmeg. Add eggs. Mix well and pour into pie shell. Bake 55 minutes in 350° oven or until knife inserted comes out clean.

Cora Rudek

Never Fail Meringue

1 Tbsp. cornstarch
2 Tbsp. sugar
½ c. water
3 egg whites

⅛ tsp. salt
6 Tbsp. sugar
1 tsp. vanilla

Mix the cornstarch, 2 tablespoons sugar and water in a saucepan and cook gently until it is thickened. Cool. Beat egg whites and salt until stiff. Add 6 tablespoons sugar gradually while beating egg whites constantly. Add vanilla and mix well. Slowly add cornstarch mixture. Continue beating mixture until it is very stiff. Pile on pie and bake in 350° oven for 15 minutes or until brown.

Frances Wyskup

New! Easy to Handle Pie Crust

5 c. flour
2½ c. Crisco
3 tsp. salt

3 Tbsp. vinegar (white)
1 egg
water

Put one beaten egg in a measuring cup. Add enough water to make one cup.
Blend flour and shortening together with pastry blender. Add salt, vinegar, egg and water mixture to flour mixture. Mix together and chill for about two hours.

This will keep in refrigerator up to two weeks.

Pat Wood

New! Easy Pie Crust

½ c. oil
¼ c. milk

1½ c. flour
pinch of salt

Mix all ingredients in pie pan with fork. Press into place with fingers. Crimp edges. Pour in filling. If top crust is desired, make another, pat out flat with hands, lay on top of filling. Bake.

Kristi Kretchmar

Pie Crust

1 c. all-purpose flour
⅓ c. (generous) butter Crisco

½ tsp. salt
3 Tbsp. ice water

Place the first 3 ingredients in a bowl. Use dough blender to blend ingredients until very well blended. (Past the pea stage usually recommended.) Add no more than 3 tablespoons of water (5½ tablespoons only for 2 crusts). Mix well with fork. Roll out dough on a floured surface. Place in pie plate. Bake a single crust or a pie in 450° oven until crust is browned. Makes a delicious crust!

Sister Bernadette Zayonc

Waldorf Astoria Pie Crust

2 c. flour
1 c. Crisco shortening

½ tsp. salt, dissolved in 6 Tbsp. cold water

Blend in flour and shortening. Dissolve salt in cold water and sprinkle over flour and shortening mixture. Mix lightly and roll out. Makes 2 (9-inch) pie shells.

Bake pie shells in 350° oven until light brown.

The secret of this tender pie crust is dissolving the salt in cold water before adding to dry ingredients.

Virginia Benedix

Zwieback Pie Crust

1 pkg. rolled Zwieback
1 c. butter

½ c. sugar
Pinch of salt

Mix well and press into pie pan. Fill with any cream filling.

The Cookbook Committee

New! *Apple Dumplings*

2 c. sugar
2 c. water
¼ teaspoon cinnamon
¼ tsp. nutmeg
¼ c. butter
6 apples

2 c. flour
1 tsp. salt
2 tsp. baking powder
¾ c. shortening
½ c. milk

Make syrup of sugar, water, cinnamon, and nutmeg. Add butter. Set aside. Pare and core apples; cut in eighths. Sift flour, salt and baking powder; cut in shortening. Add milk all at once and stir until moistened.

Roll ¼-inch thick. Cut into 5-inch squares.

Arrange four pieces of apple on each square. Sprinkle generously with additional sugar, cinnamon and nutmeg. Dot with butter. Fold corners to center and pinch edges together.

Place one inch apart in greased baking pan. Pour over syrup. Bake in moderate oven (about 375°) for 35 minutes. Serve hot with cream. Makes six dumplings.

Julia Wasik Mathewson

Bublanina Fruit Squares

1 yeast cake in pkg.
¼ c. warm water
½ c. butter
¼ c. sugar
2 eggs
½ c. milk
2 c. flour

¼ tsp. salt
½ lemon and rind
Fresh or canned fruit for topping
¼ c. flour
2 Tbsp. sugar
¼ c. cream, either sweet or sour

Dissolve yeast in warm water (according to directions on package). Let stand 10 minutes. Scald milk and cool to lukewarm. Add to yeast. Cream butter, egg yolks, salt and sugar until fluffy. To this creamed mixture add alternately the sifted flour and milk-yeast mixture, stirring well after each addition. When smooth, fold in beaten egg whites. Pour in shallow 7"x11" pan to a depth of 1 inch. Let rise until double in bulk. Cover with drained cherries, sliced Italian plums or other canned or fresh fruit. Scatter grated lemon rind and juice over all. Blend ¼ cup flour and 2 tablespoons sugar. Scatter over top. Spoon the thick cream (sweet or sour) over all. Bake at 400° for 30-35 minutes. Serve warm.

Rosie Lee Klimkowski

🐦 Apple Strudel

½ c. lard, melted
1 c. warm water
1 egg
Salt
Flour
12 apples, peeled and sliced thin

Raisins
Chopped nuts
Bread crumbs, buttered and
    browned
Sugar
Cinnamon

Melt ½ cup lard and mix with warm water, egg, salt and flour (amount of flour depends on how big a strudel you want). As you can see, my grandmother, like other good cooks, didn't always cook based on measured amounts, but on what she knew was needed to make something taste delicious. Mix the ingredients until smooth, a soft dough. Leave covered with a towel in a warm place for about 15 minutes. Peel about 12 apples and slice thin. Toast bread crumbs in butter until brown, then stretch dough on a floured dish towel until very thin. Don't leave any tears or holes.

Sprinkle with buttered crumbs, then a layer of apple slices and raisins or chopped nuts if you like those. This is usually much better without raisins or nuts, but some people seem to like strudel with "extra" ingredients. Sprinkle with cinnamon and sugar. Roll up carefully so you don't tear the dough. Sometimes it's easier to divide the dough so you can make 2. It's just a little easier to handle.

Put very carefully on baking sheet and bake at about 350°. Brush with melted lard several times. This will take about 45 minutes until golden brown. Sprinkle with sugar. Delicious.

This is a recipe given to me by my grandmother, Stephanie Balik, who emigrated to the United States from Bohemia in 1911. This takes time, but it's well worth it. My grandmother baked this in a wood stove, but it works in my electric oven.

Steve Muckala

Taven Tazeny - Apple Strudel

1 egg	½ c. butter
1 tsp. melted butter	6 large apples
½ c. warm water	½ c. raisins
½ tsp. salt	1 c. sugar
2 c. flour	½ tsp. cinnamon
½ c. dry bread crumbs	¾ c. pecans

Beat egg slightly. Add 1 tsp. melted butter, water and salt. Gradually add liquid mixture to flour. Turn out onto floured board and knead until dough is very elastic and does not stick to board. Cover with a warm bowl and let stand 1 hour. Meanwhile prepare the filling.

Use 2 tablespoons butter for browning the bread crumbs. Pare, core and slice the apples. Wash and drain the raisins. Chop the nuts.

Spread a cloth over large table and sprinkle lightly with flour. Roll dough evenly into a large square and place it in center of cloth. Begin pulling and stretching dough away from center gently to prevent tearing, until it is evenly thin as paper. Snip off thick edges. Brush dough with melted butter and sprinkle fried crumbs over ¾ of surface. Spread apple slices, raisins and nuts over crumbs. Sprinkle sugar-cinnamon mixture over all. Lifting and tilting the cloth start rolling dough from filled side toward and over the empty side. Place carefully on a greased baking sheet. Brush top with butter. Bake at 400° for 30 minutes. Reduce heat to 350° and bake another 30 minutes. Baste with melted butter.

Rosie Lee Klimkowski

Common Polish Greetings:

Dzien dobry (jean du-bree) — "Hello" or "Good Morning."
Dobry wie czo'r (du-bree- vyeh-choor) — "Good Evening."
Do widzenia (duh veed-Tzayn-ya) — "Good-bye."

🐦 Blue Plum Dumplings

Blue plums, one for each dumpling

Make pastry of:

2½ c. flour	¾ c. shortening
¾ tsp. salt	7 to 8 Tbsp. water

Syrup:

1 c. sugar	4 Tbsp. butter
¼ tsp. cinnamon	2 c. water

Mix pastry ingredients as for pie crust. Divide in half. Roll out ⅛-inch thick and cut into squares. Wrap around 1 blue plum. Seal. Place in casserole pan. Cook in syrup.

Syrup: Bring all ingredients to boil to dissolve sugar. Pour over plums. Bake in 350° oven for 45 minutes. Serve hot or cold with ice cream or whipped cream.

Bonita (Konop) Yox

Yes, sir, that's my baby ...

"Angie was the prettiest baby in the world. Momma had her all dressed up pretty. Papa and Momma were all dressed up, because we were going to a wedding. I tied a pink ribbon around Angie's wrist. Papa came in the room and saw the pink ribbon and asked what it was for. I told him it was so Momma wouldn't get her mixed up with the other babies and bring the wrong baby home. The women used to lay the babies together on the bed and let them sleep. When we got home in the wee hours of morning, I was so sleepy, I couldn't keep my eyes open, but Papa made me stand up and go look and see if we brought the right baby home before I could go to bed."

— *Agnes Czerczyk*

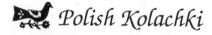 Bohemian Kolacky

1 c. warm milk	*2 tsp. salt*
½ c. warm water	*3 eggs, beaten*
2 pkg. dry yeast	*¾ c. oil*
½ c. sugar	*5 to 6 c. flour*

Combine water and milk. Add yeast. Let set until it bubbles. Add sugar, eggs, oil, salt and flour. Knead lightly. Let dough rise once and then form into small balls (walnut size). Place on greased pans. Let rise again. Press down centers with fingers. Fill with your favorite filling, poppy seed, prune, apricot, etc. Prepared filling can be purchased. Bake immediately at 375° until golden brown, about 7-12 minutes. Yields 5-6 dozen.

Bonita (Konop) Yox
Esther Konop

Polish Kolachki

1 lb. margarine	*½ c. water*
4 c. flour	*Filling*
½ tsp. salt	

Cut margarine into flour. Add salt. Add water. Refrigerate dough for several hours. Roll dough ¼ at a time on floured board. Cut in 3-inch squares. Add filling and fold. Bake at 350° for 20 minutes.

Kolachki may be frozen on cookie sheets and stored in a plastic bag. Baked as needed. Yields 3 dozen.

Bonita (Konop) Yox

🐦 Kolache

1¼ c. milk	4 c. flour
1 pkg. cake yeast	1 tsp. salt
⅓ c. sugar	Lemon rind
½ c. butter	Coconut
2 large egg yolks	Sour Cream

Filling:

1 lb. cooked prunes	1 Tbsp. lemon juice
½ c. prune juice	Grated lemon rind
½ c. sugar	

Scald milk; cool to lukewarm. Use ¼ cup of the milk to dissolve yeast. Add 1 tsp. of sugar and 1 tablespoon of flour. Let stand 10 minutes. Cream butter, egg yolks, salt and remaining sugar. Combine remaining milk with yeast mixture and add alternately with flour to creamed mixture. Knead into smooth dough.

Let rise in warm place until double in bulk. Punch down and let stand 10 minutes. Shape into balls 1 inch in diameter. Place on well-greased cookie sheet about 2 inches apart. Let rise again until doubled in size. Make depression in center of each Kolache.

Special trick: Put ¼ cup flour in corner of a clean white cloth; draw cloth up around flour. Twist cloth; tie with string or rubber band. Use this ball for making each depression. It doesn't stick and makes uniform hollow places to hold topping.

Put ½ tsp. thick sour cream in each depression. Add 1 or 2 tsps. prune or apricot mixture or poppy seed filling. Scatter shredded coconut. Brush edges of each Kolache with a mixture of 1 tablespoon milk and a slightly beaten egg (I use the egg whites). Let rise 15-20 minutes. Bake at 400° for 15 minutes. Remove from pan and sprinkle powdered sugar over each one.

Prune or apricot puree: Cook and pit 1 pound cooked prunes. Add ½ cup prune juice and ½ cup sugar. Mash and cook until smooth and thick. Add 1 tablespoon lemon juice and 1 tsp. grated lemon rind.

Poppy seed: You will need 1 cup ground poppy seed, ½ cup milk, 2 tablespoons sugar, 1 tablespoon honey or corn syrup and 1 grated lemon rind. Cook seeds and milk slowly for 5 minutes, stirring constantly. Add sugar and honey or syrup. Cook 2 minutes longer. Add lemon rind.

Rosie Lee Klimkowski

🐦 Kolache

½ pkg. fresh yeast
1 c. lukewarm water
½ c. butter
1 c. milk
⅔ c. sugar

1½ tsp. salt
2 eggs, well beaten
⅛ tsp. grated nutmeg
7 c. sifted flour or more
½ lemon (grated rind and juice)

Filling:

1 lb. prunes
Sugar to taste

⅛ tsp. cloves
Lemon rind (optional)

Simple Icing

½ lb. powdered sugar
1 tsp. vanilla

Sweet cream

Dissolve yeast, according to makers directions. Cream together butter, sugar and salt. Add eggs, lemon and nutmeg. Mix yeast with water. Add milk and blend this liquid with 3 cups of the flour. Beat smooth, then add butter mixture and enough flour to make a medium soft dough. (As stiff as can be mixed with.)

Let set in a warm place until doubled. Turn dough out on board and knead down. Let rise again for a few minutes. It will be easier to handle. Make into rolls.

Pinch or cut off with a spoon, a piece of dough the size of a large walnut. Smooth it round and lay rolls 2 inches apart on buttered cookie sheet. Let rise again until doubled, then with finger tips, stretch, do not mash, roll into the shape of a tiny pie shell. Fill with thick jam or prune filling. Brush dough edge with butter and let rise again until dough is light (about 15 minutes). Bake about 20 minutes at 375°. If desired, frost with simple icing, while warm.

Prune filling: Cook 1 pound of prunes until very tender. Remove seeds and sweeten to taste. Add ⅛ tsp. cloves and grated rind of ½ lemon, if the flavor is desired. Cook until quite thick. (A little vanilla also improves the taste.)

Simple icing: Mix powdered sugar, vanilla and sweet cream, enough to make thin enough to spread with a spoon. To be applied after Kolache is cool. For extra glamour, add few chopped pecans or shredded coconut after icing.

Minnie Nowakowski

Apricot Filling For Kolaches

Dried apricots   **Sugar to taste**

Cook 1 package of dried apricots until very tender. Add sugar to taste and cook until very thick.

Minnie Nowakowski

Poppy Seed Filling For Kolaches

1 c. ground poppy seed   *vanilla*
¼ c. butter   **¼ tsp. cinnamon**
¼ c. milk   **½ c. sugar**
1¼ tsp. lemon juice or ½ tsp.

Blend 1 cup poppy seed, butter, milk, lemon juice or vanilla, cinnamon and sugar. Blend all ingredients and simmer for 5 minutes. Let cool before filling Kolache. Will fill 1 dozen or more.

Minnie Nowakowski

Posipka - Topping For Kolaches

½ c. sugar   **⅓ c. melted butter**
¼ c. flour

Mix together until crumbly. Sprinkle on top of Kolache before baking. Much improved by adding a few chopped nuts or coconut.

Minnie Nowakowski

New! Poppy Seed Kolaches

1½ c. buttermilk
1 pkg. dry yeast
¼ c. sugar
2 eggs

½ c. butter of margarine, melted
5½ c. flour, sifted
1½ tsp. salt
½ tsp. baking soda

Filling:

½ lb. (8 oz.) poppy seed
1 Tbsp. butter
1 c. milk

1 Tbsp. corn syrup
1 c. sugar
vanilla, to taste

Melt butter and set aside to cool. Heat the buttermilk to lukewarm and add the yeast and sugar. Stir until the yeast is dissolved.

Beat the eggs slightly and add the cooled butter. Stir this into the yeast mixture. Add salt and baking soda

Add the flour gradually until you have a soft dough. (All of flour might not be used.) Turn dough into a greased bowl. Smooth the top of the dough and brush with melted butter or shortening.

Cover and let rise in a warm place until double in bulk.

Punch down the dough. Turn out on a lightly-floured surface and let rest about 10 minutes. Roll out to a little less than a half inch thick. Cut with 2 ½-inch cutter and place in greased pans. Let rise again.

Indent the centers of each kolache with your fingers by pushing the dough to one side. Fill the centers and let rise until rims are about ¾" high. Bake at 350° until light brown.

For the filling:

The day before: Grind the poppy seed, or process in a food processor. Add milk and refrigerate overnight.

The next day: Add the butter, syrup and sugar. Cook about 10 minutes or until thick, stirring constantly. Add vanilla.

In memory of Hattie Whitnah

Lulu C. Miller's Mock Mincemeat

1 box raisins	2 Tbsp. cinnamon
1 pkg. green tomatoes	2 Tbsp. nutmeg
1 peck sour apples	2 Tbsp. cloves
5 lb. brown sugar	2 Tbsp. allspice
2 lb. butter	2 c. dark vinegar
2 Tbsp. salt	

Grind and pour boiling water over green tomatoes, 3 times and drain. Cook tomatoes 15 minutes and drain again. Add all together. Let come to a boil and seal.

Doyle Miller

Nut Roll

1 c. milk	1 c. warm water
1 c. sugar	3 pkg. yeast
2 tsp. salt	4½ c. flour
½ c. shortening	3 eggs

Filling:

2 lb. ground walnuts or more	2 egg whites
2 c. sugar	Cinnamon milk (sweeten to taste)

Bring milk, sugar, salt and shortening to a boil. Cool until lukewarm. Dissolve yeast in 1 cup of warm water. Cream together well. Mix yeast mixture with flour and 3 eggs. Mix this mixture with the lukewarm mixture, being sure it's cooled. Put dough in a large, greased bowl with a lid (Tupperware works good).

Mix walnuts, sugar, egg whites and a little milk with cinnamon to taste. Roll out dough and spread with filling mixture. Roll up. Cut. Bake in moderate oven until golden.

Pauline Haynes

 Mama's Nut Rolls

8 c. flour
¾ c. sugar
1 tsp. salt
1 pkg. yeast
2 c. shortening (can use ½ butter)
1 c. milk, warmed
4 eggs, beaten

1 tsp. vanilla
6 c. ground walnuts
1½ to 2 c. milk
2 c. sugar or honey
1½ tsp. vanilla
Beaten egg
Butter

Sift flour, sugar and salt. Cut in shortening to the size of peas. Dissolve yeast in warm milk and add beaten eggs to the mixture. Add to flour mixture and knead until it comes away clean from fingers. Place in large bowl; cover and leave in refrigerator overnight.

Mix together walnuts, 1½ to 2 cups milk, sugar or honey and 1½ tsps. vanilla in saucepan. Bring to a slow boil. Take off heat when it begins to boil and let cool before spreading on dough. When ready to bake, let dough stand at room temperature to soften. Divide dough into 3 or 4 sections and roll, one at a time, on a floured surface. Spread with the cooled nut filling. Roll as for jelly roll and brush top with beaten egg. Bake for 45 minutes at 375°. This is good served warm with butter on top.

Karen Kuhns

Zelnicky

½ c. cracklings or crisp bacon
1 c. sauerkraut, rinsed once

1 c. flour
Salt, if desired

Mix crackling and kraut; add flour and salt to taste. Stir well;

Knead a bit on floured board. Form into a roll; cut into 6 pieces. Roll out each piece to about ½-inch thick. Bake on cookie sheet at 400° until light brown.

A good TV snack with a glass of beer.

Father Augustine Horne, O.S.B.

 # Egg Noodles

3 egg yolks
1 whole egg
3 Tbsp. cold water

1 tsp. salt
2 c. all-purpose flour

Beat egg and egg yolks together. Beat in water and salt. Add flour until dough is very stiff. Knead. Divide into 3 parts. Roll thin on a lightly-floured, cloth-covered board. Cover with a second towel and let set until dough is partially dry. Roll as for jelly roll. Cut into strips of desired widths. Allow strips to dry before using or storing. Makes about 6 cups.

Cora Rudek

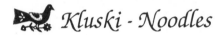 # Kluski - Noodles

2 c. sifted flour
1 tsp. salt

3 or 4 eggs

Put flour in a large bowl and add salt, mix well and add 3 or 4 eggs. Mix really well. Knead and pick up flour, forming a very thick dough. Divide in half and roll very flat on heavy floured board. Let lay until dry. Have ready extra large kettle ½ full of rapidly boiling water. Cut dough in wide strips, about 1½-inches wide and stack in stacks of 2-5. Cut in thin little slices (slivers).

Drop few at a time in boiling water and let boil hard 5-10 minutes. Fill kettle with cold water. Remove Kluski with slotted spoon into large bowl, then move Kluski back into kettle and add cold water to chill for a rinse action. Drain so Kluski won't stick to each other. Ready to serve.

Minnie Nowakowski

🐦 Polish Homemade Kluski - Noodles

1 egg, beaten
½ tsp. salt

2 Tbsp. milk or cream
1 c. flour

Mix egg, salt and milk or cream. Add flour slowly to make a stiff dough. Knead till smooth. Sprinkle flour on board and roll dough thin. Let stand 20 minutes. Cut into strips with a sharp knife. Slice strips into small pieces like Kluski. Cook in boiling salted water until tender. Drain and serve with chicken broth or hot milk or just butter.

Katie Magott

🐦 Belgian Waffles

1 box yellow cake mix
1½ c. milk or light cream

4 eggs
½ tsp. salt

Mix all ingredients in a large bowl and beat well. This makes a thick batter. Bake on a lightly-greased waffle iron. Any extras can be frozen and heated in toaster.

Judy Seikel

🐦 Buttermilk Pancakes

2 c. flour
2 tsp. baking powder
1 tsp. salt
1 tsp. baking soda

2 eggs
2 Tbsp. oil
2 c. buttermilk

Combine all ingredients. Use ¼ cup batter for each pancake. Cook until golden brown. Makes about 12 pancakes.

Diana Hanna

Heavenly Hots

2 eggs
2 Tbsp. cake flour
1½ Tbsp. sugar

½ tsp. baking soda
1 small ctn. sour cream
Pinch of salt

Beat the eggs. Add flour, sugar, sour cream, baking soda and salt. Start cooking. Make the cakes dollar size and turn quickly. Serve with melted butter and maple syrup.

Helen Dillis

New! Lithuanian Potato Pancakes

(Bulviniai Blynai)

7-8 potatoes
2 eggs
3 Tbsp. flour

1 tsp. salt
1 Tbsp. cooking oil
Sour cream

Peel and grate potatoes. Mix in eggs, flour and salt. Melt fat or heat 1 Tbsp. cooking oil in frying pan. Drop spoonfuls of mixture into hot fat. Fry until golden brown. Serve with sour cream.

Al Dilis

New! Samuel Whiskers Roly-Poly Pancakes

¾ c. unbleached white flour
¼ c. whole wheat flour
¼ c. corn meal
2 tsp. baking powder

½ tsp. salt
1 egg
1 c. milk
2 Tbsp. vegetable oil

Combine flours and corn meal, baking powder, salt into mixing bowl. Stir lightly with fork until thoroughly mixed. Blend until batter is smooth and creamy. Pour ¼ cup batter for each pancake on lightly greased griddle. When pancakes are bubbly in center and dry around edges turn over and cook about one more minute. Makes about 12 pancakes.

Diana Hanna

244

Smile Pancakes

1½ c. Bisquick mix
½ c. corn meal
1 tsp. soda

1¾ c. buttermilk
1 egg

Beat all ingredients until smooth. Pour batter on hot griddle. Bake until pancakes are dry around edges. Turn and bake other side until golden brown. Makes about 6 pancakes.

Fern Koelsch

Smorum

2 eggs
½ c. milk

2 Tbsp. flour
Salt

Beat eggs slightly; add milk, flour and salt and mix. Add more flour if too runny. It should be the consistency of runny pancake mix. Heat pan with 1 tablespoon of oil. Fry and gradually break up into pieces of varied sizes with spoon. (Somewhat like chunky scrambled eggs.) Serve with syrup, honey, fruit jam, or jelly.

Father Augustine Horne, O.S.B.
St Vincent DePaul, McLoud, OK

Chili-Cheese Corn Bread

1 pkg. corn bread mix
1 egg, beaten
1½ c. milk

1 can green chilies, chopped
8¾ oz. can corn, drained
1 c. Jack cheese

Blend corn bread mix with egg and milk until smooth. Pour ½ of batter in greased 9"x12" baking dish. Add the chilies, then corn (drained) and cheese. Top with remaining batter. Bake at 400° for 30 minutes or until done. Cut in squares.

Wonderful with barbecues.

Helen C. Nixon

Corn Bread

1 c. corn meal	1 c. flour
1 Tbsp. sugar	1 tsp. salt
2 eggs, well beaten	2 tsp. baking powder
¼ c. cooking oil	1½ c. milk

Put all dry ingredients in mixing bowl. Add eggs and shortening slowly while mixing, then add milk slowly. Use about an 8-inch square pan, oiled. Bake at 425° for 25-30 minutes.

Virginia Grinnell

Country Corn Sticks

⅓ c. butter or margarine	2 tsp. salt
2¼ c. sifted all-purpose flour	¼ c. milk
2 Tbsp. sugar	1 c. cream style corn
4 tsp. baking powder	

Preheat oven to 450°. Melt butter or margarine in pan approximately 13"x9"x2". Sift flour, sugar, baking powder and salt together. Add milk and corn. Stir until soft dough is formed. Turn out onto well-floured board. Knead dough; fold and knead about 15 times. Roll out in rectangle ½-inch thick. Cut into strips about 1-inch wide. Roll strips in melted butter in baking pan and arrange in pan. Bake 20-30 minutes or until browned and edges are crisp. Make 24 sticks. Serve warm for lunch or supper. Good with soup or salad. Delicious cold, too.

Barbara Wyskup

Spanish Corn Bread

3 eggs	1 small can jalapeno peppers
3 c. corn bread mix	1 diced onion
3 Tbsp. sugar	1 can creamed corn
2½ c. milk	1½ c. grated cheese
½ c. oil	

Mix all ingredients well. Bake in greased 10"x12" or 9"x13" pan. Bake 35-45 minutes at 350°.

Suzanne Visnieski

New! *Texas Corn Bread*

1 c. yellow corn meal
½ c. flour

1 tsp. salt

Mix above ingredients thoroughly; then add without mixing:

1 c. buttermilk
½ c. milk
1 egg

1 Tbsp. baking powder
½ tsp. soda
¼ c. oil

Grease 8"x8" pan well and heat in the oven. While pan is heating, stir the mixture thoroughly. Pour into hot pan and bake at 450° until done - about 20 minutes.

This is a very moist and delicious corn bread! I usually double the recipe and bake in a 9"x13" pan for my large family.

Diana Hanna

Shrimp Puppies

2 c. cooked and shredded shrimp
2 (6 oz.) pkg. jalapeno corn bread
   mix
1 (1 lb., 1 oz.) can cream style corn

Oil for frying
¼ c. chopped green onions and tops
1 finely-chopped jalapeno pepper

Shred cooked shrimp in a food processor or chop finely with a knife. In a large mixing bowl, combine all ingredients. Heat oil to 365°. Drop mixture by heaping teaspoonfuls into hot oil. Deep-fry until golden brown. Remove from oil and drain on absorbent paper. Makes 5 dozen puppies.

Myra Smith

Fast Cornbread

Instead of baking corn bread in oven, make it in the waffle iron for quick, crisp bread.

Banana Bread

2 c. sugar
1½ c. salad oil
5 eggs
4 medium bananas
3 c. flour, sifted

2 tsp. soda
1 tsp. salt
1 large or 2 small vanilla pudding
   and pie filling
1 c. nuts, if desired

Mix sugar, salad oil, eggs and bananas. Sift together flour, soda, salt and pudding. Add to banana mixture. Add nuts if desired. Bake at 350° for 40-45 minutes. Makes 3 loaves.

Will freeze well. This is moist.

Verna Steciak

Banana Bread

⅔ c. sugar
⅓ c. shortening
2 eggs
3 Tbsp. sour milk
1 c. fruit (bananas)

2 c. flour
1 tsp. baking powder
½ tsp. soda
½ tsp. salt
½ c. nuts, chopped

Combine sugar, shortening, flour, baking powder, soda, salt and nuts. In blender, combine eggs, milk and bananas. Pour into dry mixture. Let stand 20 minutes. Use 9"x5" loaf pan. Bake in 350° oven for 45 minutes. If recipe is doubled it makes 3 (1 pound) loaves.

Ann S. Huffman

Bubble Bread

1 pkg. frozen rolls (24)
1 (3 oz.) pkg. butterscotch pudding
   (not instant)

1 stick butter or margarine (¼ c.)
½ c. brown sugar
½ c. chopped nuts

Place frozen rolls in greased Bundt pan. Mix the pudding mix, butter, brown sugar and nuts in a saucepan and bring to a boil. Pour boiling mixture over rolls. Cover with wax paper. Let set overnight on counter top. Bake at 350° for 30 minutes. Turn out before cooling.

Judy Seikel

🕊 Banana Nut Bread

3 large bananas, mashed
½ c. soft butter
2 eggs
1 c. sugar
¼ tsp. salt
1 tsp. vanilla
2 c. sifted flour

1 tsp. vanilla
2 c. sifted flour
1 tsp. soda
1 tsp. cinnamon
½ tsp. mace
½ tsp. allspice

Sift dry ingredients together 4 times. Blend butter and sugar. Add eggs. Add flour mixture alternately with mashed bananas, then add 1 cup pecans. Spread in well greased 9½"x5½" loaf pan. Bake for 1 hour at 350°.

Mrs. B. G. Edmiston

🕊 Quick & Easy Microwave Coffee Cake

1½ c. buttermilk biscuit mix
⅓ c. sugar
½ c. chopped pecans
½ c. milk
1 egg
½ tsp. vanilla

2 Tbsp. cooking oil
⅓ c. buttermilk biscuit mix
⅓ c. brown sugar, packed
2 Tbsp. butter
1 tsp. cinnamon

Orange Glaze:

¾ c. powdered sugar
1 Tbsp. orange juice

½ tsp. grated orange rind

Combine 1½ cups biscuit mix, sugar and pecans in mixing bowl. Add milk, egg, vanilla and oil. Beat by hand, mixing well. Pour into greased 8-inch round baking dish that can be used in microwave. Combine remaining ingredients until crumbly. Sprinkle over batter. Microwave 4-7 minutes on HIGH, turning dish a half turn after 2 minutes. The cake is done when the top is almost dry and springs back when touched. Cool. Drizzle with Orange Glaze. Serves 10-12.

For glaze: Combine powdered sugar, orange juice and orange rind.

Cora Rudek

Bishop's Bread

2½ c. sifted flour
1¼ c. brown sugar, firmly packed
½ tsp. salt
½ c. butter or shortening
1 tsp. baking powder

½ tsp. soda
1 tsp. cinnamon
1 egg, well beaten
¾ c. sour milk or buttermilk

Sift flour once. Measure and add sugar and salt. Cut in shortening until mixture looks like coarse meal. Reserve ¾ cup for top. To remainder add baking powder, soda and cinnamon, then add egg and sour milk and beat until smooth. Turn into 2 greased pans, 8"x8"x2". Sprinkle with reserved ¾ cup flour-shortening mixture and additional cinnamon. Bake in 400° oven for 25 minutes.

The Cookbook Committee

New! Cranberry Orange Nut Bread

2 c. sifted flour
1 c. sugar
¼ tsp. salt (optional)
1½ tsp. baking powder
½ tsp. soda
1 egg, slightly beaten

2 Tbsp. melted butter
½ c. orange juice
2 Tbsp. hot water
1 c. cranberries, cut in half
½ c. chopped nuts.

Sift together dry ingredients; add egg, orange juice, butter and water. Mix until all are well moistened. Fold in cranberries and nuts. Pour in greased loaf pan.

Bake at 325° approximately 50 min. (Check to see if toothpick inserted comes out clean.) After cooled, top with powdered sugar glaze (optional).

Sue Nickel

Polish saying:

"Bez pracy nie ma Kolaczy." Without work, there is no bread.

submitted by Dora Kusek

Lemon Nut Bread

Bread:
¾ stick margarine
1 c. sugar
2 eggs
½ c. milk

1 lemon peel, grated
1½ c. flour
⅛ tsp. salt
1 tsp. baking powder
½ c. chopped pecans

Glaze for Lemon Bread:

Juice of 1 lemon

⅓ c. sugar

Preheat oven to 350°. Cream together margarine and sugar. Add eggs, one at a time. Sift flour, salt and baking powder together. Add the sifted ingredients alternately with milk. Add the chopped nuts and grated lemon rind. Pour into 9-inch square pan. Bake 1 hour. After removed from oven, cool 5-10 minutes.

Glaze: Mix ingredients together. Pour over bread. Let the bread stand for ½ hour in pan, then remove and place on wire rack.

Mary Camfield

Oatmeal Bread

1½ c. quick oats
½ c. raisins
½ c. finely-chopped dates
½ c. chopped pecans
1½ c. hot milk
½ c. canned pumpkin
2 beaten eggs
1 tsp. vanilla

2 c. all-purpose flour
¾ c. sugar
4 tsp. baking powder
1 tsp. salt
1 tsp. cinnamon
¼ tsp. cloves
¼ tsp. nutmeg
⅛ tsp. ginger

In a large mixing bowl, combine oats, raisins, dates, pecans and hot milk. Let stand 10 minutes. Add eggs, vanilla and pumpkin. Mix well. In medium mixing bowl, stir together remaining ingredients. Stir into oat mixture. Turn batter into a greased and floured 9"x5"x3" loaf pan. Bake in a 350° oven for 1 hour and 10 minutes or until a wooden pick inserted near the center comes out clean. Cool in pan 10 minutes. Remove from pan. Cool thoroughly on wire rack. For easier slicing and better flavor, wrap and store overnight.

Glena Jorski

Donna's Pineapple Bread

2½ c. flour
2 c. sugar
⅓ c. buttermilk
1 tsp. soda
2 eggs

½ c. Crisco oil
½ tsp. salt
15½ oz. can pineapple
½ c. nuts
¼ c. pineapple juice

Glaze:

¼ c. pineapple juice
Oleo, melted

Powdered sugar

Stir soda into buttermilk. Cream eggs, sugar and oil. Add milk and soda mixture and mix well. Add flour and salt. Drain ¼ cup of juice from pineapple. Stir in rest of pineapple and juice and mix well. Stir in nuts. Use prepared bread pan. Bake at 350° about 25 minutes or until done. Mix melted oleo, pineapple juice and enough powdered sugar to make a thin glaze if desired.

Mrs. Frank Wyskup

Orange Bread

½ c. butter
1 c. sugar
2 eggs
½ c. nuts
Rind of 1 orange, chopped

1 tsp. soda
½ tsp. salt
⅔ c. sour milk
2 c. flour
½ c. sugar

Mix all ingredients, reserving ½ cup sugar and bake 45 minutes to 1 hour at 350°. Remove from pan. Mix sugar, dissolved in juice from orange and pour on top.

Edith Sims

🐦 Pumpkin Bread

⅔ c. shortening
2⅔ c. sugar
4 eggs
1 can pumpkin
⅔ c. water
3⅓ c. flour

2 tsp. soda
1½ tsp. salt
½ tsp. baking powder
1 tsp. cinnamon
1 tsp. cloves
⅔ c. nuts

Heat oven to 350°. Grease 2 loaf pans (9"x5"x3"). Cream shortening and sugar. Add eggs, pumpkin and water. Blend in dry ingredients, except nuts. Stir in nuts. Bake 65-75 minutes until wooden pick inserted in center comes out clean.

Ina Wiedemann

🐦 Pumpkin Bread

1½ c. all-purpose flour
½ tsp. salt
½ tsp. baking soda
3 eggs, beaten
1 c. canned pumpkin
1 c. sugar

1 c. cooking oil
½ tsp. cinnamon
½ tsp. nutmeg
1 (3½ oz.) pkg. instant coconut
    cream pudding and pie filling mix
½ c. chopped pecans

Sift flour, salt and soda together. Mix beaten eggs, pumpkin and sugar together. Add flour mixture with oil. Stir in cinnamon, nutmeg and dry pie filling mix. Mix well. Fold in nuts. Pour in 5"x9" loaf pan, greased. Bake at 350° for 1 hour and 20 minutes.

Cora Rudek

🐦 Mary's Pumpkin Bread

3 c. sugar
4 eggs
1 c. salad oil
½ c. water
1 (16 oz.) can pumpkin
2¾ c. flour

2 tsp. soda
1 tsp. cinnamon
1 tsp. nutmeg
½ tsp. salt
1 c. raisins
1 c. nuts

Cream sugar with eggs. Add salad oil, water and pumpkin. Mix well. Add flour, soda, cinnamon, nutmeg and salt. Fold in raisins and nuts. Pour in greased and floured loaf pans (3). Bake at 350° for 1 hour. Wrap in foil paper while warm. Freezes well. May be served warm with butter or Dream Whip.

Mary Telowicz

🐦 Zucchini Bread

2 c. sugar
1 c. vegetable oil
1 tsp. vanilla
4 eggs
2 c. grated zucchini (unpeeled)
3½ c. flour

1½ tsp. salt
1½ tsp. soda
1 tsp. cinnamon
¾ tsp. baking powder
1 c. raisins, floured
1 c. chopped nuts

Mix sugar, oil, vanilla and eggs. Set aside. Mix zucchini, flour, salt, soda, cinnamon and baking powder. Add to first mixture. Add raisins and nuts. Bake in greased and floured loaf pans at 350° for 55 minutes. Makes 2 loaves. Can be frozen for 4 months. Check loaves with toothpick.

Becky Spaeth

Scotch Shortbread

2 c. flour
¼ tsp. baking powder
¼ tsp. salt

1 c. soft butter or margarine
½ c. confectioners' sugar

Sift flour, baking powder and salt. Cream butter and sugar until light and fluffy. Add flour mixture. Refrigerate until easy to handle. Preheat oven to 350°. On lightly floured surface, roll dough ¼-inch thick. Cut into squares, triangles, etc. Place 1-inch apart on ungreased cookie sheet. Bake 20-25 minutes or until done.

If preferred, pat unchilled dough in 9"x9"x2" pan. Bake and cut into desired shapes while warm.

If desired, before baking sprinkle with cinnamon and sugar mixture. Makes approximately 2½ dozen.

Irene Watkins

Scotch Shortbread from Edinburgh

1 c. butter
½ c. powdered sugar
2 c. flour

¼ tsp. baking powder
¼ tsp. salt

Cream butter at room temperature with sugar. Add salt and baking powder to flour and sift into bowl with butter-sugar mixture. If dough is real stiff, just keep mixing. Use your hands if you like. If it remains stiff, add a tsp. of milk. Roll dough out and cut with cookie cutter. Bake at 350° for 20-25 minutes. Makes 3 dozen cookies, depending how thick you roll the dough.

Pauline Haynes

Sweet Bread

10 c. flour
1 tsp. salt
1 tall can Milnot
1 can water
1 tsp. sugar
1 c. raisins

¼ c. lukewarm water
1 c. sugar
2 pkg. yeast
½ c. Wesson oil
3 eggs

Dissolve yeast in ¼ cup lukewarm water and 1 tsp. of sugar. Scald milk and water. Pour into a large bowl. Add sugar, salt, oil and eggs. Cool to lukewarm. Add yeast mixture. Add flour, ½ at a time. Add raisins that are blanched in hot water. Let cool a little, then add rest of flour. Mix. Knead till satiny smooth. Let rise until double. Divide dough in ½ and make 6 strips. Braid into 2 loaves. Let rise until double. Bake at 350° for 30 minutes. Reverse and cool on rack.

Helen Lukaszek

New! Babka - Polish Bread

½ c. soft butter
½ c. sugar
4 egg yolks
1 c. milk, scalded and cooled to
   lukewarm
1 pkg. yeast
1 tsp. grated lemon rind
¼ c. lukewarm water

4 c. flour
1 tsp. salt
½ tsp. cinnamon, if desired
½ c. white raisins
bread crumbs
1 egg yolk, beaten
2 Tbsp. water
¼ c. chopped almonds

Dissolve yeast in the lukewarm water and set aside. Cream together sugar and butter in a large bowl. Add salt to egg yolks and beat until thick. Add to sugar and butter. Add the yeast to the mixture. Add lemon rind and cinnamon.

Add flour alternately with milk and beat well to make a smooth batter. Add raisins and knead until batter loses stickiness and leaves the fingers.

· Let rise in a warm place until double in size. Punch down the dough and let it rise again until double in size.

Heavily grease a tube pan. Sprinkle pan with fine bread crumbs. Brush with mixture made by beating egg yolk and water. Sprinkle with almonds. Let rise and bake 30 minutes at 350°.

Katie Magott

New! Small Babka

¾ c. hot milk
2 c. flour
1 pkg. yeast or 1 yeast cake
1 Tbsp. warm water
1 tsp. sugar

2 Tbsp. soft butter
⅓ c. sugar
½ tsp. salt
2 egg yolks
½ teaspoon ground cardamon

Optional:

Raisins
Chopped nuts

Chopped cherries

In a small cup, soften the yeast in the tablespoon of warm water along with 1 teaspoon of sugar. Set aside.

On stovetop in small pan, scald the milk. Carefully stir ½ c. flour into the hot milk. When mixture is cool, add the yeast mixture.

Add salt to egg yolks and beat until thick. Pour the "sponge," or milk and yeast mixture, into a large bowl and add the butter, sugar, beaten egg yolks and cardamon. Beat with spoon thoroughly.

Slowly add the remaining 1½ cups of flour and knead with hand until dough no longer sticks to the fingers. Add the raisins, nuts and cherries, if desired.

Let rise until double in size. Punch down the dough and let it rise again for about 1 hour.

Bake in a greased loaf, tube or sheet pan. Let the dough rise again until about double in size after placing it in the pan. Bake for 30 minutes at 350°.

Katie Magott

Easter basket...

"Food baskets were blessed by the priest Holy Saturday. They contained colored eggs, smoked polish sausage, canned beets. There were also assorted sweet rolls with prunes, apricot and jelly fillings, and braided sweet bread with raisins. We had no aluminum foil, so the ham was clove studded and wrapped in a flour and water dough and baked in our wood stove oven to keep in the juices and flavor. The food smelled so good, but we couldn't eat any of it until Easter."

Mrs. Bill (Martha) Hopcus

New! Babka

1½ c. milk
¾ c. (1½ sticks) unsalted butter
2 pkgs. active dry yeast
¼ c. warm water (105° to 115°)
3 eggs
3 egg yolks
¾ c. sugar
1 tsp. salt

1 Tbsp. grated orange rind
½ tsp. grated lemon rind
1 Tbsp. orange-flavored liqueur
1 tsp. vanilla
8 to 9 c. sifted unbleached flour
½ c. slivered almonds, chopped
½ c. dark raisins
½ c. golden raisins

Streusel

¼ c. butter, softened
¼ c. sugar
½ tsp. cinnamon

½ c. chopped, blanched almonds
½ c. unsifted all-purpose flour

Mix butter, sugar and cinnamon together. Stir in almonds and flour. Mix until crumbly.

Heat milk in small saucepan until small bubbles form around the edge of the pan. Stir in butter until melted. Cool the milk to lukewarm.

Sprinkle the yeast over the yolks and sugar in medium-size bowl until smooth. Add salt, orange and lemon rinds, liqueur, vanilla and lukewarm milk mixture. Stir until well combined. Stir in yeast mixture.

Add flour, 1 cup at a time, mixing with wooden spoon until dough forms. Turn dough out onto lightly-floured surface. Knead until smooth and elastic, about 5 minutes. Knead in almonds and dark and golden raisins.

Generously butter large bowl. Place dough in buttered bowl and turn to coat. Cover with buttered wax paper and kitchen towel. Let rise in warm place, away from drafts, until doubled in volume, about 1 hour. Punch dough down. Cover with buttered wax paper and towel. Let rise a second time until doubled in volume, about 1 hour.

Butter three 9-to 10-cup kugelhopf or tube pans. Divide dough into 3 equal portions. Form each portion into 18-inch rope. Arrange evenly in bottom of prepared pans. Cover pans with towels and let rise in warm place, away from drafts, until doubled in volume, about 45 minutes.

Preheat oven to 350°. Sprinkle the Streusel over the top of each babka.

Bake in preheated, moderate (350°) oven for 30-40 minutes or until golden brown and cakes sound hollow when lightly tapped with fingers. Turn cakes out onto wire racks and let the cakes cool completely.

Judy Seikel

🐦 New! *Lemon Babka*

3 c. all-purpose flour
½ c. sugar
1 pkg. active dry or rapid-rising
    yeast
½ tsp. salt

¾ c. milk
½ c. butter or margarine
¼ c. water
3 egg yolks, at room temperature
1 c. raisins

Lemon Glaze:

¼ c. sugar
¼ c. water

2 Tbsp. lemon juice

In a large bowl, combine 1½ c. flour, sugar, undissolved yeast and salt. Heat milk, butter and water until warm. Butter does not need to melt. Gradually add to dry ingredients. Beat 2 minutes at medium speed with an electric mixer, scraping sides of bowl as needed.

Add egg yolks and ½ cup of flour; beat 2 minutes at high speed, scraping bowl as needed. With spoon, stir in remaining flour.

Cover and let rise in warm, draft-free place until doubled in size, about 1 hour. (For rapid-rising yeast, cover batter; let rest 10 minutes.) proceed with recipe.)

Stir batter down; mix in raisins. Turn into greased 3-quart kugelhopf or tube pan. Cover and let rise in warm, draft-free place until doubled in size, about 1 hour.

Bake at 350° for 35-40 minutes or until done. Remove from pan to wire rack. Brush warm cake with Lemon Glaze. Cool.

For lemon glaze: Combine sugar, water and lemon juice in a saucepan and bring to a boil. Reduce heat and simmer, stirring for 5 minutes or until syrupy.

Judy Seikel

Fizz Test for Baking Powder

If you have baking powder that has been on your shelf a long time, check it by putting a small amount in a saucer. Add a little water. If it does not fizz, it has lost its power. Throw it away and buy a new can.

No-Knead Caramel Braid

1 pkg. active dry yeast
¼ c. warm water (105° to 115°)
1 c. lukewarm milk, scalded then
    cooled
¼ c. margarine or butter, softened

¼ c. sugar
2 eggs
1½ tsp. salt
4 to 4½ c. all-purpose flour

Caramel Filling:

1 c. chopped nuts
⅔ c. packed brown sugar

⅓ c. margarine or butter, softened

Browned Butter Glaze:

¼ c. butter or margarine
2 c. powdered sugar

1 tsp. vanilla
1 to 2 tsp. milk

Dissolve yeast in warm water. Stir in milk, margarine, sugar, eggs and salt. Stir in 1 cup of the flour. Stir in remaining flour; continue stirring, scraping dough from side of bowl, until soft, sticky dough forms. Cover; let rise in warm place until double, about 1 hour. (Dough is ready if indentation remains when touched.) Stir down dough by beating about 25 strokes. Turn dough onto well floured surface. Roll or pat into rectangle, 18"x12". Spread Caramel Filling evenly over dough. Cut dough into 3 strips 18"x4". Roll each strip into rope; pinch edges and ends to seal. Place ropes diagonally and close together on lightly greased cookie sheet. Braid ropes gently and loosely. Do not stretch. Pinch ends to fasten. Tuck under securely. Cover; let rise until 1½ times original size, about 30 minutes.

Place oven rack below center of oven. Heat oven to 350°. Bake until braid is golden brown and sounds hollow when tapped, about 25-35 minutes. (If braid is browning too quickly, cover loosely with aluminum foil.) Cool slightly. Spread with Browned Butter Glaze. Note: Unbleached flour can be used in this recipe; first rising time may be slightly longer, about 1½ hours.

Caramel Filling: Mix nuts, brown sugar and margarine or butter, which has been softened in small bowl.

Browned Butter Glaze: Heat butter in 1½ quart saucepan over medium heat until delicate brown. Stir in powdered sugar and vanilla. Stir in milk, 1 tsp. at a time, until smooth and of desired consistency. If necessary, stir in few drops hot water until glaze is of desired consistency.

In memory of Ann Wallinger

New! No-Knead Sweet Bread

½ c. lukewarm water
2 pkg. yeast
2 c. milk
2 tsp. salt
2 sticks (1 c.) margarine or butter

1¼ c. sugar
4 eggs
8-9 c. flour
Raisins, to taste

Pour the ½ c. water into a large non-metal bowl and sprinkle the yeast over the water to soften. Set aside.

Bring the milk to a boil. Add margarine to melt. Add salt and sugar and set aside to cool. When cool, beat the eggs well and add to mild mixture. Pour the milk and egg mixture over the softened yeast and mix in the flour and raisins until all the dry ingredients are mixed through. Cover with a tea towel and set aside in a warm place to raise until double in size, about 2 hours.

Place in greased pans and let raise 2 hours. Bake at 300° for 1 hour. Just before baking, brush and sprinkle top with cinnamon sugar.

Katie Magott

New! Streusel Topping

1 c. flour
¼ c. very cold, hard butter
½ c. sugar

¼ c. vegetable shortening
Vanilla, to taste
Cinnamon, to taste

Combine all ingredients. This topping may be used on breads, streusel cake and coffee cakes. Any type of nuts may also be added, as desired.

Katie Magott

Christmas Eve

"The Polish meatless Christmas Eve dinner would consist of mushroom soup, a sweet poppy seed noodle dish, fish and sweet pastries galore. Needless to say, the menu in different parts of the country will vary — in Eastern Poland corn dishes and borscht soup with floating ravioli are popular."

Marian P. Opala, Justice of the Supreme Court, State of Oklahoma

New! Rumanian Almond Bread

3½ - 4 c. all-purpose flour
⅓ c. sugar
1 pkg. active dry or rapid-rising
    yeast
½ tsp. salt

½ c. milk
¼ c. plus 1 Tbsp. water
¼ c. butter or margarine
3 eggs, at room temperature
1 Tbsp. grated lemon peel

Almond filling:

⅓ c. almond paste
⅓ c. almonds, chopped and toasted

1 egg white
1 tsp. grated lemon peel

For Almond Filling, combine ⅓ cup (3 ounces) of almond paste with ⅓ cup finely-chopped and toasted almonds, egg white (save yolk for batter) and 1 teaspoon grated lemon peel. Beat with fork until blended. Set aside.

Combine 1 cup of the flour, the sugar, undissolved yeast and salt in a large bowl. Heat the milk and ¼ cup of water and butter until very warm. Gradually add to dry ingredients. Beat 2 minutes at medium speed with an electric mixer.

Separate 1 egg and reserve egg white for Almond Filling. Add 1 yolk and 1 whole egg and ½ cup of flour to the batter. Beat for 2 minutes at high speed, scraping bowl occasionally. With spoon, stir in enough remaining flour to make stiff dough.

Knead on lightly-floured surface until smooth and elastic, about 5 minutes. Cover and let rise in warm, draft-free place until doubled in size (about 1½ hours). (For rapid-rising yeast, cover kneaded dough and let rest on floured surface 20 minutes before proceeding.)

Punch dough down. Divide dough into 3 equal pieces. Roll each piece into a 24" x 4" rectangle. Spread ⅓ of filling over each rectangle to within ½-inch of edges.

Starting at long side, roll up tightly as for jelly roll. Pinch seams and ends to seal. Braid ropes. Place in greased 10-inch tube pan and pinch ends to join. Cover and let rise in warm, draft-free place until doubled in size, about 30 minutes.

Lightly beat remaining egg with 1 tablespoon water. Brush on braid. Bake at 350° for 35-40 minutes or until done. Remove from pan and cool on wire rack.

For a nice orange glaze, combine confectioner's sugar (use about a cup, or more if a lot of glaze is desired) with orange juice and beat with a fork until smooth and of a thin consistency that can be drizzled over the bread.

Judy Seikel

 Orange Frosted Braids

4 c. flour
2 tsp. baking powder
½ tsp. salt

4 Tbsp. shortening
4 Tbsp. sugar
1 egg

Frosting:

2 Tbsp. butter
3 Tbsp. orange juice

2 Tbsp. grated orange peel
Powdered sugar

Make like biscuits, but roll out and cut for braids. Bake until golden brown. Prepare frosting while braids are baking. Mix butter, orange juice and peeling with enough powdered sugar to allow it to easily spread. Spread on braids while hot out of the oven.

Mrs. A. J. Murphy
Father James Murphy's mother.

New! Fried Bread

Homemade bread dough that has
   risen and is oven ready.
Hot oil

Honey
Powdered Sugar

Pull dough up and cut off with sharp knife about golf ball size. Spread dough out lightly with fingers to about ¾-inch thick patty. Do not overwork. Fry in hot oil until brown on both sides. Serve with honey or powdered sugar.

Elizabeth Drew Magott
in memory of mother Rosa Drew

Bread

3 c. self-rising flour
5 Tbsp. sugar

12 oz. beer (room temperature)

Mix all ingredients thoroughly. Pour in loaf pan. Bake at 375° for 45 minutes. Remove from oven; split top. Fill top with butter. Return to oven. Bake another 15 minutes. Remove from oven. Ready to eat.

Mary Jo Jorski

No-Knead Bread

1 pkg. active dry yeast
1¼ c. warm water (105° to 115°)
2 Tbsp. shortening
2 Tbsp. sugar

2 tsp. salt
2⅔ c. all-purpose flour
Margarine, butter or shortening,
    melted

Dissolve yeast in warm water in large mixing bowl. Stir in shortening, sugar and 2 cups of the flour. Beat on low speed, scraping bowl constantly, 30 seconds. Beat on medium speed, scraping bowl occasionally, 2 minutes. Stir in remaining flour until smooth. Scrape batter from side of bowl. Cover; let rise in warm place until double, about 30 minutes. Stir down batter by beating about 25 strokes. Spread in greased loaf pan, 9"x5"x3". Smooth out top of batter by patting into shape with floured hands. Cover; let rise until double, about 40 minutes. Heat oven to 375°. Bake until loaf sounds hollow when tapped, 45 minutes. Brush top of loaf with margarine. Remove loaf from pan; cool on wire rack.

Cheese-Caraway Batter Bread: Add 1 cup shredded sharp Cheddar cheese (about 4 ounces) and 1 tsp. caraway seed to yeast-water mixture.

Onion-Batter Bread: Add 2-3 Tbsp. instant minced onion to yeast-water mixture.

In memory of Ann Wallinger

Bohemian Rye Bread

2 c. warm milk
1 c. warm water
2 pkg. dry yeast
2 Tbsp. honey
2 Tbsp. salt

3 Tbsp. oil
1 Tbsp. caraway seed
3 Tbsp. molasses
3 c. rye flour
5 to 6 c. white flour (or as needed)

Dissolve yeast in warm liquids. Add honey, salt, oil, molasses and caraway seed. Add rye flour and mix well. Add white flour, one cup at a time, mixing and kneading well after each cup. Let rise until doubled. Shape into 2 large round loaves and let rise again until doubled. Bake at 350° for 45 minutes, then bake at 300° for 20 minutes.

Bonita (Konop) Yox
Esther Konop

Rye Bread

2 c. milk
1 yeast cake or pkg.
2 Tbsp. sugar
2 Tbsp. shortening

1 Tbsp. salt
1 tsp. caraway seed
2 c. rye flour
4 c. white flour

Scald milk, Cool to lukewarm. Dissolve in small amount of milk, then add remaining milk. Add sugar, shortening, salt and rye flour. Stir and set aside to rise until double in bulk. Combine these 2 mixtures. Add white flour and caraway seeds. Stir and set aside until double in bulk. Punch down; shape into 2 loaves (2 pie pans are great to bake in). Let rise again until doubled. Bake at 400° for 15 minutes. Reduce temperature to 375°. Bake 45 minutes more. Remove from oven and grease tops while hot.

Rosie Lee Klimkowski

Beer Bread

3 c. self-rising flour
3 Tbsp. sugar

1 (12 oz.) can beer
¼ c. butter

Mix flour, sugar and beer with a fork. Put into greased bread pan and bake for 40 minutes at 350°. Remove from oven. Pour ¼ cup melted butter over bread. Yields 1 loaf.

Mary Keller

Boston Brown Bread

2 c. boiling water
2 c. raisins
2 c. sugar
2 eggs
1 c. chopped pecans

1 tsp. vanilla
½ c. shortening
4 c. flour
½ tsp. salt

Boil water; add raisins and boil 2 minutes. Set aside to cool. Cream sugar, shortening and eggs. Add flour, salt, pecans and vanilla. Add raisins to this mixture and pour into (unfloured) greased No. 2 tin cans. Fill ½ full. Makes 6 cans. Bake at 350° for 50 minutes. Slice in rounds for serving with coffee at breakfast. Also a good dessert bread.

Mary Keller

🐦 *New!* Lithuanian Potato Bread

(Bulvinis Ragaisis)

2 c. scalded milk
1 large raw potato
1 cake yeast
8 c. sifted flour, divided

1 egg
3 Tbsp. sour cream
1 level Tbsp. salt

Peel the potato and grate fine. Add hot milk and let stand until lukewarm. Crumble yeast into mixture. Add 4 cups flour, mix well with wooden spoon. Add egg, cream, salt and remaining flour. Beat well. Cover and let rise for 2-3 hours. Beat dough again. Grease 3 bread pans, fill half full with batter.
Cover with a towel and let stand until double in size.
Preheat oven to 450° and bake for 15 minutes. Reduce heat to 350° and bake for 45 minutes. Bread will stay moist and fresh for days.

Al Dilis

🐦 Potato Bread

1 medium potato
Hot tap water
2 pkg. active dry yeast
2 Tbsp. softened margarine

2 Tbsp. sugar
1 Tbsp. salt
1 c. milk (105° to 115°)
6½ to 7½ c. unsifted flour

Pare and dice potato; boil in water to cover until tender, about 20 minutes. Drain, reserving liquid. Add hot tap water to potato liquid to make 1 cup. Cool to warm (105° to 115°). Mash potato; set aside. Pour warm water into large warm bowl. Sprinkle in yeast; stir in mashed potato, warm milk and 3 cups flour. Beat until smooth. Stir in enough additional flour to make a stiff dough. Turn out onto lightly-floured surface and knead until smooth and elastic, about 8-10 minutes. Place in a greased bowl, turning to grease top. Cover. Let rise in warm place, free from draft, until doubled in bulk, about 35 minutes.
Punch dough down. Turn over in bowl. Cover and let rise again about 20 minutes. Punch dough down. Run out onto lightly-floured board. Divide in half. Roll each half into a 14"x9" rectangle. Shape into loaves. Place in 2 greased 9"x5"x3" loaf pans. Cover; let rise in warm place, free from draft, until doubled in bulk, about 50 minutes. Dust loaves with flour. Bake at 375° for 35-40 minutes or until done. Remove from pans and cool on wire rack.

Victoria B. Miller

Pull-Apart Bread

1 c. milk, scalded and cooled
3 eggs, beaten
1½ tsp. salt
¾ c. oleo, melted

1 pkg. dry yeast (add to milk when
  cooled)
½ c. sugar
4 c. unsifted flour

Do not knead. Mix first 5 ingredients by hand. Add ½ of flour, all of oleo, then rest of flour. Let rise 2 hours. Divide into 3 parts. Flour board and press ⅓ into 6-inch square. Cut into ½-inch strips. Dip in melted butter or oleo and coil strip from center of pan. Let rise 2 hours and bake at 350° for 25 minutes.

Rosalie Jorski

Quick Poppy Seed Bread Sticks

¾ c. soft margarine
1 c. grated Cheddar cheese

1 can refrigerated bread stick dough
Poppy seeds

Spread out dough flat. Cream margarine and cheese together. Spread the mixture over the dough. Cut into strips. Holding 1 end of a strip down with thumb, twist other end of strip 3 or 4 times to make a spiral bread stick. Roll strip in poppy seeds; place on cooking sheet, pressing ends to sheet to secure spiral. Bake as directed on can for hot bread sticks.

Judy Seikel

Soft Pretzels

1 cake yeast
1½ c. warm water
1 tsp. salt
1 tsp. sugar

4 c. flour
1 large egg, beaten
Coarse salt

Dissolve yeast in warm water. Add the salt and sugar. Blend in flour and knead dough until smooth. As soon as dough is kneaded, cut into small pieces and roll pieces into ropes. Twist into pretzel shapes onto greased cookie sheets. Brush pretzels with beaten egg and sprinkle with coarse salt. Bake immediately in a 425° oven for 12-15 minutes or until browned.

Elizabeth Hawkins

Sesame Twists

¼ c. sesame seeds
3 Tbsp. margarine, softened
½ tsp. paprika
¼ tsp. salt

2 to 4 drops liquid hot pepper or
   Worcestershire sauce
Refrigerated bread dough or bread
   dough from scratch

In a shallow skillet over medium heat, heat sesame seeds, stirring constantly until seeds are golden brown. Remove sesame seeds from pan and allow to cool. Roll out dough into a rectangle. Combine sesame seeds, margarine, paprika, salt and liquid hot pepper or Worcestershire sauce and mix well. Spread over dough evenly. Cut dough into ½-inch strips. Hold 1 end of strip and twist other end about 4 times to make a spiral. Place on ungreased cookie sheet and press each end of strip down firmly to hold. Bake in 400° oven for 12-18 minutes or until golden brown.

Judy Seikel

Noodle knowledge ...

"Mama was making noodles. I was about five. She said: 'Let me teach you how to make this.' She said to measure one cup of flour, and I measured exactly one cup of flour. She showed me what a pinch of salt was. She used just a hint of baking powder. She said: 'I will roll them out for you.' I remember that she put an egg in a bowl and told me not to touch that shell. She used the shell to measure just exactly a half shell of water and mixed it in. She told me to wash my hands again and start mixing that dough. You had to wash your hands 50 million times before you put your hands in that dough. This is my recipe. I will remember it as long as I live."

— *Agnes Czerczyk*

🐦 *New!* Strucle z Makiem

Poppy Seed Rolls

Dough:

2 pkgs. active dry yeast	½ c. butter or margarine
½ c. warm water	2 eggs
4½ c. flour (all purpose)	2 egg yolks
¾ c. sugar	½ c. dairy sour cream
½ tsp. salt	1 tsp. vanilla extract

Filling:

2 Tbsp. butter	¼ c. raisins (steamed)
10 oz. poppy seed, ground twice	2 egg whites
2 Tbsp. honey	½ c. sugar
2 tsp. lemon juice or vanilla extract	¼ c. finely-grated lemon peel

Icing:

1 c. confectioners' sugar	2 Tbsp. lemon juice

For dough, soften yeast in warm water in a bowl.

Mix flour with sugar and salt. Cut in butter with pastry blender or two knives until mixture has a fine, even crumb.

Beat eggs and egg yolks. Mix with yeast, then stir into flour mixture. Add sour cream and vanilla extract. Mix well.

Knead dough on floured surface for 5 minutes. Divide in half. Roll each half of dough into a 12-inch square. Cover.

For filling, melt butter in a large saucepan. Add poppy seed. Stir-fry 3 minutes.

Add honey, lemon juice and raisins to poppy seeds. Cover and remove from heat; let stand 10 minutes.

Beat egg whites with sugar until stiff, not dry, peaks form. Fold in orange and lemon peels. Gently fold in poppy seed mixture.

Spread half of filling over each square of dough. Roll up jelly-roll fashion, seal edges. Place on greased baking sheets. Cover and let rise until doubled in bulk — about 1½ hours.

Bake at 350° F. about 45 minutes. Cool.

For icing, blend sugar and lemon juice until smooth. Spread over rolls.

The ground poppy seed can be purchased already ground in gourmet shops.

Frances Afinowicz

Cinnamon Rolls

1 cake of yeast
¼ c. water
1 tsp. salt
2 Tbsp. shortening
¾ c. milk

1½ Tbsp. sugar
2¼ c. flour
Brown sugar (for topping)
Granulated sugar (for topping)

Soak yeast in ¼ cup water. Put sugar, salt, butter and milk in a saucepan and heat to lukewarm. Add yeast to mixture. In a large bowl, add flour to mixture. Mix with a spoon. Leave dough in the bowl and let it rise for about 20 minutes. Roll the dough out to one inch thick, just as for biscuits and cut with a biscuit cutter. Let them rise for about 20 minutes more.

Mix brown and white sugars well. Sprinkle over a greased pan. Put cut out rolls in pan on top of sugars, then bake in moderate oven until golden.

Louise Blankenship

Cinnamon Rolls

1 c. oil
1 c. sugar
1 Tbsp. salt
2 c. scalded milk
2 Tbsp. yeast

1 c. warm water
7 to 8 c. flour
1 c. butter
2 c. brown sugar
3 Tbsp. cinnamon

Dissolve yeast in water and sugar. When yeast rises, add milk, oil and salt. Add about 5 cups flour. Mix well. Add remaining flour and knead for about 10 minutes until smooth and elastic. Put in greased bowl and let rise until doubled, approximately 1 hour. Punch down. Roll out ¼-inch thick. Mix butter, brown sugar and cinnamon. Spread over dough. Roll up and cut into rolls. Bake at 400° for 15-20 minutes. When slightly warm, spread with glaze.

Mary Horn

🐦 New! Kotaczki Ze Serem

(Cottage Cheese Rolls)

1 c. milk, scalded	1 pkg. of yeast
¼ c. butter	¼ c. warm water
½ c. sugar	1 tsp. grated lemon rind
1 tsp. salt	1 tsp. grated orange rind
2 eggs	1 tsp. vanilla
4½ c. flour	

Cottage Cheese Filling:

1 lb. dry cottage cheese	1 Tbsp. lemon juice
2 eggs, separated	1 Tbsp. lemon rind
½ c. sugar	½ tsp. salt
2 Tbsp. butter	½ tsp. vanilla
1 Tbsp. flour	

Pour scalded milk over butter and sugar; stir until dissolved. Cool to lukewarm.

Dissolve yeast in warm water and add to milk mixture. Add salt to eggs, beat well and add to milk mixture. Add rinds and flavoring. Add half of the flour and beat until smooth. Add remaining flour, mix thoroughly and knead for about 10 minutes. Cover and set in a warm place to rise about one hour.

Punch down, brush with melted butter, and cover and store in refrigerator overnight.

Roll out on floured board to ¼-inch thickness and cut into small squares. On each square, place a little of the cottage cheese filling and pinch the four ends of the square over the filling crosswise to form four eyes.

Place on greased cookie sheet and brush with beaten egg yolk. Let rise until double in bulk. Bake in 350° oven for a half hour.

To make cottage cheese filling: Press cheese through sieve. Add egg yolks, sugar, butter, flour, lemon juice and rind, salt and vanilla. Mix well. Beat egg whites stiff and mix flour in carefully.

Julia Wasik Mathewson
Woodinville, Wash.
In memory of mother, Lillian Kupczynski Wasik

 Hot Bread, Rolls or Donuts

1½ c. water, boiled	2 pkg. dry yeast
½ c. Crisco	2 eggs
½ c. sugar	2 tsp. salt
½ c. warm water	6 c. flour

In large bowl, add boiling water to Crisco and sugar. Stir until melted. In glass bowl, dissolve yeast in warm water. When water mixture is cool, add yeast. Slightly beat the eggs and add salt to eggs. Add to mixture. Stir well as you add the flour. Cover with wax paper and let rise till double. Pour out on floured cabinet and work until dough can be handled without sticking. Shape into rolls or loaves and let rise again. Bake at 350° for 30-35 minutes.

Barbara Dull

Quick Dinner Rolls

Two hours before serving:

1¼ c. lukewarm water (or part milk)	1 pkg. dry yeast
2 Tbsp. sugar	2 Tbsp. soft shortening or margarine
2 tsp. salt	3 c. white flour

Mix all together. Knead on lightly-floured board. Let rise until double in size. Knead and make into rolls. Let them rise again. Bake.

Aline Honea

Refrigerator Rolls

2 c. lukewarm water	½ c. sugar
1½ tsp. salt	2 pkg. dry yeast
1 egg, beaten	¼ c. melted shortening
6 c. flour	

Mix together sugar, salt, egg and shortening. Add water until all is lukewarm. Add yeast and let stand 3 minutes. Mix in flour, 1 cup at a time. Knead until smooth. Place in a greased bowl. Spread oil or melted shortening on top. Let rise. Bake rolls at 350° for 12-15 minutes. Makes 9-10 rolls or 1 loaf of bread.

Joyce Nowakowski

Blueberry Muffins

1¾ c. flour
¾ tsp. salt
2 eggs
¾ c. milk
1 tsp. grated lemon rind

⅓ c. sugar
2 tsp. baking powder
4 Tbsp. melted butter
1 c. blueberries, drained

Sift together flour, sugar, salt and baking powder. Beat together eggs, milk and melted butter. Add blueberries and lemon rind to dry ingredients and mix. Stir liquid ingredients into dry ingredients, using as few strokes as possible; make no attempt to stir out lumps. Fill greased muffin tins about ⅔ full. Bake 15 to 20 minutes in 425 ° oven.

Suzanne Visnieski

Raisin Bran Muffins

4 c. raisin bran
1½ c. sugar
2½ c. flour
2½ tsp. soda

1 tsp. salt
2 eggs, beaten
½ c. melted shortening
2 c. buttermilk

Mix all dry ingredients well; add all others and mix well. Refrigerate if you don't want to bake immediately. Can be baked off as desired. Also it will keep up to 2 weeks in refrigerator. Bake at 400° for 15 minutes, depending on muffin tin size.

Excellent for breakfast. These are best when baked off, so you can eat while still warm.

Marilyn Tytanic

To Make Sour Milk

To make sour milk, add 1 Tbsp. vinegar or lemon juice to 1 cup of sweet milk. Let stand for a few minutes before using.

Refrigerator Muffins

½ c. margarine
½ c. brown sugar (or white)
2½ c. flour
2½ tsp. soda
½ tsp. salt

2 c. All-Bran
1 c. 100% whole bran
2 c. buttermilk
1 c. boiling water

Cream together margarine and sugar. Soak All-Bran in buttermilk. Cream all other ingredients with sugar and margarine. Add all ingredients to All-Bran and buttermilk. Put into well-oiled muffin tins. Bake at 375° for 30-35 minutes.

You can bake muffins anytime as dough will keep 4 or 5 weeks in refrigerator. This makes a lot of batter. You can use this for bread or dessert.

Gerry Lamer

New! Sour Cream Muffins

½ c. butter or margarine
1½ c. sugar
½ tsp. salt
4 eggs
1 tsp. baking soda

⅛ tsp. nutmeg
1½ c. sour cream
2¾ c. cake flour
1 to 2 c. fresh or frozen dry pack
    blueberries or raisins (optional)

Cream butter, sugar and salt until light and fluffy. Add eggs, baking soda, sour cream and flour, beating well. After each addition, put in berries or raisins. Fill greased or paper-lined muffin tins two-thirds full. Sprinkle with sugar.

Bake in preheated oven at 450° for 15 min. or until done.

Frances Afinowicz

Easy-Open Biscuits

Roll biscuit dough thin and fold before cutting. This makes biscuits crisp and flaky in the center. They split open easily for buttering.

New! Zucchini Muffins

3 eggs
1 c. vegetable oil
1 c. sugar
1 c. brown sugar
1 Tbsp. maple flavoring
2 c. zucchini (shredded)
2½ c. flour

½ tsp. baking powder
2 tsp. salt
2 tsp. baking soda
½ c. wheat germ
1 c. walnuts or pecans
Sesame seeds

In large bowl, mix eggs, oil, sugars and maple flavoring. Beat until the mixture is thick, foamy and light in color. Stir in zucchini by hand. In separate bowl, sift flour, baking powder, salt, baking soda, together. Mix wheat germ and nuts.

Stir flour mixture gently into zucchini mixture. Blend well. Fill greased and floured muffin tins two-thirds full. Sprinkle tops of muffins with sesame seeds.

Bake in a preheated oven at 350° for 20 to 25 minutes, or until a toothpick inserted in center comes out clean. Makes 24 to 30 muffins.

Keeps well in freezer, if cooled before freezing.

Frances Afinowicz

New! Corn Biscuits

1 (8 oz.) pkg. (or 2 cups) prepared
  biscuit mix

1 c. cream style corn
¼ c. vegetable margarine

Preheat oven to 450°. Melt the margarine in a jelly roll pan. Combine the biscuit mix and corn in a mixing bowl. Mix only until dry ingredients are moistened.

On a lightly-floured surface, pat the dough to about a ½-inch thickness. Cut in strips about ¾" by 4". Carefully turn the sticks in melted margarine. Bake 10 to 12 minutes, or until golden brown.

Judy Seikel

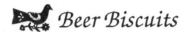 Sweet Potato Biscuits

1 c. sifted all-purpose flour
2 Tbsp. sugar
3 tsp. baking powder
¼ tsp. salt

⅓ c. margarine
1 c. cooked, mashed sweet potatoes
3 Tbsp. milk

Preheat oven to 425°. Grease baking sheet. Sift dry ingredients together. Cut in margarine. Stir in potatoes and enough milk to make a soft dough. Knead lightly; roll to ½-inch thickness. Cut in rounds. Place on prepared baking sheet and bake 15-20 minutes.

Carolyn Rudek

Beer Biscuits

3 c. Bisquick
½ tsp. salt

1 Tbsp. sugar
1¼ c. beer

Put all ingredients in together. Mix well. Grease muffin pans. Bake at 350° for 25 minutes.

Ruby Webb

Yeast Biscuits

1 pkg. yeast
1 egg
¼ c. sugar

2 c. warm water
4 c. self-rising flour
¾ c. soft or melted shortening

Sprinkle yeast over water in large bowl and dissolve. Stir in flour. Beat egg and add to sugar and shortening. Mix well and add this to the flour mixture. Mix well. Dough will be soft. Put in refrigerator. Bake in greased muffin pans 20 minutes at 400°. If covered well, rolls will keep for several days and baked as needed.

Helen Hopcus

🐦 Beer Batter

2 eggs
1 c. flour
1 tsp. salt

1 tsp. baking powder
1 tsp. oil
1 c. warm beer

Mix until smooth and creamy. Use on your favorite fish.

Bonita (Konop) Yox

🐦 Beer Batter

1 egg
½ c. flour
½ c. corn meal (white)

1 tsp. salt
1 c. warm beer

Mix all ingredients until smooth and creamy. Use on your favorite fish.

Bonita (Konop) Yox

🐦 Beer Batter

12 oz. can beer
1 to 1¼ c. flour
1 Tbsp. salt

1 tsp. paprika
½ tsp. baking powder

Pour the beer into a bowl. Add the flour (the mixture will foam). Stir in the salt, paprika and baking powder. The mixture will thicken as it stands. Make about 2½ cups. Make this at least an hour before you use it. Let it stand at room temperature. It will keep in the fridge for up to 3 or 4 days. Use batter for frying almost anything, shrimp, oysters, onion rings, mushrooms, eggplant, zucchini, fish, apple rings, fresh pineapple chunks, etc.

Irene Emmack

Desserts,
Cookies,
Cakes

 New! *Dried Fruit Compote*

½ c. dried apricots
½ c. dried peaches
½ c. dried prunes
½ c. dried pears
¼ c. raisins
2 c. water

1 Tbsp. cornstarch
½ c. sugar
⅛ tsp. salt
¼ orange and rind, sliced thin
¼ lemon and rind, sliced thin
1 Tbsp. red cinnamon candies

Pre-soak fruits only if they are very dry. Blend cornstarch with water. Combine all ingredients in pressure cooker. Use 3¾ lbs. pressure for 12 minutes or cook at 15 lbs. of pressure for 10 minutes. Reduce pressure with cool water. Chill fruit.

Judy Seikel

Apple Crisp

¾ c. sifted flour
½ c. brown sugar
½ tsp. cinnamon

6 Tbsp. butter
4 c. apples, peeled, cored and sliced

Preheat oven to 350°. Blend flour, sugar, cinnamon and butter with pastry blender or fork until flaky. Arrange apples in 8-inch square baking dish. Sprinkle flour and sugar mixture over the top of the apples. Bake for 1-1½ hours or until the apples are tender. Serves 8.

Mary Camfield

Apple Dessert

From Norway

2½ c. flour
1 heaping Tbsp. sugar
1 tsp. salt
1 c. lard
1 beaten egg yolk (plus milk to
  equal ⅔ c.)

2 handfuls corn flakes
10 chopped apples
1 c. sugar
1 tsp. cinnamon
2 whipped egg whites
1 c. powdered sugar glaze

Mix first 4 ingredients as for pie crust. Stir in the egg yolk mixture. Roll out ½ of the dough and spread in a jelly roll or edged cookie sheet. Combine 1 cup sugar and cinnamon. Sprinkle dough with crushed corn flakes, apples and cinnamon-sugar mixture. Roll out remaining crust and spread on top, being sure to pinch edges all around. Brush top with whipped egg whites. Bake at 400° for 15 minutes. Reduce temperature to 350°. Bake for 45 minutes. Dribble powdered sugar glaze on top. Add water to powdered sugar until a pouring consistency is reached to make glaze.

Joyce Rugg

Apple Kuchen

1 Pillsbury Plus yellow cake mix
½ c. coconut
1 stick butter (½ c.)
1 (20 oz.) can sliced apples, canned
  in water

½ c. sugar
1 tsp. cinnamon
1 (8 oz.) ctn. sour cream
1 egg

Mix dry cake mix with butter until crumbly. Mix in coconut. Press into ungreased 9"x13" pan. Bake for 10 minutes in a 350° oven.

Place sliced apples in a single layer (or more) over crust. Mix sugar and cinnamon. Sprinkle over the apples. Mix sour cream and egg. Pour over the apples and cinnamon sugar. Bake for 20 minutes at 350°. Serve warm or cold.

Judy Seikel

Banana Split Cake

2 c. graham cracker crumbs	5 or 6 bananas
1 stick oleo (½ c.)	1 large can crushed pineapple
2 eggs	10½ oz. Cool Whip
2 sticks oleo	½ c. pecans
2 c. powdered sugar	Maraschino cherries

Mix cracker crumbs and 1 stick melted oleo well. Pat into 9"x13" pan. Beat eggs, 2 sticks oleo and powdered sugar for 15 minutes with electric mixer. Pat onto layer 1. Spread sliced bananas over layer 2. Cover layer 3 with crushed pineapple. (Drain well.) Top with Cool Whip. Sprinkle nuts and cherries on top. Refrigerate for several hours.

Vicki Dimmer

Banana Split Cake

2 (8 oz.) pkg. cream cheese	1 c. chopped pecans
5 or 6 bananas	1 c. maraschino cherries
1 large can crushed pineapple	1 lb. box powdered sugar
1 large ctn. Cool Whip	Graham crackers, crushed

Line 8"x12" pan with graham cracker crust. Mix powdered sugar and cream cheese. Spoon onto crust. Slice bananas lengthwise and place on top of cheese mixture. (Overlap bananas.) Drain pineapple (sweeten with powdered sugar). Spoon pineapple over bananas. Cover with Cool Whip. Sprinkle with nuts and chopped cherries. Chill several hours or overnight.

Dora Lee Kusek

Bavarian Apple Torte

5 peeled and sliced apples
¼ c. slivered almonds
⅓ c. sugar
Dash of cinnamon
½ c. butter
¼ tsp. vanilla

1 c. flour
8 oz. cream cheese
¼ c. sugar
½ tsp. vanilla
1 egg

Mix sliced apples, sugar, cinnamon and almonds; toss to coat apples. Set aside. To make crust, cream butter until light and fluffy. Blend in vanilla, then flour. Roll dough into ball. Roll out in springform pan and 1½-inches up the sides. Cream together cream cheese and sugar until light and fluffy, then add vanilla and egg. Spread onto crust. Lay apple mixture on top. Bake at 450° for 10 minutes. Reduce heat to 400° and continue baking for 25 minutes. Cool before eating.

Anneliese Lancaster

Blitz Kuchen

From an Amish Dutch cookbook.

4 Tbsp. butter or margarine
10 Tbsp. sugar
2 eggs, beaten
1⅓ c. flour
1½ tsp. baking powder
¼ tsp. salt

½ c. milk
1 tsp. vanilla
½ tsp. cinnamon
¼ c. chopped nuts
4 Tbsp. sugar

Cream together first 3 ingredients. Mix well. Add next 3 ingredients alternately with milk and vanilla, mixing well. Pour into well greased pan (8"x8" or approximate). Mix last 3 ingredients and sprinkle over top. Bake at 350° for 30 minutes. This is quick, easy and bakes into a delicious, moist cake for breakfast or anytime.

Pauline Haynes

 New! Peach Kuchen

1½ c. all-purpose flour
½ c. sugar
2 tsp. baking powder
½ tsp. salt

2 eggs
2 Tbsp. milk
¼ c. butter or margarine, melted

Topping:

1 (29)oz. can cling peach slices
2 tsp. lemon juice
¼ c. sugar

½ tsp. cinnamon
1 egg yolk
¼ c. whipping cream

Combine flour, sugar, baking powder and salt in bowl. Add eggs, milk and butter. Mix to stiff batter. Spread batter in a greased 9-inch spring form pan. Drain peach slices. Arrange peaches over batter. Sprinkle with lemon juice, then sugar and cinnamon. Bake in 400° oven 25 minutes. Remove from oven. Beat egg yolk and cream together. Pour over peaches. Return to oven and bake 10 minutes longer. Serve warm.

Judy Seikel

Cherry Cherry

2 cans sour pitted cherries
1½ c. sugar
2 small boxes Jiffy vanilla cake mix

2 sticks butter (1 c.)
½ c. chopped pecans

Layer bottom of 13"x9"x2" pan with cans of cherries. Pour sugar evenly on top of cherries. Spread cake mix over sugar. Melt butter and pour on cake mix. Put pecans on top of cake mix. Bake at 350° for 1 hour.

Karen Stephenson

Cherry Delight

6 egg whites
¾ tsp. cream of tartar
2 c. sugar
2 c. crushed soda crackers

1 c. chopped nuts
2 tsp. vanilla
2 c. whipped cream
1 (21 oz.) can cherry pie filling

Preheat oven to 350°. Beat egg whites until frothy; add cream of tartar, then gradually add sugar. Beat until stiff. Fold in crushed crackers, nuts and vanilla. Spread in well buttered 9"x13" pan. Bake at 350° for 25 minutes. Cool. Whip cream and spread over top and spoon pie filling over cream. Chill several hours or overnight.

Carolyn Miles

Cherry Delight

1 can cherry pie filling
1 can sweetened condensed milk
1 (15 oz.) can crushed pineapple,
   drained

1 Tbsp. lemon juice
½ c. chopped pecans
1 (8 oz.) container Cool Whip

Combine all ingredients. Chill in refrigerator or in freezer for awhile if firmer texture is desired.

Diana Hanna

Fruit Dessert

1 (15 oz.) can fruit cocktail
1 (11 oz.) can mandarin orange
   segments

1 (13½ oz.) can pineapple tidbits
Lemon instant pudding (small)
2 sliced bananas

Blend all canned fruit with pudding. Add bananas and stir. Chill.

Suzan Schirf

Chocolate Delight

Crust:

1 c. flour
1 stick margarine
½ c. chopped pecans

Second Layer:

1 c. powdered sugar
1 (8 oz.) pkg. cream cheese,
   softened
12 oz. Cool Whip

Third Layer:

2 pkgs. instant chocolate pudding
3 c. milk

Fourth Layer:

Other ½ container of Cool Whip
Chopped pecans, toasted

For crust, combine ingredients until crumbly. Pat mixture into 9"x13" pan. Bake at 300° for 15 minutes. Cool.

For second layer, combine powdered sugar and cream cheese and mix well. Add Cool Whip and spread mixture over crust.

For third layer, combine pudding and milk. After pudding has set, spread over cream cheese layer.

For fourth layer, spread remaining Cool Whip over pudding layer and sprinkle with toasted chopped pecans. To toast pecans, bake at 250° for about 15 minutes.

Iva Nell Hanna

Mandarin Orange Dessert

1 small can mandarin oranges,
   drained
1 can Eagle Brand milk

Juice of 2 lemons
Vanilla wafers
½ pt. whipping cream

Line a glass baking dish or glass bowl with vanilla wafers. Mix Eagle Brand milk, lemon juice and drained oranges together and pour in bowl over vanilla wafers. Cover top with another layer of vanilla wafers. Whip whipping cream (unsweetened) and cover top with cream. Crush vanilla wafers and sprinkle on top. Refrigerate. Better prepared a day ahead.

Fern Koelsch

Pineapple-Apple Delight

1 (20 oz.) can pineapple chunks
3 to 4 eating apples, diced
1 c. walnuts, chopped
1 (10 oz.) pkg. miniature
    marshmallows

1 egg, beaten
1 c. sugar
2 Tbsp. flour
2 Tbsp. vinegar

Drain pineapple, reserving liquid. In a saucepan, mix the egg, sugar and flour. Add the pineapple liquid and vinegar. Cook until thick and smooth, stirring occasionally. Dice apples and mix with pineapple chunks and walnuts. Arrange marshmallows to cover top of mixture. Pour sauce over all. Do not toss. The warm sauce will partially melt the marshmallows. Refrigerate and chill several hours. Yields 8-10 servings.

Pauline Haynes

Rich Refrigerator Dessert

1 stick oleo
1 c. flour
½ c. chopped nuts
2 pkgs. instant chocolate or lemon
    pudding mix

3 c. milk
1 (8 oz.) pkg. cream cheese
1 c. powdered sugar
1 (10 oz.) ctn. Cool Whip
Chopped nuts

Mix oleo, flour and chopped nuts until crumbly. Spread over the bottom of a 9"x13" pan and press lightly. Bake at 375° for 15 minutes. Let cool completely. Mix pudding and milk and let set for a while until it thickens. Spread over first layer. Mix cream cheese, powdered sugar and Cool Whip. Spread over second layer. Sprinkle top with a few chopped nuts. Refrigerate.

Martie Wyskup

New! *Pineapple Cheesecake Squares*

Crust:

1½ c. flour
½ c. margarine, softened
½ c. almonds, finely chopped
½ c. powdered sugar

Middle Layer:

2 (8 oz.) pkg. cream cheese, softened
½ c. sugar
2 eggs
⅔ c. orange-pineapple juice

Top Layer:

¼ c. flour
¼ c. sugar
1 c. orange-pineapple juice
20 oz. can crushed pineapple, well drained
1 c. Cool Whip
½ c. coconut

Mix flour, margarine, almonds and powdered sugar for crust until crumbly. Press firmly in bottom of ungreased 9"x13" pan. Bake at 350° until set — about 15-20 minutes.

Make middle layer by beating cream cheese until fluffy. Add sugar and eggs. Stir in juice. Pour onto hot crust and bake at 350° until center is set, about 20 minutes. Let this cool completely.

To make the top layer, mix flour and sugar in a microwave-safe bowl. Stir in juice. Microwave at full power for a few minutes until thickened, stirring occasionally. (Or, cook over stove on medium heat, stirring constantly. Boil and stir one minute. Remove from heat.) Fold in well-drained pineapple. Let cool completely. Then fold in coconut and Cool Whip. Spread carefully over dessert. Cover loosely and refrigerate until firm, about four hours. Makes one dozen 3-inch squares.

Kathy Small

Whipping Cream Tricks

Cream will whip faster and better if you'll first chill the cream, bowl, and beaters well.

Soupy whipped cream can be saved by adding an egg white, then chilling thoroughly. Re-beat for a fluffy surprise!

A few drops of lemon juice added to whipping cream helps it whip faster and better.

Cream whipped ahead of time will not separate if you add ¼ teaspoon unflavored gelatin per cup of cream.

A dampened and folded dish towel placed under the bowl in which you are whipping cream will keep the bowl from dancing all over the counter top.

 Shamrock Gelatin Surprise

1 pkg. lime gelatin
1½ c. hot water

1 pt. vanilla ice cream

Mix gelatin with the hot water. Stir in vanilla ice cream. Set in refrigerator until solid. Serves 4.

Mary Camfield

Apple Pudding

1 c. sugar
½ c. butter
2 eggs
½ c. milk

1½ c. flour
1 tsp. baking powder
½ tsp. lemon extract
8 apples

Pare and core 8 apples carefully and place close together in a deep pan. Beat the batter very lightly and pour over apples and bake in moderate oven. Serve with hot sauce.

Mrs. A.J. Murphy
Mrs. A.J. Murphy is Father James's mother.

Fruit Pizza

8 oz. cream cheese
¾ c. powdered sugar
1 tsp. vanilla
Sugar cookie dough
½ c. sugar
3 Tbsp. cornstarch

¾ c. water
¼ c. lemon juice
1 c. orange juice
Banana, pear, kiwi, strawberries,
*   peaches, grapes, pineapple or any*
*   assorted sliced fruit*

Spread cookie dough on pizza pan and bake until brown. Mix cream cheese, powdered sugar and vanilla. Spread on crust. Top with sliced fruit of your choice. Cook sugar, cornstarch, water, lemon and orange juice until thick. Cool and spread on top when ready to serve.

Kay Brown

Date Pudding Or Cake

Cake:

1 c. sugar
1 Tbsp. butter
1 egg
1 c. boiling water

1 tsp. soda
1 c. chopped dates
½ c. nuts
1¼ c. flour

Topping:

1 c. chopped dates
½ c. nuts

1 c. sugar
½ c. water

Cut up dates. Pour boiling water over them. Add soda and let stand while getting other ingredients ready. Add other ingredients (dough will be quite thin). Bake about 45 minutes at 350°.

Topping: Put on stove and cook until thick. Spread on cake while still hot.

Gerry Lamer

Steamed Pumpkin Pudding

6 Tbsp. butter
¾ c. packed brown sugar
¼ c. granulated sugar
2 eggs
1½ c. all-purpose flour
½ tsp. salt
½ tsp. baking soda

½ tsp. ground cinnamon
½ tsp. ground nutmeg
¾ c. mashed, cooked pumpkin or
    canned pumpkin
½ c. buttermilk
½ c. chopped walnuts

Cream butter and sugars together until light. Beat in eggs. Stir together flour, salt, soda, cinnamon and nutmeg. Mix pumpkin and buttermilk. Add to creamed mixture alternately with dry ingredients, mixing well after each addition. Fold in nuts. Spoon into greased and floured 6½ cup ring mold. Cover tightly with foil. Bake at 350° for 1 hour. Let stand 10 minutes. Unmold. Serve with whipped cream if desired. Serves 12-16.

Pauline Haynes

🐦 Sweet Noodle Kugle

1 lb. pkg. broad noodles	1 c. raisins (golden)
1 (8 oz.) pkg. cream cheese	½ stick melted butter (¼ c.)
1 can crushed pineapple	1 tsp. cinnamon
1 can drained fruit cocktail	1 c. sugar
1 pt. cottage cheese	3 c. Frosted Flakes, crushed or
1 pt. sour cream	S'Mores cereal, crushed
7 eggs	

Cook noodles as directed on package. Drain and mix with all ingredients, except Frosted Flakes, ½ cup sugar and teaspoon cinnamon. Mix these 3 remaining ingredients together and top casserole with the mixture. This will make 2 casseroles in 9"x13" pans. Bake at 400° for 10 minutes, then reduce heat to 350° for 1 hour. Serve warm or at room temperature.

Delicious served cold, too.

Evelyn Saxton

🐦 Three-Layer Dessert

First layer:

1½ c. flour
1½ sticks margarine
¾ c. nuts

Third Layer:

1 large pkg. chocolate instant
    pudding
Nuts

Second Layer:

1 c. sugar
1 (8 oz.) pkg. cream cheese
12 oz. Cool Whip

For first layer, cream margarine and flour. Add nuts and spread in a 9"x13" pan. Bake for 15 minutes at 350°. For second layer, cream sugar and cream cheese together. Fold in ½ of the Cool Whip. Spread on the baked crust. Prepare pudding as directed on package. Spread on top of second layer. Spread the remaining Cool Whip over this. Sprinkle with nuts and chill.

Jean Maddox

Lemon Squares

1 c. sifted flour
1 stick (¼ c.) butter
1¼ c. sugar
2 eggs, lightly beaten
1 tsp. grated lemon rind

3 Tbsp. lemon juice
2 Tbsp. flour
½ tsp. baking soda
¼ tsp. salt

Blend 1 cup flour, butter and ¼ cup of the sugar in a small bowl until smooth. Press mixture into an 11"x7"x1½" baking pan. Bake at 325° for 20 minutes or until lightly browned. Combine the remaining cup of sugar, eggs, lemon rind, lemon juice, salt, remaining flour and baking soda in a medium bowl. Beat until well blended. Spread mixture over the hot shortbread crust. Bake an additional 25 minutes. Remove from oven and cool in pan. Cut into squares.

Judy Seikel

Banana Split Ice Cream

4 eggs
1 c. sugar
2 Tbsp. vanilla
½ pt. whipping cream
¼ tsp. salt
2 cans Eagle Brand milk
Dairy milk (about ½ to 1 qt.)
2 ripe bananas, chopped
1 bottle maraschino cherries,

drained
1 (15 oz.) can crushed pineapple, drained
2 c. marshmallow fudge, chopped (without nuts)
Chopped pecans
1 c. very ripe strawberries, sliced
¾ c. miniature marshmallows

Combine eggs, cream, sugar, salt and vanilla in a bowl and mix thoroughly with mixer. Pour into freezer can. Add condensed milk and stir well. Add bananas, cherries, pineapple, fudge, nuts, strawberries and pecans. Add dairy milk to the "fill" line on freezer can and stir well.

Won second place in 1987 Harrah Memorial Day Ice Cream Crank Off.

The Pray Team
Becky Spaeth
Kay Brown
Judy Seikel

Butterfinger Ice Cream

4 eggs
1 large pkg. instant vanilla pudding
2 small cans Carnation evaporated
   milk

32 oz. milk
1 tsp. vanilla
1 c. sugar
5 Butterfingers

Beat eggs. Add pudding, milk, Carnation milk, sugar and vanilla. Mix
well. Add crushed Butterfingers. Freeze in ice cream maker.

Becky Spaeth

Golden Glow Ice Cream

2 qt. milk
1 Tbsp. flour
1 c. grated pineapple
2 c. sugar

2 oranges
1 c. hot water
1 qt. can apricots

Boil the sugar and water together 5 minutes. Add the grated pineapple,
apricots, cut fine with juice and juice and pulp of the oranges. Scald the milk.
Add the flour moistened with 2 tablespoons of milk and cook 2 minutes.
Blend the milk and fruit mixture. Cool and freeze. This recipe makes a gallon.

Our Lady's Cathedral Cookbook
Circa 20s or 30s

Homemade Ice Cream

4 eggs
1 c. sugar
1 can Eagle Brand milk
1 tsp. vanilla

1 qt. milk
Fruit, if desired
Milk

Beat with mixer, the eggs and sugar. Add Eagle Brand milk and vanilla.
Add 1 quart of milk. Pour in freezer can and fill to "fill line" with more milk
and fruit, if desired.

Linda Beam

Old-Fashioned Homemade Ice Cream

3 eggs
2½ c. sugar
½ tsp. salt
2 tsp. vanilla
2 tall cans Milnot
6⅓ c. milk

2 or more c. drained, mashed and
   diced fruit or 1 Tbsp. lemon juice
   with 1 tsp. vanilla (optional)
1 Tbsp. unflavored gelatin with
   ¼ c. water (optional)

Beat eggs well. Add sugar, salt and vanilla. Beat thoroughly. Add Milnot and milk. Freeze.

Fruit: Add 2 or more cups of drained fruit, mashed or diced.

Lemon: 1 tablespoon lemon juice added with only 1 tsp. vanilla.

To prevent quick melting: 1 tablespoon unflavored gelatin in ¼ cup water. Melt over hot water and add to the milk.

Carolyn Rudek

One-Two-Three Sherbet

1 c. orange juice
1 c. lemon juice
1 c. pineapple juice

1½ c. sugar
1½ c. Milnot
2 c. water

Combine juices and sugar and place in the icebox until cold. Pour in milk and water and stir well. Return to refrigerator. Stir 1 time and freeze. Can be made in ice cream mixer.

Minnie Nowakowski

Orange Sherbet

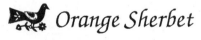

7 bottles orange pop
2 cans Eagle Brand

1 can crushed pineapple

Mix in ice cream freezer.

Robert Nowakowski

Oreo Ice Cream Dessert

1 small bag Oreo cookies
½ stick melted butter
½ gal. vanilla ice cream (soft)
1 small can chocolate syrup

8 oz. Cool Whip
Chopped pecans
Cherries, drained on paper towel
  (optional)

In 9"x13" glass pan, crumble Oreos. Pour on butter. Spread ice cream, the chocolate syrup, then Cool Whip. Sprinkle pecans. Freeze. Add cherries when ready to serve.

Suzan Schirf

Snow Ice Cream

2 c. milk
2 eggs
1½ c. sugar

½ tsp. salt
3 tsp. vanilla

Mix 2 cups milk, 2 eggs, 1½ cups sugar, ½ tsp. salt and vanilla. Whip together and add clean snow (not packed) until no more can be added, then eat! Can be stored in freezer.

Judy Seikel

Vanilla Ice Cream

1 can Eagle Brand milk
1 medium Cool Whip
1 small vanilla instant pudding

1 c. sugar
4 eggs
Add milk to fill line

Blend all ingredients. Add milk to fill line. Freeze. Makes 1 gallon.
Tastes like Braum's French vanilla ice cream.

Jeri Schuessler

Banana Bars

½ c. butter
1½ c. sugar
2 eggs
¾ c. sour cream or milk
1 tsp. vanilla

2 or 3 small bananas
2 c. flour (scant)
1 tsp. salt
1 tsp. soda

Cream butter and sugar. And eggs and beat. Add sour cream or milk and mashed bananas and vanilla. Beat until mixed. Add flour, salt and soda. Beat until well mixed. Pour on cookie sheet and bake at 375° for 20 minutes or until done. Frost if desired and cut while still warm. Can be frozen.

Becky Spaeth

Creamy Brownie Frosting

3 Tbsp. butter or margarine,
    softened
3 Tbsp. cocoa
1 Tbsp. light corn syrup or honey

½ tsp. vanilla
1 c. confectioners' sugar
1 to 2 Tbsp. milk

Cream butter or margarine, cocoa, corn syrup or honey and vanilla in small mixer bowl. Add sugar and milk. Beat to spreading consistency. Makes 1 cup frosting.

Carol Brookes

Zupusti

"In the old days, there was always a big dance the Saturday night before Lent. It was called Zupusti, which means Mardi Gras. We would dance no more until after Easter."

Veronica Kupczynski

Best Brownies

½ c. vegetable oil or melted butter
1 c. sugar
1 tsp. vanilla
2 eggs
½ c. unsifted all-purpose flour

⅓ c. cocoa
¼ tsp. baking powder
¼ tsp. salt
½ c. chopped nuts (optional)

Blend oil or melted butter, sugar and vanilla in large mixer bowl. Add eggs; beat well, using spoon. Combine flour, cocoa, baking powder and salt. Gradually add to egg mixture. Stir in nuts if desired. Spread into a greased 9-inch square pan. Bake at 350° for 20-25 minutes or until brownie begins to pull away from edge of pan. Cool in pan. Frost with Creamy Brownie Frosting if desired. Cut into squares. Makes 16 brownies.

Carol Brookes

Candied Fruit Bars

¾ c. melted butter
1½ c. graham crackers
1 c. flaked coconut
2 c. candied fruit (red cherries,
    green cherries)

1 c. chopped dates
1 c. nuts
15 oz. can sweetened condensed
    milk

Mix butter and crackers. Pat into 9"x13" pan. Mix remaining ingredients and pour into crust. Bake at 350° for 20-25 minutes.

Kay Brown

Caraway Seed Cookies

2 eggs
1 c. sugar
1 c. butter
½ c. sour milk
½ tsp. soda

½ tsp. cream of tartar
1 tsp. vanilla
Flour
Caraway seeds

Mix ingredients and add enough flour for a very soft dough. Roll very thin. Sprinkle generously with caraway seeds. Bake in moderate oven.

Our Lady's Cathedral Cookbook, Circa 20s or 30s

Congo Bars

⅔ c. butter
2¼ c. brown sugar
3 eggs
2¼ c. flour

2 tsp. baking powder
½ tsp. salt
2 c. chocolate chips
1 tsp. vanilla

Melt butter and brown sugar on low heat, one at a time. Measure dry ingredients together in large mixing bowl. Add melted butter and sugar. Add eggs, one at a time. Mix together at low speed. Add chips and vanilla last. Bake in greased 9"x13" pan at 350° for 30 minutes.

Anita Craiger

Delicious Bars

1 stick butter (½ c.)
1 c. vanilla wafers
1 c. coconut
1 c. chocolate chips

¾ c. walnuts
1 can Borden's Eagle Brand
   evaporated milk

Preheat oven to 375°. Melt butter in large Pyrex dish. Arrange ingredients in order listed. Pour milk over the top. Bake for 30 minutes. Cool and cut in squares.

Irene Watkins

New! Coconut Crisps

1 pkg. yellow cake mix
½ c. cooking oil
¼ c. water
Vanilla
1 egg

1 (3½) oz. can flaked coconut
Whole unblanched almonds,
   maraschino cherry pieces, or
   chocolate sprinkles (if desired)

Preheat oven to 325°. Blend dry cake mix, oil, water, vanilla extract and egg. Stir in coconut. Drop from a teaspoon onto ungreased cookie sheets. If desired, press a whole almond or a piece of maraschino cherry on the center of each cookie.

Bake at 325° for 8-10 minutes, or until light golden brown. Makes about six dozen 2¼-inch cookies.

Josephine Russell

Cowboy Cookies

1⅛ c. white sugar
1⅛ c. brown sugar
1⅛ c. margarine
3 eggs
1⅛ tsp. vanilla
2¼ c. flour

1¼ tsp. soda
Scant tsp. salt
2¼ c. oats
1 (16 oz.) pkg. chocolate chips
1 c. pecans
1 c. coconut, if desired

Cream sugars, margarine, eggs and vanilla. Add dry ingredients, except oats. Cream together; stir in oats, chocolate bits, pecans and coconut. Use ice cream scoop for large cookies. Bake at 350° for about 12 minutes. Makes a lot.

Joyce Nowakowski

Crunchy Coconut Cookies

½ c. margarine
½ c. packed brown sugar
½ c. granulated sugar
1 egg
1 c. flour
½ tsp. soda
½ tsp. baking powder

¼ tsp. salt
½ tsp. vanilla
1⅓ c. Angel Flake coconut
1½ c. Post Raisin Bran or 40%
    Bran Flakes or Wheaties
⅛ c. milk (optional)

Stir together ingredients with mixer. If dough is too thick, add milk. Drop on ungreased cookie sheet and press with a fork that has been dipped into water. Bake 12 minutes at 350°. Makes 3 dozen.

Verna Steciak

Frank's Cookies

½ c. oleo
½ c. brown sugar
¼ c. buttermilk
½ c. sugar
1 tsp. vanilla
1 egg

1 c. flour
½ tsp. soda
¼ tsp. salt
2 c. oats
¾ c. nuts
¾ c. raisins

Cream oleo and sugars together. Stir soda in buttermilk, then add egg and vanilla. Add this mixture to oleo and sugar mixture. Stir in flour, salt, oats, pecans and raisins. Drop by teaspoon onto greased cookie sheet. Bake 15 minutes at 350°.

Dorothy Wyskup

God Bless Them Cookies

1 tsp. soda
2 Tbsp. hot water
1 c. shortening
1 c. Total or Bran Flakes
1 c. coconut

2½ c. flour
1 c. chopped pecans
2 c. cut up dates
1 tsp. vanilla
3 eggs

Mix dry ingredients. Cream sugar, eggs and shortening. Add to dry ingredients. Add pecans, dates and vanilla. Bake in moderate oven until golden.

Louise Olive

Keep Sugar Soft

Brown sugar won't harden if an apple slice is placed in the container.

If your brown sugar is already brick hard, put your cheese grater to work and grate the amount you need.

A slice of soft bread placed in the package of hardened brown sugar will soften it again in a couple of hours.

Soften brown sugar by placing it in the microwave for several seconds. Start with a small increment of time to soften a large bag or box of brown sugar in the microwave and test for desired softness frequently.

A sack of lumpy sugar won't be if you place it in the refrigerator for 24 hours.

Chocolate Crinkles

1 c. shortening
1½ c. sugar
2 tsp. vanilla
2 c. flour
2 tsp. baking powder
½ c. chopped nuts

2 eggs, beaten
2 (10 oz.) sq. unsweetened
   chocolate, melted
½ tsp. salt
⅓ c. milk

Cream shortening, sugar, vanilla, eggs and chocolate. Sift flour, baking powder and salt. Add alternately with milk to batter. Add nuts and chill 3 hours. Form into 1-inch balls. Roll in powdered sugar. Place on greased cookie sheet 2-3 inches apart. Bake in moderate 350° oven for 15 minutes. Cool slightly. Remove from pan.

Fern Koelsch

Ginger Crinkles

⅔ c. cooking oil
1 c. sugar
1 egg
4 Tbsp. molasses (⅓ c.)
2 c. flour

2 tsp. soda
½ tsp. cinnamon
1 tsp. ginger
¼ c. sugar

Mix oil and sugar. Add egg and beat well. Stir in molasses and sift dry ingredients and add. Drop by teaspoon into sugar and form into balls and coat with sugar. Cook on ungreased cookie sheet. Bake in 350° oven for 15 minutes.

Helen Brown

 Gingersnaps

¾ c. shortening
1 c. brown sugar, packed
1 egg
¼ c. molasses
2¼ c. flour
2 tsp. soda

1 tsp. cinnamon
1 tsp. ginger
½ tsp. cloves
¼ tsp. salt
Granulated sugar

Cream shortening, brown sugar, egg and molasses. Mix in remaining ingredients, except granulated sugar. Cover and chill 1 hour. Heat oven to 350°. Shape dough by rounded teaspoonsful into balls. Dip in sugar. Place balls 3 inches apart on lightly-greased baking sheet. Bake 10-12 minutes or just until set. Immediately remove from baking sheet. Makes 4 dozen.

Josephine Russell

Golden Carrot Cookies

1 c. shortening or oleo
¾ c. sugar
1 c. mashed cooked carrots
2 c. flour
2 tsp. baking powder

½ tsp. salt
1 tsp. vanilla
1 c. coconut
½ c. nuts
2 eggs

Icing:

1 box powdered sugar
Grate of 1 orange on outside for
   orange peeling

½ c. juice
1 tsp. vanilla

Mix shortening or oleo, sugar and eggs. Add carrots. Sift flour, baking powder and salt. Mix into batter mixture. Add coconut, nuts and vanilla. Bake 8-10 minutes. Do not over bake. Ice while hot.
Icing: Add all ingredients to powdered sugar and ice cookies while hot.

Fern Koelsch

🐦 Honey Drop Cookies

3¼ c. sifted all-purpose flour
3 tsp. baking powder
1 c. (2 sticks) butter
½ c. honey
1 c. seedless raisins
1 tsp. vanilla

½ tsp. salt
½ tsp. nutmeg
1⅓ c. firmly-packed light brown
   sugar
1 egg
1 c. coarsely chopped nuts

Sift together flour, salt, baking powder and nutmeg. Cream butter and sugar. Beat in honey and egg. Stir in dry ingredients. Add raisins, nuts and vanilla. Mix well. Chill dough. Drop by level tablespoons onto greased baking sheet. Bake in moderate 350° oven for 10-12 minutes. Makes about 6 dozen cookies.

Gerry Roller

🐦 New! Chruscik or Crullers

4 egg yolks
1 egg white
¼ c. powdered sugar
½ tsp. salt

1 tsp. vanilla
1 tsp. rum
1 c. flour

Mix salt and eggs and beat 10 minutes. Add sugar. Mix with plenty of flour. Separate into two pieces and roll thin. Cut 2-inch by 1½-inch wide. Cut a slit in center about a ½-inch long and take one end and pull through center and then do the same with the other side.

Deep fry in deep Crisco. Let them float, brown on one side. They brown very fast; you have to watch them carefully. Lay on brown paper. When cool, sprinkle with powdered sugar.

Helen Lukaszek

New! Kipfels

1 pkg. dry yeast
¼ c. warm water
¾ c. cream, scalded and cooled
1 c. butter, melted
Juice and grated rind of ½ lemon

3 egg yolks, slightly beaten
4 c. sifted all-purpose flour
Fruit filling, purchased or pureed
 from dried fruit

Soften yeast in the warm water. Mix cooled, scalded cream, melted butter, lemon juice, rind and yolks. Add yeast. Gradually add flour. Beat until smooth. Cover and let stand one hour. Turn out onto floured pastry cloth and shape into 48 balls. Dough will be buttery and soft. Cover and let stand for one hour. Press balls flat.

Add your favorite filling and roll into crescents. Canned fruit filling such as apricot or prune may be purchased for use, or you can make the filling.

Bake at 375° about 15 minutes.

I purchase prunes and puree them in the blender to make the filling. I add a little of the cookie mixture to help thicken and hold it together.

Helen Lukaszek

Lebkuchen Or Christmas Cookies

1 lb. brown sugar
3 eggs
½ c. citron, finely chopped
1 tsp. baking soda
1 Tbsp. water

1 tsp. baking powder
3 c. flour
1 tsp. cloves
1 tsp. allspice

Mix brown sugar and eggs. Dissolve baking soda in water and add. Add remaining ingredients and mix. Bake in a layer pan in moderate oven. Cut into squares and ice separately.

Our Lady's Cathedral Cookbook
Circa 20s or 30s

New! Lithuanian Butter Cookies

(Sviesto Sausainiai)

½ lb. cream cheese
½ lb. butter (two sticks or 1 cup)
2 c. flour

Apricots, pureed and stewed
Prunes, pureed and stewed
Confectioner's sugar

Instead of ½ pound of butter, you can mix ¼ pound of butter and ¼ pound of margarine, if desired.

Cream butter and cheese and then sift in flour. Mix and chill overnight. Roll thin and cut into squares. Fill squares with pureed, stewed apricots, prunes or jam may be substituted.

Bake in 450° oven until lightly browned. Remove from pan, sprinkle with confectioner's sugar.

Al Dilis

New! Meltaway Cookies

1 c. butter or margarine, softened
½ c. powdered sugar
1 tsp. vanilla

2 c. flour
¼ tsp. salt

Heat oven to 400°. Mix butter, sugar and vanilla thoroughly. Stir in flour and salt. Drop dough by rounded teaspoons 1-inch apart on ungreased cookie sheet. Bake until set but not brown (approx. 8-9 minutes). While warm roll in powdered sugar. Cool. Makes about 4 dozen.

Diana Hanna

🐦 Million Dollar Cookies

2 c. shortening	1 tsp. soda
1 c. sugar	1 tsp. salt
1 c. brown sugar	1 tsp. vanilla
2 eggs	1 c. coconut
4 c. flour	1 c. chopped pecans

Cream shortening, sugar and eggs. Sift flour, soda and salt. Add this to creamed mixture. Add vanilla, coconut and pecans. Roll into small balls and press down with a glass that has been dipped in flour (do this for each cookie). Bake at 350° for 7 minutes.

Pauline Drew

🐦 Fruit Roll

1 lb. pecans	1 lb. vanilla wafers
1 lb. walnuts	½ lb. candied fruit
1 lb. dates	½ lb. marshmallows
1 lb. raisins	½ lb. softened butter (to be added
1 lb. dried apricots	last)
1 lb. coconut	

Grind fruits, etc. Add butter. Mix and knead like dough on bread board. Shape into roll. Wrap well and store in refrigerator. To serve, slice like cookies and place on plates or trays.

Aline Honea

🐦 No Bake Cookies

½ c. margarine	3 c. oatmeal (quick cook)
½ c. canned milk	½ c. chunky peanut butter
2 c. sugar	1 tsp. vanilla
4 Tbsp. cocoa	

Boil margarine, milk, sugar and cocoa for 2 minutes. Remove from heat. Stir in oatmeal and peanut butter. Add vanilla. Drop on wax paper. Cool until firm.

Rosalie Marino

No Bake Cookies

2 c. sugar
½ c. margarine
½ c. milk

¼ c. cocoa
1 tsp. vanilla
3 c. oatmeal (not instant)

Boil sugar, margarine, milk and cocoa together for 3 minutes. Remove from heat and add other dry ingredients. Drop by teaspoonfuls on wax paper.

Mary Camfield

New! No Bake Peanut Butter Honey Cookies

¼ c. honey
¼ c. margarine
½ tsp. vanilla

½ c. peanut butter
Dash salt
1½ c. oats

Bring honey and margarine to a boil. Remove from heat and stir in peanut butter, vanilla, salt and oats. Drop large spoonfuls onto wax paper.

I set them in the freezer for a few minutes and my kids enjoy them cold.

Diana Hanna

Polish saying:

"Krowa co du'zo ryczy, malo mleka daje." A noisy cow gives little milk. (Great talkers are little doers.)

submitted by Dora Kusek

Oatmeal Chocolate Refrigerator Cookies

1 c. shortening	¾ c. cocoa
2 c. brown sugar	1 tsp. soda
2 eggs	1 tsp. salt
2 tsp. vanilla	2 c. oatmeal
2 c. flour	1 c. chopped nuts

Cream shortening, sugar, eggs and vanilla. Add flour, cocoa, oats and nuts. Make 2-inch rolls and chill. Cut ¼ inch and place on ungreased cookie sheet; or drop by teaspoonfuls and press with fork dipped in water. Or, roll small balls and press with finger. Bake at 375° for 10-12 minutes. Makes approximately 6 dozen.

Substitute 1 cup white sugar and 1 cup brown sugar. You can also substitute 1 tsp. vanilla and 1 tsp. mint flavoring.

Ann S. Huffman

Orange Icebox Cookies

1 c. shortening	2¾ c. flour
½ c. brown sugar, packed	¼ tsp. salt
½ c. granulated sugar	¼ tsp. soda
1 egg	1 c. chopped pecans
1 orange, grated	

Cream shortening and sugars. Add well-beaten egg, juice of orange and grated rind. Mix. Sift flour, salt and soda. Add to creamed mixture with pecans. Roll in wax paper. Chill ½ hour. Slice. Place on greased baking sheet. Bake 12-15 minutes in 350° oven.

Josephine Russell

Uncooked Cookies

2 c. sugar
¼ c. cocoa
¼ lb. butter
½ c. milk

2 tsp. vanilla
½ c. peanut butter
3 c. raw oatmeal

Bring sugar, cocoa, butter and milk to a boil. Add vanilla, peanut butter and oats. Remove from fire and mix all ingredients thoroughly. Drop by spoonfuls on wax paper.

Ina Wiedemann

Oatmeal Rocks Cookies

1 c. shortening
1 c. sugar
2 c. flour
2 eggs, beaten
2 c. 3-Minute oats
¼ c. sweet milk
1 tsp. baking powder

½ tsp. soda
1 tsp. cinnamon
¼ tsp. salt
1 c. chopped nuts
1 c. chopped raisins or dates
    (optional)

Cream shortening and sugar. Add eggs. Mix the rest of dry ingredients. Sprinkle over nuts and raisins. Combine the mixtures, adding only enough milk to make a stiff dough. Drop onto a greased pan, 1 inch apart. Bake 10-12 minutes at 350°. Makes 4 dozen.

Ruby Webb

Oatmeal Cookies

¾ c. soft shortening
1 c. brown sugar
½ c. sugar
1 egg
¼ c. water
1 tsp. vanilla

1 c. flour, sifted
1 tsp. salt
¼ tsp. soda
3 c. oats (uncooked)
1 c. nuts (optional)

Mix shortening, sugars, egg, water and vanilla. Beat thoroughly. Sift together flour, soda and salt. Add shortening mixture to flour mixture and mix well. Blend in oats and pecans if used. Drop by teaspoon on greased cookie sheet. Bake in 350° oven for 12-15 minutes.

Robert Nowakowski

Oatmeal Cookies

1 c. shortening
1 c. brown sugar
1 c. granulated sugar
2 beaten eggs
1 tsp. vanilla
1½ c. sifted all-purpose flour

1 tsp. salt
1 tsp. baking soda
3 c. quick cooking oats
½ c. chopped nuts
Raisins (optional)

Cream shortening and sugars until fluffy. Add eggs and vanilla. Beat well. Sift flour with dry ingredients and add to creamed mixture. Add oats and nuts. Form into long rolls. Wrap in wax paper and chill thoroughly. Slice ¼-inch thick. Bake on ungreased cookie sheet at 350°, approximately 10 minutes.

To be successful, this recipe must be beaten with mixer and must be chilled or frozen. Makes 5 dozen.

Ann Kubiak Jones

Aunt Lena's Oatmeal Cookies

2 c. sifted flour	1 c. brown sugar
1 tsp. baking soda	2 eggs
1 tsp. salt	1 tsp. vanilla
1 c. shortening	2 c. quick oats
1 c. sugar	1 c. nuts, chopped fine or ground

Beat sugar, shortening and eggs until fluffy. Add dry ingredients that have been sifted together. Add oats, nuts and vanilla. Mix well. Drop by rounded teaspoonfuls or preferably make small teaspoon-size balls. Place on greased cookie sheets. Flatten to 1/8-inch with bottom of floured glass. Bake at 325° or until lightly browned. Remove from sheets immediately. Cool on baking racks. Makes approximately 3 dozen.

Joan Taulbee

Chocolate Oatmeal Cookies

2 c. sugar	3 c. quick oats
1/4 c. cocoa	1 tsp. vanilla
1/4 lb. oleo	1/4 c. nuts or coconut or peanut
1/2 c. milk	butter (optional)

Mix sugar, cocoa, oleo and milk in saucepan. Boil 2 minutes (begin timing when bubbles are all over surface). Stir constantly to keep from burning. Take pan off heat. Stir in oatmeal, vanilla and nuts (etc.). Drop by spoonful onto wax paper.

Suzanne Visnieski

Keep Cookie Dough Light
To roll out cut-out cookies, use powdered sugar instead of flour and dough will not become heavy from "extra" flour.

🐦 Peanut Butter Cup Cookies

**1 roll prepared peanut butter
cookie dough**

**1 pkg. peanut butter cups candy
(Reese's)**

Preheat oven to 350°. Cut dough into 9 (1-inch) slices. Cut each section into 4 equal pieces. Roll each piece into a ball and place in ungreased miniature muffin tins. Bake 10 minutes. As the cookie dough bakes, remove foil from peanut butter cup candy. Immediately upon removing cookies from oven, press peanut butter cups into each cookie. Cool 8-10 minutes in pan before removing. Makes 36 cookies.

Ina Wiedemann

🐦 Peanut Butter Fingers

**1 pkg. active dry yeast
2 Tbsp. warm water (105°-115°)
½ c. granulated sugar
1 egg
½ c. peanut butter (crunchy or
smooth)**

**¼ c. margarine or butter
¼ c. shortening
1½ c. all-purpose flour or wheat
flour
¾ tsp. baking soda
¼ tsp. salt**

Cocoa Glaze:

**1½ c. powdered sugar
¼ c. cocoa**

**3 Tbsp. milk
1 tsp. vanilla**

Dissolve yeast in warm water in large bowl. Mix in sugars, egg, peanut butter, margarine and shortening until smooth. Stir in flour, baking soda and salt. Cover and refrigerate until chilled, about 30 minutes. Heat oven to 375°. Shape dough by teaspoonfuls into 2½-inch fingers on ungreased cookie sheet. Bake until light brown, about 8 minutes. Cool. Dip 1 end of each cookie into Cocoa Glaze. Makes about 6 dozen cookies.

Cocoa Glaze: Mix powdered sugar and cocoa in medium bowl. Stir in milk and vanilla until smooth. Stir in additional milk, ½ teaspoon at a time, until of desired consistency.

Elenora Jarvis

Polish Butter Cookies

1 c. sweet butter
½ c. sugar
2 egg yolks
1 tsp. vanilla
2 c. unsifted flour (all-purpose)

2 egg whites, beaten
1 c. finely chopped walnuts or
   pecans
Currant or grape jelly

With wooden spoon beat butter, sugar, egg yolks and vanilla until smooth. Stir in flour just until combined. Refrigerate 30 minutes. Meanwhile, preheat oven to 375°. Using hands, roll dough into balls 1 inch in diameter. Dip in egg whites, then roll in chopped nuts. Place 1 inch apart on ungreased cookie sheet. With thumb, press center of each cookie. Bake 8 minutes or just until delicate golden brown. Remove to wire rack and cool. In center of each cookie, place a dot of jelly. Makes about 6 dozen.

Rosie L. Klimkowski

Polish Ring Cookies

5 unbroken egg yolks
1 c. butter or margarine, softened
3 eggs
2 tsp. grated lemon peel

3 c. unsifted all-purpose flour
2 Tbsp. lemon juice
1 egg white, slightly beaten
1 c. sugar

Gently drop egg yolks into boiling water; simmer, uncovered, 20 minutes. Drain. Preheat oven to 350°. Lightly grease cookie sheets. In medium bowl beat butter and 1 cup sugar until smooth and fluffy. Add hot hard cooked egg yolks, one at a time, beating well after each addition. Add lemon peel. Stir in flour and lemon juice; mix until smooth. Chill several hours. On slightly floured surface with palms of hands, roll 1-inch balls of dough into 4-inches long. Shape into rings. Place on prepared cookie sheets 1 inch apart. Brush with egg whites. Sprinkle with sugar. Bake 12-15 minutes until lightly golden brown. Cool on wire rack. Yields 6½ dozen.

Rosie L. Klimkowski

Ciastka Z Konserwa

Polish Tea Cakes

½ c. butter
½ c. sugar
1 egg yolk, slightly beaten
1 c. flour
½ tsp. salt

½ tsp. vanilla
Egg whites
Chopped nuts
Preserves

Cream the butter and sugar until fluffy. Add the slightly beaten egg yolk and mix in well. Add the flour, sifted with the salt. Mix. Roll the dough into small balls; dip in unbeaten egg whites and roll in chopped nuts. Place on buttered baking sheets and press down the center of each with a thimble or your thumb. Bake at 325° for 5 minutes. Remove from oven and press down again with thimble and return to oven for 10-15 more minutes. Remove from oven and while still warm, fill indentation with preserves.

Victoria B. Miller

Power Cookies

2 c. brown sugar
2 c. granulated sugar
¾ c. butter, softened
1 c. vegetable shortening
4 eggs
2 tsp. vanilla
3 c. all-purpose flour

2 tsp. salt
2 tsp. baking soda
3 c. uncooked oats
2 c. coconut
2 c. raisins
1 c. chocolate chips
1 c. chopped nuts

Cream together the sugars, butter and shortening. Beat in eggs and vanilla. Combine flour, salt and soda and beat into first mixture. Add remaining ingredients and knead into first mixture.

Drop by heaping teaspoon, 2 inches apart, on greased baking sheet. Bake in preheated 350° oven about 8 minutes or until nicely browned. Let cookies cool on baking sheet about 1 minute before removing to rack to cool. Store in airtight container. Makes 7 dozen cookies. For best results, shape dough into rolls. Wrap and chill several hours. Slice and bake as above.

Carolyn Werchan

Quick Macaroons

1½ c. fine grated coconut
3 Tbsp. Tang instant breakfast
   drink

¾ c. sweetened condensed milk
1 tsp. vanilla
¼ tsp. almond extract

Combine all ingredients and blend well. Drop by teaspoonsful 1 inch apart on greased baking sheets. Bake at 325° for 15 minutes or until golden brown. Remove from baking sheets at once and cool on racks. Makes about 2½ dozen.

Victoria Miller

Roskies - Filled Cookies

1 (8 oz.) pkg. cream cheese
1 lb. butter (may use 2 sticks butter
   and 2 sticks margarine)

½ c. powdered sugar
4 c. flour
Pinch of salt

Filling:

1 lb. dried fruit (prunes, apricots,
   etc.)

Sugar to taste

Cream softened butter and cheese. Add powdered sugar. Combine flour and salt and add to cheese mixture. Divide dough into 4 balls and wrap each in wax paper or plastic wrap. Refrigerate a couple of hours or overnight. If dough becomes too soft and hard to handle, refrigerate for 30 minutes. Roll dough on a floured board or wax paper (the thinner, the better) and cut into 2-2½-inch squares. Put about 1 tsp. of fruit filling on each square. Fold 2 opposite ends over filling, overlapping slightly and press to seal. Bake at 375° until lightly browned, about 12-15 minutes. Remove from pan and cool. Sprinkle with powdered sugar.

Fruit Filling: Cook fruit with sugar and water until done. Drain fruit, saving liquid. Put fruit through blender and add just enough of the reserved juice to make a very thick consistency.

Dorothy Zurbriggen

Rocky Road S'mores Bars

½ c. Parkay margarine
½ c. packed brown sugar
1 c. flour
½ c. graham cracker crumbs

2 c. miniature marshmallows
16 oz. pkg. semi-sweet chocolate
pieces
½ c. chopped walnuts or pecans

Beat margarine and sugar until light and fluffy. Add combined flour and cracker crumbs. Mix well. Press onto bottom of greased 9-inch square pan. Sprinkle with remaining ingredients. Bake at 375° for 15-20 minutes or until golden brown. Cool and cut into bars. Serves 16.

Cindy Garrett

Seven Layer Bars

½ c. melted butter
2 c. crushed graham crackers
2 c. coconut
2 c. butterscotch chips

2 c. chocolate chips
2 c. chopped walnuts
2 cans sweetened condensed milk

Layer ingredients as stated in large cookie sheet. Bake at 350° for 20-30 minutes. Let cool before slicing into bars.

Bonita (Konop) Yox

Toasted Almond Slices

6 eggs
1 stick oleo
2 c. sugar
6. c. flour

6 tsp. baking powder
1 tsp. almond flavor
1 tsp. vanilla
1½ c. chopped nuts

Cream eggs, oleo and sugar. Add remaining ingredients. Form loaf shapes (4). Place 2 on 2 cookie sheets. Bake at 325° for 20 minutes till cookie shapes test done with toothpick. Remove from oven. Slice 1-inch slices and turn on side. Return to oven to toast, then remove and turn over to toast other side.
Good dunking cookie.

Ann S. Huffman

🐦 New! *Almond Toffee Triangles*

½ c. packed brown sugar
⅔ c. margarine or butter, softened
½ c. light or dark corn syrup
1 egg

1 tsp. vanilla
2 c. all-purpose flour
¼ tsp. salt

Heat oven to 350°. Grease jelly roll pan (15½" x 10½" x 1"). Mix brown sugar, margarine, corn syrup, egg and vanilla. Stir in flour and salt. Spread dough in pan. Bake until light golden brown, 18 - 20 minutes. Prepare topping. Pour over hot baked layer; spread evenly. Bake until light brown and set, 15 to 20 minutes; cool. Cut into 2½-inch squares; cut each square diagonally into halves. Makes about 48 triangles.

Topping

⅓ c. packed brown sugar
⅓ c. light or dark corn syrup
¼ c. margarine or butter

¼ c. whipping cream
1 tsp. vanilla
1 c. almonds

Cook and stir brown sugar and corn syrup over low heat until sugar is dissolved. Stir in margarine and cream. Heat to boiling; remove from heat. Stir in vanilla and almonds. This is a great holiday treat!

Dianna Hanna

🐦 New! *Vanillekipfel*

Almond Vanilla Crescents

1 c. (two sticks) butter or
    margarine, softened
¾ c. powdered sugar
½ tsp. almond extract (or substitute
    with 2 tsp. vanilla)

1¾ c. all-purpose flour
¼ tsp. salt
1 c. oats
½ c. finely-chopped almonds
Powdered sugar

Heat oven to 325°. Beat margarine, sugar and almond extract until well blended. Add flour and salt; mix until well blended. Stir in oats and almonds. Using level measuring tablespoonfuls, shape dough into crescents.

Bake on ungreased cookie sheet 14-17 minutes or until bottoms are light golden brown. Remove to wire rack. Sift additional powdered sugar generously over warm cookies. Cool completely. Store tightly covered. Makes about three dozen.

Judy Seikel

New! Tea Time Tassies

Crust:

1 (3 oz.) pkg. cream cheese
½ c. butter or margarine

1 c. all-purpose flour

Filling:

2 eggs
1 c. light brown sugar
2 Tbsp. butter or margarine

1 tsp. vanilla extract
Salt (pinch)
1 c. chopped nuts

To make the crust, soften cream cheese and butter. Stir in flour and mix well. Chill for one hour or longer. Shape in 24 balls. Press into tassie muffin pans. Press into each cup to look like pie crust.

For filling, beat eggs slightly. Add the brown sugar and butter and mix well. Add the other ingredients and blend. Put one tablespoon of filling into each pie crust. Bake at 325° for 30 minutes. Use non-stick Tassie pans or spray the pans with oil.

Lila Dilis

Sugar Cookies

2 c. flour
½ tsp. soda
½ tsp. salt
½ c. shortening or margarine

1 c. white sugar
1 egg
½ c. buttermilk
½ tsp. vanilla

Sift flour, soda and salt. Cream remaining ingredients and add dry ingredients. Bake at 375° for approximately 8 minutes.

This recipe freezes well. You can add anything you wish: nuts, raisins, chocolate chips, or coconut, etc.

Mary Williams

Festival Fare

The members of the Catholic Daughters run a "Piekarnia" (pronounced: p-yekarn-ya), or bakery, at the Polish Festival held the second Saturday in May each year where you can sample Polish butter cookies, Vanillekipfel and other traditional Polish treats.

🐦 Sugar Cookies & Frosting

½ tsp. baking soda
1 c. Crisco shortening
1 c. sugar
1 c. milk, mixed with 1 tsp. vinegar
3 egg yolks

1 tsp. vanilla
3 c. flour
1 tsp. salt
1 tsp. baking powder

Frosting:

⅔ c. Crisco
1 tsp. salt
1 lb. powdered sugar

¼ c. water
1 tsp. vanilla
Food coloring, optional

Cookies: Mix all ingredients. Using ½ of the mixture, put on floured surface and knead until no longer sticky, using a few cups of flour. When dough isn't sticky, roll out to ⅛ inch thick (will rise to twice this size) and cut out with floured cookie cutters.

Bake on ungreased cookie sheet at 350° for 8 minutes, or until lightly browned on bottom. Cool completely on racks before frosting.

Frosting: Mix ingredients. Decorate with knife or frosting bags with tips. If knife is used, double recipe. If using bags, divide into non-plastic bowls to add 2 drops food coloring. Leave cookies spread out for a few hours to dry. Makes 8 dozen.

Dolly Conley

🐦 New! Melt-In-Your-Mouth Sugar Cookies

1 c. butter or margarine, softened
1 c. vegetable oil
1 c. sugar
1 c. sifted powdered sugar
2 eggs

1 tsp. vanilla extract
4½ c. all purpose flour
1 tsp. baking soda
1 tsp. salt
1 tsp. cream of tartar

Combine butter, oil and sugar in a large mixing bowl; beat well at medium speed of an electric mixer; add eggs one at a time, beating after each addition. Stir in vanilla. Combine flour, soda, salt and cream of tartar in a medium mixing bowl; add to creamed mixture, beating well.

Shape dough into 1-inch balls; place on ungreased cookie sheets. Flatten with the bottom of a glass dipped in sugar. Bake at 350° for 8-10 minutes or until done. Cool on wire racks. Yield 8 dozen

Helen Morin

Minnesota Sugar Cookies

1 c. shortening
1 c. brown sugar
2 eggs
3½ c. flour
2 tsp. soda

1 tsp. salt
2 tsp. salt
2 tsp. cream of tartar
1 tsp. vanilla
Sugar and cinnamon

Cream shortening and sugars. Add other ingredients and mix well. Shape into balls and roll in sugar and cinnamon. Bake at 350° about 10 to 12 minutes.

Anita Craiger

Sugar Cookies

1 c. butter
1½ c. powdered sugar
2½ c. flour
½ tsp. salt

1 tsp. soda
1 tsp. cream of tartar
1 tsp. vanilla
1 egg

Mix all ingredients. Roll out on a floured surface to about ¼-inch thick. Use cookie cutters or rim of drinking glass to make shapes. Bake in a 350° oven until lightly brown, about 10 minutes.

Joyce Nowakowski

New! Pat Wood's Sugar Cookies

1 c. Crisco
2 c. sugar
2 eggs
1 c. sour cream
1 tsp. vanilla

½ tsp. soda
4 tsp. baking powder
4½ c. flour
½ tsp. salt

Cream Crisco and sugar together. Add eggs, one at a time. Continue to beat until smooth. Add sour cream and the rest of the dry ingredients. Continue to stir until smooth.

Roll out on floured canvas or board, fairly thick. Cut with large round cutter. (I use a water glass.)

Bake at 350° 12-15 minutes on an ungreased cookie sheet. These are a soft, thick sugar cookie. Sprinkle with sugar or cinnamon before baking.

Pat Wood

New! Valentine Cookie

1 lb. butter, or use ½ lb. butter and
  ½ lb. oleo
1½ c. sugar

2 Tbsp. vanilla
5 c. flour
Very little water

    Cream sugar and butter. Add flavoring, flour and water. Mix well. Put 1" ball on ungreased cookie sheet. Press out cookie using flat bottom glass. Bake at 350° for 8-10 minutes.

Josephine Russell

Snickerdoodles

1 c. margarine or Crisco
1½ c. sugar
2 eggs
2¾ c. flour
Small pinch of salt
1 tsp. cream of tartar

1 tsp. soda

Coating Mix:
2 Tbsp. sugar
1 tsp. cinnamon

    Cream margarine and sugar together. Add eggs and mix well Add the rest of the ingredients and mix well. Refrigerate for 10 minutes or more. Shape dough into 1-inch balls. Mix sugar and cinnamon well. Roll balls in the mixture. Bake at 400° until golden.

Frances Wyskup

Snickerdoodles

1 c. shortening or oleo
1½ c. sugar
2 eggs
¼ tsp. salt
2 Tbsp. powdered sugar

2¾ c. flour
1 tsp. soda
2 tsp. cream of tartar
2 tsp. cinnamon

    Cream shortening and sugar. Add eggs. Sift flour, soda and salt. Add to mixture. Chill and roll into 1-inch balls. Mix powdered sugar and cinnamon. Roll balls in sugar mixture. Bake in 350° oven.

Fern Koelsch

Apple Cake

2 c. sugar
1½ c. oil
3 eggs
2 Tbsp. vanilla
3 c. flour

1 tsp. soda
1 tsp. salt
1 tsp. cinnamon
3 c. chopped apples
1 c. walnuts or pecans

Topping:

1 c. brown sugar
¼ c. milk

½ c. butter

Cream sugar, oil and eggs together. Add vanilla. Sift dry ingredients and add to creamed mixture. Stir in apples and nuts. Mix well. Pour into oiled and floured pan, 9"x13"x2". Bake at 350° for 40 to 50 minutes or until done. While cake is warm, spread on topping.
Topping: Boil together ingredients for 3 minutes. Cool. Beat until thick.

Sharon Barker

Applesauce Cake

2 c. sugar
½ c. shortening
2 whole eggs
2 c. flour
½ tsp. salt

1 tsp. soda
1 tsp. cinnamon
1 tsp. nutmeg
1 tsp. cloves
4 c. diced apples

Mix all ingredients together, then add the diced apples. Mix well. Bake in a 350° oven for about 45 minutes.

Bena Meany

Applesauce Cake

1 c. shortening	½ tsp. nutmeg
1 c. sugar	⅛ tsp. cloves
2 c. applesauce	½ tsp. allspice
2½ c. flour	1 c. raisins
2 tsp. soda	1 c. chopped nuts
1 tsp. cinnamon	½ tsp. salt

Cream shortening and sugar together. Combine applesauce, flour, soda, cinnamon, nutmeg, cloves, allspice, raisins, nuts and salt. Mix into shortening mixture. Mix well. Bake in greased and floured tube pan at 325° for 45 minutes to 1 hour or until well done. Test cake with a folded broom straw.

Mickey Wyskup

Moma's Applesauce Cake

2 c. applesauce	1 tsp. nutmeg
2 tsp. soda	1 tsp. mixed spices
¾ c. Crisco	1 c. chopped nuts
2 eggs	1 c. raisins
1½ c. sugar	3 c. flour
1 tsp. cinnamon	1 c. chopped dates (optional)

Mix soda in applesauce and let stand while you mix the other ingredients. Cream sugar and shortening. Add eggs and beat well. Sift flour with the spices added. Mix part of the flour with raisins. Combine all ingredients together and mix well. Bake in large angel food cake pan in moderate 350° oven for 1 hour.

Pat Bacon

German Apple Cake

4 c. apples, diced	1 c. pecan pieces
2 c. sugar	2 tsp. soda
3 c. flour	1 c. oil
½ tsp. cinnamon	1 tsp. vanilla
½ tsp. nutmeg	2 eggs, well beaten
½ tsp. salt	

Mix apples, sugar and pecans. Let stand 1 hour. Sift or mix together flour, spices, salt and soda. Add to apple mixture alternately with the oil, vanilla and eggs. Mix by hand. Bake at 350° for 1 hour, 15 minutes or less, if done. Makes 2 loaves or 1 ring cake. Stays moist if wrapped in foil.

Joyce Nowakowski

Apple Cake

3 eggs	1 tsp. soda
2 c. honey (or sugar)	1 c. salad oil
3 c. flour	1 tsp. cinnamon
3 c. fresh, shredded apples	1 tsp. baking powder
2 tsp. vanilla	1 c. chopped nuts
1 tsp. salt	1 c. coconut

Beat eggs, salad oil, honey (or sugar) and vanilla. Sift dry ingredients together and add to egg mixture. Fold in apples, nuts and coconut. Bake in Bundt pan or angel food cake pan for an hour at 350°. Some pans may take longer.

Linda Beam

New! *Banana Cake*

2½ c. cake flour
1⅔ c. sugar
1¼ tsp. baking powder
1¼ tsp. baking soda
1 tsp. salt
⅔ c. shortening

⅔ c. butter milk or sour milk,
  divided
1¼ c. ripe mashed bananas
  (about 3)
2 eggs

Sift the first five ingredients together into a bowl. Add the shortening, the bananas and half of the buttermilk (⅓ c.). Beat the mixture for 2 minutes with an electric mixer and add the remaining ⅓ cup of buttermilk. Add the eggs. Beat 2 more minutes.

Pour the batter into either two 9" round pans or a 13"x9" casserole. Bake at 350° for 30-35 minutes for the round layer cakes or about 45 minutes for the oblong cake.

Sour milk may be made by adding 1 tablespoon of vinegar to regular milk.

Katie Magott

Banana Cake

2 c. cake flour (or Gold Medal
  flour)
1⅔ c. sugar
1¼ tsp. soda
1 tsp. salt

1¾ tsp. baking powder
⅔ c. shortening
⅔ c. buttermilk
3 eggs
Cool Whip

Filling:

1 small box Jell-O pudding or pie
  filling (make as directed)

1¼ mashed ripe bananas

Preheat oven to 350°. Grease and flour 2 (9-inch) round pans. Measure all ingredients into large mixing bowl. Blend ½ minute on low speed, scraping bowl constantly. Beat 3 minutes or more on high speed. Pour into pans. Bake 35-40 minutes. Cool cake.

Filling: Split the 2 cakes. Make pudding as directed. Spread the pudding on the cakes; slice bananas on the cake. Put layers together and frost with Cool Whip.

Vernie Visnieski

Mashed Banana Cake

½ c. shortening
1¼ c. sugar
1 tsp. soda
1 tsp. baking powder
2 eggs
¼ tsp. salt

2 c. cake flour
⅓ c. sour milk
1 c. mashed ripe bananas
1 tsp. vanilla
½ tsp. lemon extract
Pecan pieces, if desired

Mix as for any batter cake. Bake at 350° - layers 25-30 minutes. Makes 2 layers and is very good. Ice as desired.

Aline Honea

Sour Cream Banana Cake

¼ c. shortening
2 eggs
2 c. flour
1 tsp. soda
1 c. sour cream
½ c. chopped nuts

1⅓ c. sugar
1 tsp. vanilla
1 tsp. baking powder
¼ tsp. salt
1 c. mashed bananas

Frosting:

Powdered sugar
Cream cheese

Small amount mashed bananas
Vanilla

Cream shortening and sugar. Add eggs and beat until fluffy. Combine dry ingredients. Add to creamed mixture. Alternate with sour cream, beginning and ending with dry ingredients. Add bananas and nuts, mixing until just blended. Spoon batter into greased and floured 13"x9"x2" pan. Bake 35-40 minutes at 350°. Cool and frost with powdered sugar, cream cheese and small amount of mashed bananas and vanilla. Mix well.

Mary Keller

Blackberry Wine Cake

Cake:

1 box white cake mix
1 (3 oz.) box blackberry Jell-O
½ c. cooking oil

4 eggs
1 c. blackberry wine
½ c. chopped pecans

Topping:

½ c. blackberry wine
1 c. powdered sugar

½ c. butter

Combine cake mix and dry Jell-O in mixing bowl. Add eggs, oil and wine. Mix on low speed until moistened. Beat at medium speed for 20 minutes. Generously grease Bundt pan. Sprinkle nuts in bottom of pan. Pour in batter. Bake at 325° for 45-55 minutes (until cake pulls away from sides). Mix ½ cup wine, powdered sugar and butter in saucepan. Boil 1 minute. While cake is hot (still in pan) pour ½ of topping over cake. Let set for 30 minutes. Turn cake out of pan and pour rest of topping over cake.

Kathy Visnieski

Carrot Cake

2 c. flour
2 c. sugar
4 eggs
3 c. grated carrots
1 tsp. vanilla

1½ c. oil
2 tsp. cinnamon
½ tsp. salt
1 tsp. baking powder
2 tsp. baking soda

Frosting:

1 box powdered sugar
1 (8 oz.) pkg. cream cheese
1 stick butter or margarine

1 tsp. vanilla
1 c. chopped pecans

Mix all dry ingredients together. Add oil, eggs and vanilla. Blend well. Add carrots and blend. Bake in 3 (9-inch) greased and floured pans at 350° for 30 minutes or until done.

Frosting: Cream the cheese and butter. Add sugar, vanilla and pecans. Blend well.

Diana Hanna

New! *Carrot Cake*

3 c. flour	*1⅓ c. corn oil*
2 tsp. baking powder	*4 eggs, well beaten*
2 tsp. baking soda	*1 c. chopped nuts*
2 c. sugar	*3 c. grated carrots*

Mix sugar and oil. Blend in carrots, beaten eggs and mix thoroughly. Add sifted dry ingredients. Add the nuts.

Grease loaf or tube pans. Bake at 350° for 1 hour to 1 hour and 15 minutes.

Katie Magott

Cherry Nut Cake

2 c. flour	*2 eggs*
2 c. sugar	*2 Tbsp. butter*
2 tsp. soda	*1 can cherries and juice*
½ tsp. salt	

Icing:

¾ c. sugar	*1 tsp. vanilla*
¾ c. water	*1 c. nuts*
1½ Tbsp. butter	

Mix all ingredients together in large bowl and beat till all blends into thin mixture. Bake in rectangular pan at 350° for 35-45 minutes or knife inserted in center comes out clean.

Icing: Cook icing for 7 minutes. Place nuts on top of cake and pour or spoon icing over nuts while cake is hot.

Ruby Webb

Pineapple Carrot Cake

1½ c. all-purpose flour
1 c. sugar
1 tsp. baking powder
1 tsp. baking soda
1 tsp. ground cinnamon
½ tsp. salt

⅔ c. cooking oil
2 eggs
1 c. finely shredded raw carrot
½ c. crushed pineapple (with syrup)
1 tsp. vanilla

Frosting:

3 oz. cream cheese
4 Tbsp. butter or margarine
1 tsp. vanilla

Dash of salt
2½ c. powdered sugar
½ c. chopped pecans

Cream Cheese Frosting:

1 (3 oz.) pkg. cream cheese
4 Tbsp. softened butter or
   margarine
1 tsp. vanilla

Dash of salt
2½ c. sifted powdered sugar
½ c. chopped pecans

In large mixer bowl, stir together dry ingredients. Add oil, eggs, carrot, pineapple and vanilla. Mix till all ingredients are moistened. Beat with electric mixer 2 minutes at medium speed. Pour batter into greased and lightly floured 9"x9"x2" baking pan. Bake at 350° for about 35 minutes. Cool. Frost with Cream Cheese Frosting.

Frosting: Cream together cream cheese and butter or margarine. Beat in vanilla and dash of salt. Gradually add powdered sugar. Blend well. Stir in chopped pecans.

Marsha Nation

Make Baking a Piece of Cake
To cut a fresh cake, use a wet knife.

Cinnamon Supper Cake

¾ c. sugar
¼ c. shortening
1 egg
1 tsp. vanilla
½ c. milk
1 c. flour

1½ tsp. baking powder
¼ tsp. salt
1 Tbsp. butter or margarine
3 Tbsp. powdered sugar
1 tsp. cinnamon

Add sugar to shortening and cream till fluffy. Add egg and beat. Add vanilla and milk. Sift flour, baking powder and salt. Add to mixture and beat. Bake in greased pan at 375° for 20-25 minutes. Spread butter on top of cake and then sift powdered sugar mixed with cinnamon over cake.

Mary Winters

Chocolate Sheet Cake

1 c. water
1 c. butter
4 Tbsp. cocoa
2 c. flour
2 c. sugar

1 tsp. baking soda
½ tsp. salt
½ c. buttermilk
2 eggs, beaten
1 tsp. vanilla

Frosting:

½ c. butter
4 Tbsp. cocoa
1 tsp. vanilla

6 Tbsp. buttermilk
1 box powdered sugar

Combine water, butter and cocoa in saucepan and bring to a boil over medium heat. Combine flour, sugar, baking soda and salt in mixing bowl. Add cocoa mixture to flour-sugar mixture. Add buttermilk, eggs and vanilla. Mix well. Pour into greased and floured 15"x10" jelly roll pan. Bake at 350° for 15-20 minutes. Frost after cooling.

Frosting: Combine all ingredients. Stir until thick and glossy, but spreadable.

Joyce Nowakowski

New! *Chocolate Sheet Cake*

2 c. granulated sugar
2 c. all-purpose flour
⅓ c. cocoa
1 tsp. baking soda
½ tsp. salt

1 c. (2 sticks) margarine
1 c. water
½ c. buttermilk
2 eggs
1 tsp. vanilla

Combine sugar, flour, cocoa, baking soda and salt in a large mixing bowl. Mix well. Heat margarine and water in saucepan until boiling. Pour over dry ingredients and mix. Beat in buttermilk, eggs, and vanilla. Pour thin batter in greased and floured 10"x15" (jelly roll) pan. Bake in 400° oven for 20 minutes.

Frosting:

½ c. (1 stick) margarine
¼ c. cocoa
6 Tbsp. milk

4 c. powdered sugar
1 c. chopped pecans

Combine margarine, cocoa and milk. Heat to boiling. Pour over sugar and nuts. Mix well. Spread on hot cake. This cake is very moist and very easy to make.

Diana Hanna

Chocolate Sheet Cake

2 c. flour
2 c. sugar
½ tsp. salt
2 sticks oleo
1 c. water
6 Tbsp. cocoa
2 eggs, well beaten

1 tsp. soda
½ c. buttermilk
1 Tbsp. vanilla
½ c. canned milk
1 lb. powdered sugar
1 c. chopped nuts

Sift together flour, sugar and salt. In 2-quart saucepan, bring 1 stick oleo, water, oil and 3 tablespoons cocoa to a boil. Mix with flour mixture. Mix eggs, soda, buttermilk and vanilla. Add to flour mixture. Pour into well-greased and floured 10"x15" cookie sheet. Bake at 350° for 20 minutes. During last 5 minutes of baking, bring 1 stick oleo, milk and 3 tablespoons cocoa to a boil. When boiling, remove from stove and stir in powdered sugar and nuts. Pour over warm cake. Serves 15.

Barbara Witte

Red Velvet Cake

½ c. shortening
1½ c. sugar
2 eggs
1 tsp. vanilla
1 tsp. butter flavor
1 oz. bottle red food coloring

3 Tbsp. cocoa (level Tbsp.)
2¼ c. flour
1 c. buttermilk
1 tsp. salt
1 Tbsp. vinegar
1 tsp. soda

Frosting:

3 Tbsp. flour
½ tsp. salt
1 c. milk
1 c. shortening

1 c. sugar
2 tsp. vanilla
¼ tsp. butter flavor

Preheat oven to 350°. Cream shortening, sugar, eggs and flavors. Make a paste of cocoa and food coloring. Add to first mixture. Alternately add flour and buttermilk. Mix soda and vinegar in a small bowl. Add to batter mixture. Bake in 3 (9-inch) pans for 20-25 minutes.

Frosting: Cook milk, flour and salt until thick, stirring constantly. Let cool (make sure it is cool). Cream shortening and sugar very well. Add flavor. Combine with first mixture. Heat well.

Rosalie Marino

Wacky Cake

3 c. flour
6 Tbsp. cocoa
2 c. sugar
2 tsp. soda

1 tsp. salt
2 c. water
¾ c. oil
2 Tbsp. vinegar

Sift all dry ingredients together and mix in water, oil and vinegar. Bake at 350° for 30 minutes. Do grease and flour pan.

Linda Beam

Mexican Chocolate Cake

½ c. margarine (1 stick)
½ c. vegetable oil
2 sq. unsweetened chocolate (or 4
   Tbsp. cocoa)
1 c. water
2 c. flour
1 tsp. baking soda

2 c. sugar
½ c. sour milk (1½ tsp. vinegar to
   ½ c. milk)
2 eggs, beaten
1 tsp. cinnamon
1 tsp. vanilla

Mexican Chocolate Frosting:

½ c. margarine
2 sq. chocolate (or 4 Tbsp. cocoa)
6 Tbsp. milk

1 (1 lb.) box powdered sugar
1 tsp. vanilla
½ c. chopped nuts

Combine margarine, oil, chocolate and water in heavy saucepan and heat until chocolate is melted. Mix flour, sugar, soda, milk, eggs, cinnamon and vanilla, then combine both mixtures. Pour in greased 18"x12" pan. Bake 25-30 minutes. Frost while still warm.

Mexican Chocolate Frosting: Combine chocolate, margarine and milk in saucepan and heat until bubbles form around edges. Remove from heat. Add powdered sugar, vanilla and nuts. Beat and frost cake while warm.

Carolyn Werchan

Black Chocolate Cake

2 c. flour
6 Tbsp. cocoa
1 tsp. soda
1 tsp. baking powder
2 c. sugar

2 cubes oleo
4 eggs, beaten
1 c. buttermilk
1 c. boiling water
2 Tbsp. vanilla

Sift together flour, cocoa soda and baking powder. Mix sugar, oleo, eggs and buttermilk and add to flour mixture. Add boiling water and vanilla and pour into greased and floured cake pan. Bake at 350° until done (inserted toothpick comes out clean). Makes a 3-layer cake. Top with your favorite icing after cake has cooled.

Mary Ellen Fortelney

Marvel's Chocolate Cake

2 c. each sugar and flour
1 c. shortening (I use oleo)
1 c. water
4 Tbsp. cocoa

½ c. buttermilk
2 eggs
1 tsp. soda
1 tsp. vanilla

Icing:

½ c. oleo
4 Tbsp. cocoa
6 Tbsp. milk

2½ c. powdered sugar
1 tsp. vanilla
1 c. chopped pecans

Sift together flour and sugar. In a saucepan bring to boil, oleo, water and cocoa. Pour over flour mixture while hot. Add remaining ingredients. Pour into greased and floured 11"x14"x1" pan. Bake 20 minutes at 400°. Ice while hot.

Icing: Bring to boil the oleo, cocoa and milk. Add remaining ingredients. Spread while hot over hot cake.

Ina Wiedemann

Chocolate Soda Cake

½ c. butter
1½ c. sugar
2 eggs (unbeaten)
2 c. flour
½ tsp. salt

1 c. sour milk or buttermilk
1 tsp. vanilla
2 sq. bitter chocolate
1 tsp. soda
1 tsp. vinegar

Mix cake as usual, using all ingredients but soda and vinegar. Dissolve soda in vinegar and add last. Bake in 350° oven for 30 minutes.

Mrs. A. J. Murphy
Mrs. A.J. Murphy is Father James' mother

Grandma Hattie's Perfect Chocolate Cake

Part 1:

¾ c. sugar
¾ c. cocoa

1½ c. milk
1 tsp. vanilla

Part 2:

¾ c. butter
1½ c. sugar
3 eggs
1½ tsp. soda

4 Tbsp. cold water
¾ c. milk
3 c. cake flour

Fudge Icing:

1½ c. sugar
3 Tbsp. chocolate
¼ c. corn syrup

½ c. milk
1½ Tbsp. butter
½ tsp. vanilla

Cook the first 3 ingredients of Part 1 to medium thick syrup and allow to cool, then add vanilla. Cream butter and sugar until light and fluffy. Add eggs, well beaten, not separated. Dissolve soda in water. Add soda water to mixture and mix well. Add flour and milk alternately and beat lightly. Add the Part 1 mixture and beat again. Pour into prepared cake pans. Bake at 350° for 40 minutes.

Fudge Icing: Melt chocolate. Add to sugar, corn syrup and milk. Stir over low heat until sugar is dissolved. Continue to cook to soft ball stage (test in cold water). Remove from fire and add butter. Cool to lukewarm and add vanilla. Beat until it is of right consistency to spread. It should not be as firm as fudge, but soft and creamy.

Judy Seikel

Clean cut

When I plan to cut an entire cake for a whole crowd, I use dental floss pulled tightly to slice even slices without tearing up the cake. The design remains intact and it's easy to use a spatula to lift the individual pieces of cake and place them onto a serving plate. — Judy Seikel

Beulah's Chocolate Sheet Cake

2 c. sugar
2 c. flour
¼ c. oleo (1 stick)
½ c. oil
1 c. water

4 Tbsp. cocoa
2 eggs
½ c. buttermilk
1 tsp. soda
1 tsp. vanilla

Icing:

1 stick oleo
6 Tbsp. canned milk
4 Tbsp. cocoa

1 box powdered sugar
½ to 1 tsp. vanilla
Pecans (optional)

Mix sugar and flour in a large bowl. Mix oleo, oil, water and cocoa in a saucepan and heat to boiling. Pour hot mixture into flour-sugar mixture and mix well. Beat eggs, buttermilk, soda and vanilla together. Add to mixture. Pour into prepared sheet cake pan. Bake at 400° for 20 minutes.

Icing: Mix oleo, milk and cocoa in saucepan until oleo is melted. Remove from heat and add powdered sugar and beat well. Add vanilla and nuts if desired. Pour on cake while still hot.

Joyce Nowakowski

Chocolate Miracle Whip Cake

1 c. white sugar
2 c. flour
4 level Tbsp. cocoa
1½ tsp. baking powder
1½ tsp. soda

½ tsp. salt
1 c. Miracle Whip salad dressing
2 tsp. vanilla
1 c. hot water

Sift first 6 ingredients together and add Miracle Whip and vanilla. Mix well and bake in 325° oven until done. Use oblong glass pan sprinkled with a little flour.

Aline Honea

Red Devil's Food Cake

2 c. pastry flour	1 tsp. soda
½ c. cocoa	½ c. buttermilk
¾ c. shortening	1 tsp. vanilla
1½ c. sugar	½ c. boiling water
2 eggs	

Seven Minute Icing:

1½ c. sugar	¼ tsp. cream of tartar
5 Tbsp. water	2 egg whites
1 tsp. vanilla	

Sift flour once. Measure and resift twice with cocoa. Cream shortening and sugar thoroughly. Add well beaten eggs and beat until light and fluffy. Add soda to buttermilk. Add dry ingredients alternately with buttermilk to creamed mixture, beating hard after each addition. Add vanilla. Pour in boiling water and beat until smooth. Bake in 2 (8-inch) greased tins in a moderate 350° oven for 30-35 minutes. Spread between layers and top with Seven Minute Icing.

Icing: Put in top of double boiler and beat with rotary beater for 7 minutes. Remove from heat and add vanilla. Beat until cool. Spread on cake.

Copied from "Harrah Herald" Friday, October 20, 1944.

Rosie L. Klimkowski

Emergency Chocolate

3 Tbsp. powdered cocoa equal 1 square of baking chocolate. To add richness, add 1 Tbsp. butter.

Dorothy's Chocolate Cake

Cake:

1 stick oleo, cut into 8 pieces
4½ Tbsp. cocoa
¾ c. Crisco oil
1 c. boiling water
2½ c. flour (all-purpose)

2½ c. sugar
½ c. buttermilk
1 tsp. soda
2 eggs, beaten
1 tsp. vanilla

Frosting:

½ stick oleo (¼ c.)
4½ Tbsp. cocoa
¼ c. milk

1 tsp. vanilla
2½ c. powdered sugar
1 c. pecans

Put oleo, cocoa and oil into bowl. Pour boiling water into bowl. Let set until oleo melts. Pour boiling mixture over flour and sugar and mix. Dissolve soda in buttermilk. Add beaten eggs and vanilla. Add to cake mixture. Pour into a 12-inch round greased and floured pan. Bake at 375° for 25 minutes or until done.

Frosting: Melt oleo, cocoa and milk. Stir in sugar to desired thickness. Add remaining ingredients. Cake may be iced warm. Cherry pie filling may also be used as topping.

Dorothy Wyskup

The last pioneer ...

Selena Kusek of Harrah, died December 29, 1994, at the age of 105. Her death marked the close of an era. She was the last of the original settlers who made the land run of 1891 to settle what is now Harrah. Selena was age two at the time. Her parents were Ike and Victoria (Olejniczak) Jezewski (now spelled Jorski).

🐦 Saucepan Fudge Cake

1½ oz. unsweetened chocolate,
   grated
½ c., boiling water
¼ c. butter
1 c. cake flour
¾ tsp. baking powder

½ tsp. salt
1 c. granulated sugar
¼ c. sour cream
1 egg
1 tsp. vanilla

Frosting:

1 c. confectioners' sugar
1 egg
¼ c. milk

½ tsp. vanilla
3 or 4 sq. chocolate, melted
1 tsp soft butter

Assemble all ingredients before beginning to work. Place chocolate, water and butter in medium saucepan. Stir and let cool. Saucepan must be hot. Sift flour, soda, salt and sugar 3 times. Sift once more into saucepan and stir until smooth. Stir in sour cream, beaten eggs and vanilla. Pour mixture into small, well-buttered cake pan and bake 45 minutes in a 350° oven. When cool, frost as follows.

Frosting: Sink a bowl into a large bowl of ice cubes. Beat 3 minutes the confectioners' sugar, egg, milk, vanilla and chocolate (which you have melted in a double boiler and cooled). Add 1 tsp. soft butter. Beat until fairly stiff and spread thickly over the top of cake.

This cake keeps well and stays moist. Is easy to make. You will never have a failure. Try your luck. You can't fail.

Rosie Lee Klimkowski

🐦 Coconut Cream Cake

3 layers.

½ c. shortening
½ c. oleo
2 c. sugar
5 eggs, separated
2 c. sifted flour

1 tsp. soda
1 c. buttermilk
1 (7 oz.) can coconut (reserve 1 c.
   for filling)

Filling:

½ c. oleo
1 (8 oz.) pkg. cream cheese
1 box confectioners' sugar
1 tsp. vanilla

½ tsp. salt
½ c. chopped nuts (optional)
1 c. coconut (for garnish)

Beat egg whites and set to side. Cream shortening and oleo. Add sugar. Beat until fluffy. Add egg yolks, one at a time, beating well. Stir in flour and soda. Add alternately with buttermilk beginning and ending with flour. Add coconut. Fold in egg whites. Makes 3 layers. Pour into 8-or 9-inch cake pans. Bake at 350° for 35-45 minutes.

Beat filling ingredients together (except nuts and coconut). After beating other ingredients add nuts. Spread between cake layers. Garnish with coconut.

Helen Hopcus

The extra plate ...

The old custom of setting the extra plate at the Christmas dinner table proved to be a part of one of my most special memories. We were living in Long Beach, Calif., in the mid-70s. I had all of my family at my house. We ended up with an extra place at the table and I decided that we were just going to leave it there. "It will be for the Christ child," I told everyone.

Just before we were ready to sit down to dinner, my dear cousin, Father Eugene Marshall, called and said he was coming over. I knew he was in Los Angeles going to school at the University of Southern California, because we had been in touch earlier in the year. He had finished all of the masses for the day and he said he knew he could always call his Cousin Dorothy. His place was already set — the extra plate that according to custom, is for the Christ child or a weary stranger. It was just so special.

After dinner we sat in the kitchen and he was telling me how close his mother and my mother, Sophia Jorski, were. My mother wrote love letters for his mother to send to his father. It was one of the most wonderful Christmases.

— Dorothy (Jorksi) Towne

Serowiec

Cottage Cheese Cake

8 large graham crackers
1 Tbsp. sugar

⅓ c. melted butter
¼ tsp. cinnamon

Cheese Filling:

1 lb. dry cottage cheese
4 eggs
1 c. sugar
½ tsp. salt
¼ c. flour

½ tsp. vanilla
1 c. heavy cream
Juice of 1 lemon
Grated rind of 1 lemon

Roll graham crackers fine. Mix with butter, sugar and cinnamon. Press into sides and bottom of 8"x11" cake pan. Keep 2 tablespoons crumbs to sprinkle over top.

Filling: Press cheese through sieve. Add salt to eggs and beat thoroughly. Add sugar, vanilla and cream. Carefully fold in the cheese and flour. Mix well. Pour onto crumbs in pan. Sprinkle crumbs on top. Bake 1 hour in 250° oven. At end of 1 hour, turn oven off and leave the cake in oven for another hour. Chill and serve.

Dora Lee Kusek

Dump Cake

1 can cherry pie filling
1 can crushed pineapple and juice
1 yellow cake mix (dry)

1 c. coconut
Nuts if desired
½ c. oleo

Dump into baking dish all ingredients in order given, reserving oleo. Melt oleo and drizzle over all dumped ingredients. Bake at 350° for 30-35 minutes.

Lila Dilis

Apple-Spice Dump Cake

20 oz. can pineapple
20 oz. can apple pie filling
1 pkg. 2 layer spice cake mix

¼ c. margarine
½ c. chopped nuts

Set oven at 350°. Grease and flour 13"x9" pan. Dump and spread, one at a time: pineapple, pie filling and the cake mix. Dot margarine over top and sprinkle on the nuts. Bake 50-55 minutes.

For blueberry-spice, substitute blueberry pie filling for the apple.

Lila Dilis

Cherry-Chocolate Dump Cake

20 oz. can pineapple
21 oz. can cherry pie filling
1 pkg. 2-layer chocolate cake mix

¼ c. margarine
½ c. chopped nuts

Set oven at 350°. Grease and flour a 13"x9" pan. Dump and spread, one at a time, the pineapple, pie filling and cake mix. Dot the top with margarine. Sprinkle on nuts. Bake for 50-55 minutes.

Lila Dilis

Cherry Dump Cake

2 cans cherry pie filling
1 can pineapple
1 Duncan Hines yellow cake mix

1¼ c. cutter
Pecans, if desired

Pour cherries in pan and spread evenly. Pour pineapple on top and spread. Pour cake mix on and smooth out evenly. Cut butter in thin squares all over cake mix till whole cake is covered. Bake at 350° for approximately 45 minutes or till lightly browned crust is on top. If pecans are used, sprinkle over cake mix and then add butter. Extra pineapple and cherries can be added.

Becky Spaeth

New! *Earthquake Cake*

1 c. chopped pecans
1 c. coconut
A box German Chocolate Cake Mix
8 oz. pkg. cream cheese

1 tsp. vanilla
½ c. margarine
1 lb. powered (confectioner's) sugar

Grease a 9"x13" pan. Mix pecans and coconut and spread into the bottom of the pan. Prepare cake mix following the package directions. Pour cake batter over the pecans and coconut.

Combine cream cheese, vanilla, margarine and powdered sugar. Spoon in dollops over batter.

Bake at 350° for 45-50 minutes.

Suzan (Russell) Schirf

Polish Easter Cake

½ c. butter
½ c. sugar
6 egg yolks
1 pkg. active dry yeast
¼ c. warm water (110° to 115°)
Grated rind of 1 lemon
Grated rind of 1 orange

1 tsp. salt
1 tsp. cinnamon
1 c. lukewarm milk
4 c. all-purpose flour
1 c. golden seedless raisins
¼ c. sliced almonds

In large bowl, cream butter and sugar until light and fluffy. Add 5 of the egg yolks, one at a time, beating well after each addition. Soften yeast in warm water. Add this mixture, with the lemon and orange rinds, salt and cinnamon. Add lukewarm milk and only enough flour to make a soft dough. Stir in raisins. Knead the dough about 10 minutes. Cover; let the dough rise until it has doubled in bulk, about 2 hours.

Butter a 3-quart Bundt pan and shape the dough to fit it. Cover and let rise until doubled in bulk. Beat remaining egg yolk with 2 tablespoons of cold water. Brush on dough generously and sprinkle with sliced almonds. Bake in preheated oven at 350° for 30 minutes. Mix sugar, water, lemon rind and juice. Pour over cake.

Patti Visnieski

 Easy Cool Cake

1 pkg. regular white cake mix
1 pkg. strawberry banana Jell-O

1 (12 oz.) container Cool Whip
1 c. coconut

Bake cake as directed on package in a glass baking dish. After removing cake from the oven, let it cool and then poke holes all over the cake with a fork. Mix Jell-O as directed on package. Pour Jell-O liquid over cake. Cover cake with Cool Whip. Sprinkle coconut over Cool Whip. Cover with plastic wrap and refrigerate overnight. You can vary the flavor if you like. Colors can be coordinated for specific holidays such as orange Jell-O for Halloween.

Pat Hopcus

Eggnog Cake

1 c. butter, softened
2 c. powdered sugar
5 egg yolks
¼ c. brandy
¾ c. slivered almonds, toasted

1 10 oz. angel food cake
1 c. whipping cream, whipped
  (or Cool Whip)
¼ c. slivered almonds, toasted

Cream butter and powdered sugar until light and fluffy. Add egg yolks, one at a time, beating well after each. Stir in brandy and ¾ c. almonds. Slice cake into 4 layers. Spreading mixture between layers. Chill 24 hours. Before serving, spread whipped cream on top and sides. Sprinkle with remaining almonds.

Barbara Dull

Hummingbird Cake

3 c. flour
1 tsp. salt
1½ c. vegetable oil
2 c. sugar
2 medium bananas

1 tsp. soda
1 tsp. butter flavoring
1 (8 oz.) can pineapple
1 c. chopped nuts
1 tsp. cinnamon

Mix all ingredients by hand until all dry ingredients are moist. Don't beat too much. Bake in greased and floured Bundt pan for 1 hour and 5 minutes at 325°. Let cool 1 hour in pan.

Lila Dilis

Graham Cracker Cake

½ c. butter or shortening
1 c. sugar
3 eggs
¾ c. milk

½ c. coconut or chopped nuts
28 graham crackers, rolled fine
2 tsp. baking powder

Orange Icing:

2 Tbsp. butter
1¾ c. powdered sugar

Grated rind of 1 orange
Orange Juice

Cream butter and sugar until light and fluffy. Add egg yolks which have been beaten until light and lemon colored. Add milk and rolled sifted crackers alternately. Fold in stiffly-beaten egg whites and baking powder. Bake in 2 greased (8-inch) pans in moderate 350° oven for 30 minutes. Of all the cakes that have been developed, the one which is always ready to go over with a bang is Graham Cracker Cake with Orange Icing.

Orange Icing: Cream butter and sugar. Add grated rind and enough orange juice to make a spreading consistency. Place in between the layers and ice top and sides.

Recipe copied from "Harrah Herald," Friday, October 20, 1944

Rosie L. Klimkowski

Hawaiian Wedding Cake

1 box white cake mix

Icing:

1 (9 oz.) Cool Whip
1 (8 oz.) Philadelphia cream cheese
1 (3 oz.) pkg. instant vanilla
  pudding

1 c. milk
1 (20 oz.) can crushed pineapple
1 c. flake coconut

Bake cake as directed on box. For icing, cream your cream cheese with milk. Add pudding and drained, crushed pineapple, Cool Whip and coconut. Ice cake when cool. Keep in refrigerator.

Victoria B. Miller

🐦 Italian Cream Cake

1 c. buttermilk
½ c. shortening
5 eggs, separated
2 c. flour
1 c. coconut

1 tsp. soda
½ c. butter
2 c. sugar
1 tsp. vanilla
1 c. pecans

Frosting:

1 (8 oz.) pkg. cream cheese
1 lb. powdered sugar

½ c. butter or margarine
1 tsp. vanilla

Combine buttermilk and soda. Let stand for a few minutes. Beat egg whites until stiff. Cream sugar, butter and shortening. Add egg yolks, one at a time, beating well after each addition. Add buttermilk alternately with flour to cream mixture. Stir in vanilla. Fold in egg whites. Gently stir in chopped nuts and coconut. Bake at 350°. Put in 3 (8-or 9-inch) pans and bake for 25-30 minutes. Frost when cool.

Frosting: Cream cheese and butter. Add vanilla. Beat in sugar, a little at a time until, blended to right consistency.

Rosalie Marino

🐦 Italian Cream Cake

2 c. sugar
1 stick butter or margarine
½ c. Crisco
5 egg yolks
2 c. sifted flour

1 c. buttermilk
1 tsp. baking soda
1 tsp. vanilla
5 egg whites, whipped
1½ c. coconut

Frosting:

1 (8 oz.) pkg. cream cheese
1 stick margarine
1 box powdered sugar

1 tsp. vanilla
1 c. chopped pecans

Cream sugar, butter and Crisco. Add egg yolks, one at a time and cream well. Add flour and buttermilk alternately. Blend well. Add baking soda and vanilla. Fold in egg whites and coconut. Bake in 3 greased and floured 9-inch cake pans at 350° for 25 minutes or until done.

Frosting: Cream cheese and butter. Add sugar, vanilla and pecans. Blend.

Diana Hanna

Italian Cream Cake

Cake:

2 sticks oleo (1 c.)
2 c. sugar
5 eggs, separated
2 c. flour
1 tsp. soda
½ tsp. salt

1 c. buttermilk
2 c. coconut
Cherries
2 (6 oz.) jars maraschino cherries
3 tsp. vanilla butternut flavor
1 c. pecans

Frosting:

1½ sticks oleo (4 c.)
3 Tbsp. milk
1 (8 oz.) pkg. cream cheese
1 c. pecans

3 tsp. vanilla butternut flavor
Powdered sugar to thicken
1(6 oz.) jar maraschino cherries

Cream oleo, sugar and egg yolks. Add yolks, one at a time. Mix flour, soda and salt together. To creamed mixture add buttermilk, alternating with dry ingredients. Beat well. Add coconut, cherries, vanilla, butternut flavor and pecans. Fold in stiffly beaten egg whites. Makes 4 layers or 12"x18"x2".

Frosting: Mix all ingredients and frost cake. This makes a very large cake good for holidays or Easter.

Louise Olive

Spring Sprinkling

"Every Easter season, a small jar of Holy Water was brought home. With the sign of the cross, each outside corner of the house was sprinkled with the Holy Water as was throughout the inside of the house. If you moved to another house, it too was blessed the same way."

Mrs. Bill (Martha) Hopcus

Bible Cake

1 c. Judges 5:25 (butter)
2 c. Jeremiah 6:20 (sugar)
½ c. Judges 4:19 (milk)
6 Jeremiah 17:11 (eggs)
4½ c. 1 Kings 4:22 (flour)
2 tsp. Amos 4:5 (baking powder)
Pinch of Leviticus 2:13 (salt)

1 Samuel 14:25 (honey)
2 c. Nahum 3:12 (figs)
1 c. Numbers 17:8 (almonds)
2 c. 1 Samuel 30:12 (raisins)
1 c. 1 Kings 4:22 (flour)
11 Chronicles 9:9 (all spice to taste)

Mix butter, sugar, milk, eggs, 4½ cups flour, baking powder and salt until well blended. Add honey and stir well. Toss the figs, almonds and raisins together with the flour. Add to cake mixture. Season with 11 Chronicles 9:9 (allspice). Stir together and bake in a deep pan in 375° oven for 45 minutes.

The Cookbook Committee

Milkless, Eggless, Butterless World War 1 Cake

2 c. light brown sugar
2 c. raisins
2 c. hot water
1 c. shortening
2 tsp. cinnamon
1 tsp. cloves

½ tsp. nutmeg
½ tsp. salt
2 tsp. soda
3½ c. flour
1 tsp. vanilla (optional)
1 c. nuts (optional)

Mix all but flour and soda in a saucepan and boil for 2 minutes. Cool. Sift flour and soda together and add to cooled mixture. Mix and beat well by hand. Add 1 tsp. vanilla and a cup of nuts if desired. Bake in slow 300° oven about 1 hour or until toothpick comes out clean.

Makes a large cake. Can be made in layers. Can be iced or is good plain. Half recipe makes 8'x10' cake.

Barbara Wyskup

Lump Eliminator
Sifting cake mixes before adding liquid saves overtime beating to get the lumps out.

New! Mazurkas – Apricot Cake

1 frozen 10¾ oz. all butter pound
  cake, thawed
¼ c. apricot preserves

¼ c. sliced almonds, toasted
  confectioners' sugar

Cut pound cake into 16 slices. Spread 8 slices with apricot preserves using about 1½ teaspoon per slice of cake.

Sprinkle about 1½ tsp. almonds over preserves. Top with remaining 8 slices of cake. Cut each cake sandwich in half. Sprinkle with confectioners' sugar. Makes 16 cake mazurkas.

Rosalie Jorski

Lady Baltimore Cake

½ c. shortening
1¼ c. granulated sugar
2 c. cake flour, sifted
2½ tsp. baking powder

½ tsp. salt
1 tsp. almond extract
⅔ c. milk
5 egg whites

Frosting:

1½ c. sugar
⅓ c. boiling water
⅓ c. hot maraschino cherry juice
½ tsp. light corn syrup
¼ tsp. grated orange rind
1 Tbsp. Lemon juice

15 to 20 maraschino cherries, cut
  in eighths
2 egg whites, beaten stiff
¾ c. chopped blanched almonds,
  toasted

Cream shortening and sugar until light. Add sifted dry ingredients and milk alternately. Last fold in stiffly beaten egg whites and flavoring. Bake in 3 (8-inch) layers in a moderate 375° oven for 25 minutes.

Frosting: Combine sugar, water, fruit juices and syrup and bring to a boil quickly, stirring only until sugar is dissolved. Boil rapidly without stirring until syrup spins a thread when dropped from a spoon and forms a soft ball in cold water (238°). Pour syrup into a stream over egg whites, beating constantly. Continue beating until of a consistency to spread. Fold in remaining ingredients and spread in between and on top of layers of Lady Baltimore Cake.

Recipe copied from Harrah Herald, October 20, 1944.

R. L. Klimkowski

 New! Polish Orange Nut Torte

1 10¾ oz. frozen all butter pound
  cake, thawed
½ c. dairy sour cream

¼ c. orange marmalade
½ c. chopped walnuts

Glaze:

½ c. confectioners' sugar
2 to 3 tsp. milk or orange juice
½ tsp. grated orange peel

Garnish

2 orange slices, quartered

Cut pound cake lengthwise into 4 layers. Place bottom layer on serving plate. Spread with about 2½ Tbsp. sour cream. Top sour cream with about 1 Tbsp. orange marmalade. Sprinkle 2 Tbsp. chopped walnuts over marmalade.

Repeat with 2 more layers of cake and filling. Reassemble cake using plain layer on top.

To make more glaze: Combine confectioners' sugar, milk and orange peel. Spread over top of cake and drizzle down side of cake. Sprinkle with remaining 2 Tbsp. of nuts. Arrange quartered orange slices down center top of cake. Makes 10-12 servings.

Rosalie Jorski

Neiman Marcus Cake

1 pkg. butter cake mix
1 stick butter (½ c.)

2 eggs
2 Tbsp. vanilla

Icing:

8 oz. cream cheese
1 box powdered sugar
2 eggs

2 tsp. vanilla
Pecans

Mix cake mix, butter, 2 eggs and 2 tsp. vanilla together and pour in a 9"x13" greased pan.

Icing: Mix cream cheese, powdered sugar, 2 eggs and 2 tsp. vanilla and spread on top of cake mixture. Sprinkle with pecans. Bake for 50 minutes at 350°.

Rosalie Marino

Maudie's Oatmeal Cake

1 c. quick cooking oats
1½ c. boiling water
1 stick oleo (½ c.)
1 c. brown sugar
1 c. white sugar
½ tsp. salt
2 eggs

1 tsp. vanilla
½ tsp. soda
1 tsp. cinnamon
1½ c. flour
½ c. coconut
Pecans, if desired

Pour boiling water over oats and let stand. Cream oleo, sugars, salt, eggs and vanilla. Mix soda, cinnamon and flour. Fold into oleo mixture. Add oats and coconut and pecans if desired. Bake at 350° for 1 hour.

Mary Keller

Cranberry Orange Cake

2¼ c. flour
1 c. sugar
¼ tsp. salt
1 tsp. baking powder
1 tsp. baking soda
1 c. chopped pecans
1 c. chopped dates

1 c. whole fresh cranberries
Grated peel of 2 oranges
2 eggs
1 c. buttermilk
¾ c. oil
1 c. orange juice
1 c. sugar

Combine flour in bowl with sugar, salt, baking powder and soda. Stir in nuts, dates, cranberries and orange peel. Combine eggs, buttermilk and salad oil. Stir into flour mixture until blended. Pour into greased and floured Bundt pan. Bake at 350° for 1 hour. Let stand 15 minutes.

Heat sugar and orange juice until sugar is dissolved. Pour over cake and catch drippings. Repeat several times. Wrap in foil and refrigerate overnight.

Elfriede Raught

Orange Raisin Cake

½ c. butter
1 c. sugar
1 c. raisins, ground
1 whole orange, ground (rind too)
2 eggs

2 c. flour
1 tsp. soda
½ c. buttermilk
1 tsp. vanilla
½ c. nuts (optional)

Cream butter and sugar; add ground orange and raisins. Add 2 beaten eggs, then add flour and soda sifted together, alternately with buttermilk. Add vanilla and nuts. Pour into greased 9"x13" pan. Bake at 300° for 35-40 minutes.

Linda Bradley

Orange Spice Cupcakes

½ c. shortening
1 c. sugar
1 Tbsp. grated orange rind
2 beaten eggs
2 c. flour
½ tsp. salt
1 tsp. soda

1 tsp. cinnamon
½ tsp. cloves
½ tsp. allspice
⅔ c. buttermilk or sour milk
⅓ c. orange juice
½ c. walnuts
1 c. raisins

Thoroughly mix shortening, sugar and rind. Add eggs and beat well. Sift dry ingredients and add alternately with liquids. Add walnuts and raisins. Fill cupcakes pans ⅔ full. Bake in moderate 350° oven for 25-30 minutes. Makes 2 dozen.

Mrs. A.J. Murphy
Mrs. A.J. Murphy is Father James' mother.

Family rosary...

"*During Lent and Advent, our family knelt on the cold, hardwood floor every night while Mother led the rosary in Polish. We were not allowed to go to a dance or show during Lent. Weddings were not held in Lent. In case of hardship, a small wedding could be performed, but no music or car horn blowing was permitted. Only a small family dinner.*"

Mrs. Bill (Martha) Hopcus

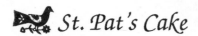 New! Pumpkin Pie Cake

1 38 oz. can pumpkin
1 12 oz. can evaporated milk
3 eggs, slightly beaten
1 c. sugar
½ tsp. salt
1 tsp. vanilla

4 tsp. pumpkin pie spices
  (or, 2 tsp. cinnamon, 1 tsp. ginger,
  ½ tsp. ground cloves)
1 18 oz. box yellow cake mix
½ c. margarine
1 c. chopped pecans

Preheat oven to 350°. Grease 9"x13" pan.

Mix pumpkin, milk, eggs, sugar, salt, spices and vanilla. Pour into prepared pan.

Cut margarine into cake mix to consistency of pie crust. Mix with pecans and sprinkle over top of filling. Bake for 50-55 minutes.

Cut in squares to serve. Serve with prepared whipped topping, whipped cream or ice cream.

Can be made in advance and stored in refrigerator. It also freezes well.

Vi Deacon

St. Pat's Cake

1 pkg. white cake
1 pkg. lime Jell-O

1 pkg. shredded coconut

Put coconut in glass jar with 1 rounded tablespoon dry Jell-O. Shake to coat coconut. Make cake mix as directed on package and add the remainder of the Jell-O to the mixture. Bake in a moderate oven. Frost with white frosting and sprinkle with prepared coconut.

Red can be used for Christmas and Valentine's, orange for Halloween.

The Cookbook Committee

Linda's Pig Cake

1 box yellow cake mix (Betty
  Crocker Super Moist)
4 large eggs
1 tsp. vanilla

½ c. orange juice (pulpless)
1 (11 oz.) can drained mandarin
  oranges, chopped

Icing:

½ c. powdered sugar
1 small (3¾ oz.) instant vanilla
  pudding

1 large can crushed pineapple with
  juice
1 small ctn. Cool Whip

Beat cake mix, eggs and vanilla for 4 minutes. Add orange juice; beat until well mixed. Add oranges and beat 15 seconds. Bake in greased and floured pan 35 minutes at 325°. Mix ingredients for icing and frost cake.

It's called Pig Cake because after one bite, you will make a pig of yourself.

Becky Spaeth

Pineapple Sheet Cake

Cake:

2 c. flour
2 c. sugar
2 eggs
2 tsp. soda

½ tsp. salt
1 tsp. vanilla
1 (No. 2) can unsweetened crushed
  pineapple

Frosting:

1 (8 oz.) pkg. cream cheese
½ stick margarine (¼ c.)

½ box powdered sugar
1 tsp. vanilla

Mix in order given and pour into a greased cookie sheet (one with raised sides). Bake 25-30 minutes in 350° oven or until lightly browned.

Frosting: Mix all ingredients. Let cake cool slightly and frost.

Mary Keller

🐦 **New!** *Orange & Poppy Seed Bundt Cake*

3 large oranges	*1 tsp. salt*
2 c. all-purpose flour	*1 tsp. vanilla extract*
¾ c. margarine or butter, softened	*3 large eggs*
⅔ c. milk	*Sugar*
2½ tsp. baking powder	*½ c. poppy seeds*

About 4 hours before serving or early in the day: Preheat oven to 325°. Grease and flour 10-inch Bundt pan.

From 2 oranges, grate 1 tablespoon peel and squeeze enough juice to equal ⅓ c. Reserve juice in refrigerator for use on top of cake later.

Into large bowl, measure flour, margarine or butter, milk, baking powder, salt, vanilla, eggs, and 1½ cups sugar. With electric mixer at low speed, beat ingredients until well blended, scraping sides as needed with spatula. Beat on high 2 minutes. Stir in poppy seeds and grated orange peel.

Pour batter into pan. Bake 55 minutes or until toothpick inserted in center of cake comes out clean. Cool cake in pan on wire rack 15 minutes. With spatula, loosen cake from pan and invert onto wire rack to cool completely.

Meanwhile, with vegetable peeler, cut peel from remaining orange into 1-inch-wide strips; with knife, trim white membrane, if any. Cut orange-peel strips diagonally into match stick-thin strips.

When cake is cool, in small saucepan over high heat, heat reserved orange juice with orange-peel strips and ⅓ c. sugar to boiling. Reduce heat to medium; boil 8 minutes or until mixture thickens slightly. With fork or slotted spoon, remove orange-peel strips from syrup to waxed paper.

Place rack with cake over plate. With toothpick, make vertical holes about ½-inch apart in cake. Brush warm orange syrup in saucepan over cake, allowing excess syrup to drip onto plate. Return any syrup in plate to saucepan and repeat brushing until all syrup is absorbed by cake. Sprinkle orange-peel strips over cake for garnish.

Judy Seikel

🐦 Bohemian Poppy Seed Cake

½ c. butter
1½ c. sugar
2 c. flour
2 tsp. baking powder
1 c. milk

½ c. poppy seed
Dash of salt
4 egg whites, beaten to hold peaks
   (but not dry)

Pour milk over poppy seed and soak for 1 hour or more. Sift flour, baking powder and salt. Cream butter and sugar. Mix flour mixture and creamed butter and sugar. Add dry ingredients alternately with milk mixture. Fold in egg whites. Bake at 350° for 30-35 minutes in 9"x13" pan or 2 round cake pans. Frost with your favorite frosting.

Optional: Filling - 1 cup milk. Pour slowly over ½ cup sugar and 1 tablespoon flour and 2 beaten egg yolks. Cook until thick. Cool. Spread between layers.

Bonita (Konop) Yox

🐦 Seven-Up Cake

1 yellow cake mix
1 pkg. lemon instant pudding
4 eggs

¾ c. cooking oil
1 (10 oz.) bottle 7-Up

Icing:

1 stick oleo
1 c. sugar
2 eggs

1 Tbsp. flour
1 small can crushed pineapple

Mix all ingredients and bake in well greased and floured 12"x15" pan for 30 minutes at 350°.

Icing: Mix all ingredients and cook until slightly thick. Pour over cake while it is still warm.

Dora Lee Kusek

Spice Cake

½ c. butter or substitute
2 c. brown sugar
4 eggs
3 bananas, mashed fine
1 c. milk

2 tsp. cinnamon
1 tsp. each cloves, nutmeg and
  allspice
2½ c. flour
3 tsp. baking powder

Cream together sugar and butter. Add beaten egg yolks and mashed bananas. Add alternately the sifted dry ingredients and milk. Fold in the egg whites. Bake in a large square pan which has been well greased in a moderate 350° oven for 35 minutes. Ice with Marshmallow Icing or 7-minute frosting. See Red Devil's Food Cake for 7 Minute Frosting Recipe.

Recopied from "Harrah Herald" Friday, October 20, 1944.

Rosie L. Klimkowski

Strawberry Cake & Frosting

Cake:

1 box white cake mix
¾ c. oil
3 Tbsp. flour
1 box. strawberry Jell-O

4 whole eggs
½ c. water
½ box frozen strawberries, thawed

Frosting:

½ box frozen strawberries, thawed
1 stick margarine, melted

1 box powdered sugar

Mix cake ingredients. Bake in 9"x13" pan at 350° for 30-35 minutes. Mix frosting ingredients. Frost and refrigerate.

LouAnn Spaeth

A flavor trick for frosting

Tint your cake frosting any shade by using ¼ teaspoon of flavored gelatin for taste and color. Vary the amount to make the shade you desire.

New! Texas Tornado Cake

1½ c. granulated sugar
2 eggs
2 c. fruit cocktail, undrained
2 c. all-purpose flour

2 tsp. baking soda
¼ c. brown sugar
1 c. nuts

Icing:

½ c. butter
¾ c. granulated sugar

½ c. evaporated milk
1 c. flake coconut

Mix and cream together sugar, eggs, fruit cocktail, flour and baking soda. Pour into lightly-greased and floured 9"x13" cake pan.

Mix brown sugar and nuts. Sprinkle on batter. Bake in a preheated 325° oven for 40 minutes. Spread icing on cake while hot.

To make icing, boil the butter, sugar and milk for two minutes. Add coconut. Spoon icing over the cake as soon as cake is removed for the oven. Cut into squares when cool.

Josephine Russell

Yum Yum Cake

2 c. sugar
2 c. flour
2 eggs

2 tsp. soda
1 large can crushed pineapple
1 tsp. salt

Icing:

1 c. sugar
1 stick oleo
1 small can milk
1 c. coconut

3 Tbsp. flour
Pinch of salt
1 c. chopped pecans
1 tsp. vanilla

Mix all ingredients. Bake 30-35 minutes in a 350° oven.

Icing: Cook sugar, oleo, milk, flour and salt until thick. Add pecans, coconut and vanilla. Pour over cake while hot.

Dora Lee Kusek

🐦 Zucchini Cake

3 c. zucchini, grated
4 eggs, well beaten (fluffy)
3 c. sugar
1½ c. oil
3 c. flour

1½ tsp. baking powder
1 tsp. salt
1½ tsp. cinnamon
1½ c. chopped nuts

Frosting:

2 c. powdered sugar
1 small pkg. cream cheese

2 Tbsp. butter
Vanilla

Mix eggs, sugar and oil. Add dry ingredients to egg mixture alternately with grated zucchini and nuts. Bake in well-greased and floured Bundt pan. Bake at 350° for 1½ hours or preferably 1 hour and 15 minutes. Don't bake too long. Turn out when a little warm. Cream frosting ingredients together and spread on cake.

Geneale Nowakowski

🐦 Cake Decorating Icing

3 c. powdered sugar
5 Tbsp. shortening
⅓ c. water

1 tsp. white vanilla
¼ tsp. salt
½ c. cocoa (for chocolate icing)

Beat all ingredients with a mixer until light and fluffy.

The Cookbook Committee

🐦 Judy's Easy Cream Icing

Ready-to-use frosting

Cool Whip

Choose any flavor of ready-to-spread frosting in a can. In a large bowl, blend with a medium size container of Cool Whip. Makes enough to cover a large sheet cake.

Judy Seikel

New! *Mom's Strawberry Icing*

2 c. sifted confectioners' sugar
Dash of salt
2 tsp. lemon juice

¼ c. crushed or sieved fresh
    strawberries

Crush strawberries and stir in sugar and salt. Mix well. Add the lemon juice. More lemon juice can be used if a thinner consistency is needed. You should be able to thinly spread the icing on cake. This makes enough icing to cover the top and sides of a tube sponge cake.

Judy Seikel

Mexican Fruit Cake

2 c. sugar
2 c. all-purpose flour
2 eggs, beaten
2 tsp. baking soda

½ tsp. salt
1 (20 oz.) can crushed pineapple
    (undrained)
1 c. chopped nuts

Frosting:

1 (8 oz.) pkg. cream cheese
½ c. margarine or butter
2 c. powdered sugar

2 Tbsp. milk
1 tsp. vanilla

Mix all ingredients for cake and bake in a greased and floured 9"x13" pan in a preheated 350° oven for 30-45 minutes.

Frosting: Have cream cheese and margarine at room temperature. Whip all ingredients together and use to frost baked cake.

Fern Koelsch

Smooth Icing
    Add one packet of plain gelatin to boiled icing to increase bulk and to make it stand in peaks and swirls. Dissolve the gelatin in 2 Tbsp. of cold water and add to hot syrup before removing from the heat.

Fruit Cake Gems

Cakes:

⅓ c. softened butter
⅓ c. light brown sugar
½ tsp. vanilla extract
2 eggs
1 c. flour
1 tsp. baking powder

½ tsp. salt
1 c. orange juice
2 Tbsp. brandy
1 c. (½ lb.) mixed candied fruit
⅔ c. chopped dates

Glaze:

⅓ c. sugar
⅓ c. orange juice

2 Tbsp. brandy

Preheat oven to 350°. Grease muffin cups with butter. In mixer bowl, cream together the softened butter, brown sugar and vanilla. Add eggs, one at a time, beating well after each addition. Mix together flour, baking powder and salt. Add alternately with the orange juice and brandy to the creamed mixture. Stir in fruits. Fill cups with about ¼ cup of batter. Place a pan of hot water on bottom rack of oven. Bake gems on middle rack for 25 minutes.

Meanwhile, make the glaze. Combine sugar, orange juice and brandy in saucepan. Heat. When cakes are done, remove from oven and cool for about 10 minutes. Prick tops with a 2-tined fork. Spoon glaze over. Make 12 little fruit cakes. These are delicious and quick.

Irene Emmack

Uncooked Fruit Cake

1 lb. graham crackers
1 lb. marshmallows
1 lb. raisins
1 lb. coconut
1 lb. pecans or walnuts

½ tsp. salt
1 small can condensed milk
1 small jar maraschino cherries
¼ c. milk

Mix all dry ingredients together. Melt marshmallows in milk over low heat. Pour over dry ingredients. Mix well with hands. Pack in tube pan. Let set 2-3 hours. Turn out on plate. Do not refrigerate. Better if made 2 or 3 days before serving.

Rosie Klimkowski

Mom's Unbaked Fruitcake

1 lb. marshmallows
1 c. sugar
1 c. Milnot (or Carnation milk)
1 lb. graham crackers, crushed
1 lb. pecan halves

½ lb. mixed candied fruit
1 lb. candied cherries
1 lb. coconut
½ lb. candied pineapple
2 tsp. vanilla

Mix marshmallows, sugar and Milnot together and cook until marshmallows are melted. Stir occasionally to keep from sticking. Add graham crackers, pecans, mixed fruit, cherries, coconut, pineapple and vanilla.

Wash hands thoroughly and mix by hand. Dip hands in cold water occasionally to keep mixture from sticking to hands. After all is well mixed, put in oblong pan lined with foil. Refrigerate for a few hours. Very rich cake.

Beverly Fortelney Winstead

Black Fruit Cake

1 lb. butter
1 lb. sugar
1 lb. flour
8 egg whites, beaten
1 large c. molasses
1 c. tea or cold water
1 tsp. soda
10 lb. raisins
4 lb. currants

½ lb. candied lemon peel
1 lb. citron
½ lb. candied orange peel
1 lb. candied cherries
1 lb. blanched almonds
1 pt. Madeira wine
1 pt. good whiskey
Cloves to taste
Cinnamon to taste

Stir tea or cold water into well beaten egg whites, carefully. Heat the molasses and stir in soda. Cream butter and sugar. Mix in flour and molasses. Fold in egg white mixture. Flour fruit well. Mix into dough. Bake in moderate oven until tests done.

Our Lady's Cathedral Cookbook
Circa 20s or 30s

🐦 White Fruit Cake

12 egg whites, stiffly beaten
2 c. powdered sugar
1 c. butter
1 c. sweet cream
5 c. flour
1½ tsp. soda
4 tsp. cream of tartar

2 lb. chopped, blanched almonds
1 lb. citron, cut fine
1 lb. shredded coconut
2 Tbsp. rose water
2 lb. white raisins
1 tsp. lemon extract
¼ c. sugared orange peel

Cream butter and sugar. Add cream, flour, cream of tartar, soda and fruit. Fold in egg whites and add flavoring. Bake in moderate oven until well done.

Our Lady's Cathedral Cookbook
Circa 20s or 30s

🐦 White Fruit Cake

1 lb. fresh pineapple or 1 (20 oz.)
  can and 1 (8 oz.) can, well drained
2 c. sugar
1 lb. butter or margarine
2 c. sugar
8 eggs

2 oz. lemon extract
4 c. flour
½ tsp. salt
1 tsp. baking powder
1 lb. candied cherries
1 lb. nuts, chopped

Add sugar to pineapple and mix well. Cook until clear. Cool. Cream butter and sugar together. Add eggs, one at a time and beat well after each. Add lemon extract. Mix flour, salt and baking powder. Add to creamed mixture. Chop cherries. Add cherries and nuts to mixture. Add the candied pineapple, saving some for garnish. Bake at 250° for 2½ hours or until done.

Aline Honea

Very Best Fruit Cake

1 lb. candied cherries
1 lb. candied pineapple
1 lb. pitted dates (light in color)
1 lb. pecan pieces
¼ lb. butter
1 c. white sugar
4 eggs
1 Tbsp. vanilla

6 Tbsp. orange juice or grapefruit
  juice
1 tsp. finely-grated orange peel, or
  to taste
2 c. sifted flour
1 Tbsp. baking powder
½ tsp. salt

Prepare pans. Line pans (and stem of angel food pan if using) with 2 layers of oiled, brown paper. First oil the pan or pans. Cut up candied fruit and dates. Add pecan meats and sprinkle 3 tablespoons of flour from the 2 cups total over the fruits and nuts. Cream butter, sugar and eggs, one at time, beating well after each. Add vanilla and fruit juice and blend well. Sift together flour, baking powder and salt. Blend into flour mixture, then add fruit and nuts, folding them in carefully. Add small amounts of spices if desired. Pack into prepared pans and place a double layer of oiled brown paper over the top of the pan. Bake at 250° on center rack.

Place pan of hot water on bottom rack (oblong preferred). Keep pan filled. Remove paper from top of pan during the last 30 minutes of baking. Raise temperature to 300° if desired. (I do not.) Bake 1-2 pound cakes for 2½-3 hours in a 225° oven. Bake 3-6 pound cakes for 3-6 hours in a 250° oven.

The cakes are done when tester comes out of cake clean. Let cool slightly in pan. Remove papers. If making 1-pound cakes, use a 225° oven and test frequently. If making 3-pound cakes, use a 250° oven and bake 3 hours, testing frequently. Yields 6 pounds of cake.

Aline Honea

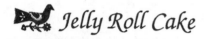 Christmas Fruit Cake

1 c. sugar
1 c. flour
½ tsp. salt
2 tsp. baking powder
4 eggs (whole)

1 tsp. vanilla
½ lb. cherries
½ lb. pineapple
1 lb. dates
1 lb. pecans

Mix all ingredients and bake 1½ hours in 300° oven. Try to use White Swan cherries and pineapple. This cake is not like an ordinary fruit cake. It's delicious!

Louise Olive

Jelly Roll Cake

3 eggs, separated
1½ c. sugar
1 tsp. orange or lemon juice
1½ c. cake flour
1 Tbsp. grated orange or lemon rind

½ c. boiling water
¼ tsp. salt
1½ tsp. baking powder
Powdered sugar

Beat egg yolks until thick. Add sugar gradually. Add fruit juice, rind and hot water, stirring constantly. Sift four. Measure and sift with baking powder and salt. Fold into egg mixture. Fold in stiffly whipped egg whites. Pour into oiled, shallow pan. Bake at 375° for about 12 minutes.

Remove and turn onto board covered with cloth. Spread with jelly or jam. Roll. Wrap tightly with cloth. Leave until cold. Unwrap and sprinkle with powdered sugar.

Virginia Grinnell

Cream Cheese Roll

Roll:

1 c. sour cream
½ c. sugar
1 tsp. salt
½ c. melted butter

2 pkg. dry yeast
½ c. warm water
2 eggs, beaten
4 c. flour

Filling:

2 (8 oz.) pkg. cream cheese
1 beaten egg
¾ c. sugar

⅛ tsp. salt
2 tsp. vanilla

Glaze:

2 c. powdered sugar
4 Tbsp. milk

2 tsp. vanilla

Heat sour cream on low heat. Stir in sugar, salt and butter. Cool to lukewarm. Sprinkle yeast in warm water, stirring until yeast dissolves. Mix in sour cream mixture, eggs and flour. Cover; refrigerate overnight. Next day, divide dough into 4 equal parts. Roll each on floured surface into 12"x8" rectangle. Make cream cheese filling by combining cream cheese and sugar. Add egg, salt and vanilla. Mix well. Spread ¼ of cream cheese filling on each rectangle. Roll beginning with long side. Pinch and fold ends under slightly. Place rolls seam side down on greased sheets. Split each roll at 2-inch intervals ⅔ of way through dough to resemble braid. Cover. Let rise in warm place until double. Bake at 375° for 15 minutes. Spread with glaze while warm. To make glaze, combine powdered sugar with milk and vanilla.

Elenora Jarvis

🐦 Pumpkin Roll

¾ c. flour
2 tsp. cinnamon
1 tsp. baking powder
1 tsp. ginger
½ tsp. salt
½ tsp. nutmeg

3 eggs
1 c. sugar
⅔ c. pumpkin
1 tsp. lemon juice
½ to 1 c. chopped nuts
Powdered sugar

Filling:

6 oz. pkg. cream cheese
¼ c. butter

½ tsp. vanilla
1 c. powdered sugar

Mix flour, cinnamon, baking powder, ginger, salt and nutmeg in a large bowl. With a small hand mixer beat the eggs on high for 5 minutes. Gradually add sugar to eggs. Stir in pumpkin and lemon juice. Fold into dry ingredients. Spread in a jelly roll pan on greased wax paper. Sprinkle chopped nuts and bake 8 minutes at 350°. Turn out on a towel sprinkled with powdered sugar. Roll it up and let cool.

Filling: Mix cream cheese, melted butter and vanilla together. Add powdered sugar. Gently unroll cake and carefully spread with filling. Reroll.

Joyce Nowakowski

🐦 Gingerbread

½ c. sugar
½ c. lard
1 c. molasses
2½ c. flour
1½ tsp. soda
1 tsp. ginger

½ tsp. cloves
½ tsp. cinnamon
¼ tsp. salt
2 eggs
1 c. boiling water

Cream sugar, lard and molasses together. Sift dry ingredients together and add to creamed mixture along with 2 beaten eggs. Add boiling water. Bake about 30 minutes in 350° oven. Use a 9"x12" prepared pan or 2 smaller ones.

Helen Jorski Pate

🐦 Pumpkin Roll

3 eggs
1 c. sugar
⅔ c. pumpkin
1 Tbsp. lemon juice
¾ c. flour
1 c. nuts
1 tsp. baking powder

1 tsp. cinnamon
½ tsp. ginger
½ tsp. nutmeg
½ tsp. salt
Nuts
Powdered sugar

Filling:

1 c. powdered sugar

2 (3 oz.) pkgs. cream cheese

Beat eggs 5 minutes at high speed. Stir in pumpkin and lemon juice. Sift flour, spices and salt. Add to egg mixture. Spread in greased and floured jelly roll pan. Top with nuts. Bake at 350° for 15 minutes. Turn out on towel sprinkled with powdered sugar. Roll as for jelly roll. Leave 2-3 minutes.

Mix together ingredients for filling. Unroll pumpkin roll and spread with filling. Roll again and refrigerate until ready to serve.

Barbara Dull

🐦 Bohemian Coffee Cake

1 c. Wesson oil
1 c. brown sugar
1 c. white sugar
1 c. buttermilk
2 eggs
2½ c. flour

1 tsp. soda
1 tsp. nutmeg
1 tsp. cinnamon
1 tsp. vanilla
1 c. chopped pecans

Mix well and pour into buttered and floured tube cake pan. Bake at 350° for 45 minutes to 1 hour.

Father Augustine Horne, O.S.B.

Streusel Coffee Cake

1½ c. flour
3 tsp. baking powder
¼ tsp. salt
¾ c. white sugar

¼ c. shortening
1 egg
½ c. milk
1 tsp. vanilla

Filling:

½ c. brown sugar
2 Tbsp. flour
2 tsp. cinnamon

2 Tbsp. melted butter
½ c. chopped nuts

Sift dry ingredients together. Cut in shortening. Blend in beaten egg mixed with milk and vanilla. Beat just enough to mix well. Put ½ of batter into greased and floured pan (6"x10"). Mix together ingredients for streusel filling. Sprinkle batter with ½ of streusel filling. Add remaining batter and sprinkle remaining streusel over top. Bake 25-30 minutes at 375°.

Kay Brown

Strawberry Shortcake

½ c. Crisco
½ c. sugar
1 c. flour
1 egg

Pinch of salt
Fresh sliced strawberries
Cool Whip

Make a dough with first 5 ingredients. Divide and press into 2 round cake pans. Bake at 350° until golden brown. Cool. Layer the cake, fresh sliced strawberries and Cool Whip and repeat. Refrigerate. These cookie-type cakes will soften to make a delicious shortcake!

Leta Overton

Glorious Sponge Cake

¾ c. egg yolks
1 whole egg
1¾ c. sugar
1 c. boiling water
1 Tbsp. grated orange rind

1 Tbsp. strained orange juice
½ tsp. lemon flavoring
2 c. sifted flour
½ tsp. baking powder
½ tsp. salt

Beat eggs until they are thick and lemon colored, about 5 minutes. Gradually beat in sugar. Beat in part of water, the flavoring, salt, juice, orange rind and flour with baking powder. Add remaining water. Bake in ungreased tube center pan for 1 hour at 325°.

Mrs. A.J. Murphy (Father James' mother)

Brown Sugar Pound Cake

1 lb. light brown sugar
½ c. granulated sugar
1½ c. butter flavor Crisco
5 eggs, separated
3 c. flour, sifted

½ tsp. baking powder
1 c. milk
1 c. pecans, chopped
1 tsp. vanilla

Cream shortening and sugar well. Add beaten egg yolks. Sift flour with baking powder. Add alternately with milk to shortening and sugar mixture. Add nuts and vanilla. Beat egg whites till stiff and fold into mixture. Bake in greased and floured tube pan at 325° for 1½ hours.

Carolyn Werchan

Buttermilk Pound Cake

1 c. butter
3 c. sugar
4 eggs

1 c. buttermilk
3 c. cake flour
½ tsp. baking soda

Cream butter. Add sugar and eggs, one at a time. Beat well. Add flour and soda with buttermilk. Pour into greased and floured 10-inch tube pan. Bake in 350° oven for 1 hour and 10 minutes.

For added color, you could put strawberries or blackberries in the cake.

Vernie Visnieski

Cream Cheese Pound Cake

3 sticks butter
3 c. sugar
3 c. all-purpose flour
1 tsp. almond extract

1 (6 oz.) pkg. cream cheese
6 eggs
1 tsp. vanilla

Cream butter and cream cheese together until fluffy. Add sugar gradually. Beat eggs in, one at a time. Mix flour into mixture, little at a time, mixing until smooth after each addition. Pour into a greased and floured tube pan. Place cake in cold oven and bake at 275° about 1½ hours or until tests done. Cool in pan. Yields about 20 slices.

Pauline Haynes

Easy Chocolate Pound Cake

½ c. butter
1 c. shortening
3 c. sugar
6 eggs (room temperature)
3 c. flour

¼ tsp. baking powder
4 Tbsp. cocoa
1 c. milk (room temperature)
1 tsp. vanilla

Cream butter and shortening together. Blend in sugar. Add eggs, one at a time, beating well after each.

Sift dry ingredients together. Add slowly to the batter, alternately with milk and vanilla just until well blended.

Pour into a 10-inch tube pan that has been lined with wax paper. Bake 1½ hours at 325°. Cool a few minutes and remove from pan. May be dusted with powdered sugar or frosted. Delicious plain, too.

Mary Keller

🐦 Yellow Pound Cake

1 egg
6 to 8 egg yolks
1 c. butter
2 c. sugar
1 c. milk

3 c. cake flour
½ tsp. salt
¾ tsp. baking powder
1 tsp. vanilla
1 tsp. lemon

Beat egg. Cream together butter, sugar and the egg. Beat egg yolks until thick and add to creamed mixture. Stir dry ingredients. Add alternately with milk and flavoring. Bake in floured tube pan approximately 1 hour at 325°. When done, cake shrinks from pan edges. Leave in pan for 5 minutes. Remove and cool on rack. Cover with Lemon Butter Icing or serve plain.

If made along with the White Pound Cake, all of the eggs can be used.

Virginia Morton

🐦 White Pound Cake

1 c. butter
2 c. sugar
6 egg whites
1¼ c. milk
3½ c. flour

½ tsp. salt
3 tsp. baking powder
1 tsp. vanilla
1 tsp. lemon extract

Cream butter and sugar. Combine dry ingredients. Add to butter and sugar mixture alternating with the milk. Add flavoring. Fold in beaten egg whites. Bake in greased and floured tube pan at 300° for 1-1½ hours. When done, cake will break away from sides of pan. Use favorite icing.

If made along with Yellow Pound Cake, all of the eggs can be used.

Virginia A. Morton

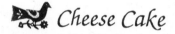 Surprise Cheese Cake

2 (8 oz.) pkg. cream cheese
⅔ c. sugar
1 tsp. almond extract
3 large eggs (if not large use 4)
1 pt. sour cream

6 Tbsp. sugar
1 tsp. vanilla
Fresh strawberries, blueberries and
   blackberries

Preheat oven to 325°. Place cream cheese, ⅔ cup sugar, almond extract and eggs in blender or food processor. Blend well. Pour mixture into 9-inch metal pie tin which has been well greased. Bake for 50 minutes.

Remove from oven. Place on cake rack and cool 15 minutes. Mix sour cream, 6 tablespoons sugar and vanilla. Spoon into crust. Bake 15 minutes. Cool 15 minutes. Serve with topping of fresh berries.

Denniece Knapp

Cheese Cake

Filling:

1 lb. cottage cheese, drained
½ pt. sweet cream
4 eggs

¾ c. sugar
3 Tbsp. flour

Crust:

9 graham crackers
½ c. melted butter

¼ c. sugar

Make powder of graham crackers. Add melted butter and sugar. Mix and press to sides and bottom of pan. Mix cheese with cream and force through a colander or ricer. Beat eggs and add to cheese. Add sugar, flour and vanilla. Mix well. Bake 45 minutes at 375° or until done.

Lila Dilis

New! *Amaretto Cheesecake*

Crust:

2 c. graham cracker crumbs
¼ lb. butter

¼ c. sugar

Filling:

4 (8 oz.) pkgs. cream cheese
1½ c. sugar
4 large eggs
1 Tbsp. amaretto

1 Tbsp. vanilla
1 Tbsp. almond extract
pinch of salt

Topping:

2 c. sour cream
¼ c. sugar
1 Tbsp. amaretto

1 tsp. almond extract
slivered, toasted almonds

Preheat oven to 350°. For crust, melt butter and mix in sugar and graham cracker crumbs. Work melted butter in with a fork until all crumbs are moist.

Blend cream cheese with sugar in large bowl on low speed. Add eggs, one at a time, one low speed so as not to whip any air into the filling. Blend in flavorings.

Bake 40 minutes in an ungreased 10-inch springform pan. Remove and let stand 10 minutes.

While cheesecake is standing, mix ingredients for the topping. Smooth over top of cheesecake and top with slivered, toasted almonds. Return to oven for 10 minutes. Refrigerate immediately to keep top from cracking. Sets up overnight.

Vicki Ledet
In memory of Mrs. A. C. Ledet

New! Cheese Cake

Filling:

1 c. sugar
5 eggs
2 c. cottage cheese
1 tsp. vanilla

1½ c. sour cream, thick
2 Tbsp. cornstarch
¼ c. milk
2 Tbsp. lemon juice

Crust:

¾ c. flour
1 tsp. sugar
1 egg

1 egg yolk
pinch of salt
½ stick butter (¼ cup)

Mix ingredients for the crust. Roll out dough and fit it into an 8x8" square pan.

Mix cornstarch with ¼ cup milk until smooth. Mix all other ingredients for filling and beat until smooth. Pour into the crust.

Bake at 375° for 50-60 minutes.

Al Dilis

Cheesecake

1¾ c. fine crushed graham cracker
    crumbs
¼ c. chopped walnuts or pecans
½ Tbsp. cinnamon
½ c. melted butter
3 eggs
2 (8 oz.) pkg. cream cheese

1 c. sugar
¼ tsp. salt
2 tsp. vanilla
¼ tsp. almond extract
3 c. sour cream
Cherry or blueberry pie filling

Combine graham cracker crumbs, nuts, cinnamon and butter for crust. Press into 9"x13" pan. Beat eggs. Mix with cream cheese, sugar, salt, vanilla and almond extract. Blend in sour cream. Pour into crust. Bake at 375° for 35 minutes or until done. Chill 4-5 hours. Top with cherry or blueberry pie filling.

Muriel Lachance

Chocolate Malt Cheese Cake

*⅓ c. butter or margarine, unsalted
  and melted*
*1 c. pretzel or graham cracker
  crumbs*
¼ c. sugar
*3 (8 oz.) pkg. cream cheese,
  softened*

*1 (14 oz.) can Dairy Sweet
  sweetened condensed milk*
*1 c. semi-sweet chocolate chips,
  melted*
¾ c. chocolate malt powder
4 eggs
1 tsp. vanilla

Stir butter, pretzel crumbs and sugar well. Pat in bottom of 9-inch springform pan. Beat cheese in large bowl until fluffy. Blend in condensed milk. Add other ingredients and beat thoroughly. Pour into crust. Bake in 300° oven for 65 minutes or until cake springs back when lightly touched. Cool, then chill. Garnish as desired.

Carolyn Rudek

Lemon-Pineapple Cheese Cake

2 pkg. (8 oz.) cream cheese
2 c. sugar
2 tsp. vanilla
2 small pkg. lemon Jell-O
2 c. boiling water

*2 (No. 303) cans drained crushed
  pineapple*
1 large tub Cool Whip
½ to 1 c. chopped nuts

Cream sugar, cream cheese and vanilla. Mix Jell-O with boiling water until well dissolved, then mix with creamed mixture. Add pineapple and Cool Whip. Mix well in large bowl. Pour into graham cracker crust and sprinkle top with chopped nuts. Refrigerate several hours or overnight. This makes large recipe, 1 (8"x12") cake pan and 1 (8"x8") cake pan.

Suzanne Visnieski

Spices for Desserts

Allspice

Use allspice on plum puddings; fruit cakes; fruit compotes; baked bananas; cranberry dishes; spice cake; molasses cookies; tapioca pudding; chocolate pudding and mincemeat.

Anise

Use the fragrant licorice-like flavor of anise for coffee cake; sweet breads; cookies; fruit compotes; stewed apples; fruit pie fillings; and licorice candies.

Cardamon

Use cardamon, also called cardamom, on danish pastries; buns; coffee cake; baked apples; fruit cup; pumpkin pie; cookies and frozen ice cream pudding.

Cinnamon

Use this popular spice on buns; coffee cake; spice cake; molasses cookies; butter cookies; custards; tapioca; chocolate pudding; rice pudding; fruit pies; stewed fruit; hot cocoa and chocolate drinks and over vanilla ice cream.

Cloves

Use cloves on stewed fruit; apple, mince and pumpkin pies; spice cake; rice pudding; chocolate pudding, tapioca.

Fennel

Use fennel to add flavor to coffee cake; sugar cookies and apples in any form.

Ginger

Use ginger for cookies; spice cake; pumpkin pie; pudding; baked, stewed and preserved fruits; applesauce and custard.

Mace

Use mace on gingerbread batter; stewed cherries; doughnuts; cakes; pound cakes and fruit pies.

Three Fruit Marmalade

1 cantaloupe
1 (15½ oz.) can crushed pineapple
Fresh peaches

2 Tbsp. lemon juice
1 pkg. Sure-Jell
8 c. sugar

Peel and remove seeds from cantaloupe. Chop in food chopper. Drain pineapple and cantaloupe. Grind peaches, enough to make a total of 6 cups of fruit. Add Sure-Jell and lemon juice. Bring to boil. Add sugar and boil 8 minutes. Skim off foam. Pour into hot jars. Seal with paraffin.

LouAnn Spaeth

Plum Jam

4 lb. plums or 6 c. juice
1 box Sure-Jell

1 bar paraffin wax
8 c. sugar

Wash fruit. Put in pan and cover with water. Bring to boil (skins will split). Drain juice through colander. Mash pulp through colander into juice. Measure 6 cups juice into pot. Add Sure-Jell. Bring to boil, stirring constantly. Meanwhile, melt 1 bar paraffin wax. Run hot water into jelly jars. Measure sugar and set aside. When juice boils, add sugar, stirring constantly, bring to a rapid boil that cannot be stirred down. Boil 1 minute, stirring constantly. Scrape off foam with metal spoon. Pour into hot jars. Seal with ⅛ inch wax. Pop wax bubbles with toothpick.

Becky Spaeth

Old-Fashioned Strawberry Preserves

2 qt. small ripe strawberries,
    washed and stemmed
6 c. sugar
¼ tsp. salt

2 Tbsp. light corn syrup
¼ c. lemon juice
Few drops red food coloring
    (optional)

Place whole stemmed strawberries in a large 8 quart saucepan with sugar, salt, corn syrup and lemon juice. Gently mix until berries are coated with sugar. Let stand 5-6 hours. Prepare home canning jars and lids according to manufacturer's instructions. Slowly heat strawberry mixture until sugar dissolves. Shake pan occasionally, but do not stir. Boil rapidly for 12-15 minutes or until strawberries are translucent and syrup is thick. Add a few drops of red food coloring if desired. Skim foam. Carefully ladle berries into hot jars, leaving ¼ inch head space. Adjust caps. Process 15 minutes in a boiling water bath canner. Yields about 4 (8 ounce) jars.

Rosie L. Klimkowski

New! Pineapple Glaze

1 c. brown sugar
1 Tbsp. cornstarch
Small can crushed pineapple, with
    syrup

¼ tsp. salt
2 Tbsp. lemon juice
1 Tbsp. prepared mustard

Cook over medium heat, stirring constantly until mixture thickens and boils. Boil and stir one minute. Make 1¾ cup. Serve over ham.

Becky Spaeth

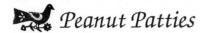 *Peanut Patties*

2¼ c. sugar
⅔ c. white corn syrup
1 c. milk
2 c. raw peanuts

1 tsp. vanilla
1 Tbsp. butter
⅛ tsp. salt

Mix sugar, syrup, milk and peanuts. Cook until temperature of 234° to 240° or soft ball stage is reached. Add vanilla, butter and salt and heat until creamy. Pour out in patties on buttered cookie sheet or wax paper.

Lila Dilis

 **New!** *Cinnamon Pecans*

1 egg white
4 c. pecan halves

½ c. sugar
2 Tbsp. cinnamon

Beat egg white. Add four cups of pecan halves and stir.
In a separate bowl, combine ½ c. sugar and 2 Tbsp. cinnamon. Pour over pecan mixture and stir. Bake on cookie sheet at 300° for 30 minutes.

Becky Spaeth

Spiced Pecans

1 c. sugar
1 tsp. salt
½ tsp. cinnamon
½ tsp. cloves

½ tsp. nutmeg
¼ c. water
3 to 4 c. pecan halves

Cook all ingredients but pecans until it makes a syrup that forms a soft ball in cold water. Add pecans. Remove from fire and stir until it becomes sugary. Cool, then spread on wax paper. Break apart any pecans that are stuck together and allow to cool completely.

Frances Wyskup

Peanut Brittle

2 c. sugar
½ c. water
1 c. white Karo syrup
2 c. raw peanuts

2 Tbsp. soda
1 Tbsp. butter
1 Tbsp. vanilla

Cook sugar, water and Karo until it spins a thread. Add raw peanuts and stir until mixture turns a golden brown and peanuts are cooked. Take from fire and add soda, butter and vanilla previously mixed together. Stir well and pour on buttered cookie sheet and as it cools, stretch out to desired thinness.

Ina Wiedemann

Microwave Toffee

2 sticks butter (1 c.)
1 c. sugar
2 Tbsp. water

½ c. chopped pecans
1 (10 oz.) pkg. chocolate chips

Heat butter, sugar and water on HIGH to boiling for 4-5 minutes. Sprinkle bottom of 9"x9" buttered pan with chopped pecans. Pour toffee mixture over pecans. Sprinkle chocolate pieces over mixture and spread evenly with spatula as they melt. Cool and break into wedges. Take out a corner chunk and the rest will flip out.

Judy Seikel

Peanut Butter Bonbons

1 c. creamy peanut butter
½ c. butter
1½ c. Rice Krispies

½ lb. powdered sugar
12 oz. chocolate chips
¼ bar paraffin (canning wax)

Melt 1 cup creamy peanut butter and ½ cup butter. Pour over Rice Krispies and powdered sugar. Mix well. Form into 1-inch balls and chill 2 hours. Melt chocolate chips and paraffin. Dip balls by toothpick into chocolate. Chill 1 hour. Makes 50.

Becky Spaeth

 # Bonbons

2 boxes powdered sugar	3 c. chopped nuts (optional)
1 can Eagle Brand milk	1 (12 oz.) pkg. chocolate chips
1/4 lb. butter (1 stick)	3 oz. paraffin wax
1 large Angel Flake coconut	

Mix together and form into balls. Put in refrigerator to harden, a few hours. Melt in double boiler the chocolate chips and paraffin wax. Dip mounds or balls in chocolate mixture and dip in cold water, then place on wax paper.

Linda Beam

Buttermilk Brown Candy

Mock Aunt Bill's Brown Candy

2 c. white sugar	1 tsp. soda
1 c. buttermilk	1 c. broken pecans
1/2 stick butter (1/4 c.)	1 tsp. vanilla

Cook first 4 ingredients over low flame, stirring constantly, to form firm soft ball. Add pecans and cook 1 minute. Add vanilla and beat until ready to pour in buttered pan or pans. This candy foams very much, so use large stewer when making.

Originally this was made in Florida. This recipe was given to me by a friend in Oklahoma City. Very good and easier than regular Aunt Bill's Brown Candy.

Aline Honea

 *Caramels*

2 c. brown sugar
2 c. cream
1 c. light corn syrup

2 Tbsp. butter
Nuts

Cook sugar, cream and syrup together to soft ball. Remove from stove. Add butter and nuts. Beat by hand until candy begins to stiffen. Place in butter greased cake pan. Allow to fully cool. Cut in pieces (size you wish) and wrap individually in wax paper.

Kay Brown

 *Divinity*

3 c. sugar
⅔ c. water

½ c. white corn syrup
3 egg whites

Cook sugar, water and corn syrup to hard ball. Add cooked ingredients slowly to beaten egg whites. Egg whites must be stiff peaks. I add them with the mixer on lowest speed. Add nuts if desired. After adding all the cooked ingredients, mix by hand until gloss begins to disappear. Put in buttered, greased pan or drop individual portions on wax paper.

Kay Brown

 *Chocolate Candy*

2 bars German chocolate
2 (6 oz.) pkg. butterscotch bits

1 lb. salted peanuts

Melt chocolate and butterscotch bits in a double boiler and then add peanuts. Mix well. Drop by teaspoons on wax paper.

Mary Ann Padgett

 New! *Clara's Potato Candy*

1 medium potato, peeled	*Crunchy peanut butter*
1 lb. powdered sugar	

Boil potato (no salt). Drain off water and mash. Add at least one pound of powdered sugar until consistency to knead. Knead out stickiness by adding more powdered sugar.

Roll out as pie dough and spread generously with crunchy peanut butter. Roll as for jelly roll and slice. Chill overnight.

Becky Spaeth

 *Fudge*

1½ c. white sugar	*2 Tbsp. cocoa*
1½ c. brown sugar	*1 Tbsp. butter*
1 c. cream	*1 tsp. vanilla*
¼ c. white corn syrup	*Nuts*

Cook ingredients to soft ball stage. Remove from stove. Add butter, vanilla and nuts. Beat by hand until gloss begins to disappear. Put in butter-greased pie plate.

Kay Brown

 *Fudge*

4½ c. sugar	*1 large pkg. chocolate chips or 12*
1 large can evaporated milk	*small Hershey bars*
¼ lb. butter or oleo	*2 c. pecans*
1 jar marshmallow creme	*2 tsp. vanilla*

Heat sugar, milk and butter to soft ball stage, while stirring. Take off heat and add remaining ingredients. Mix well and pour into large oblong glass dish. Makes 5 pounds.

Ina Wiedemann

 New! *"Oh Fudge"*

2 c. sugar
1 small can evaporated milk (5 oz.)
12 large marshmallows
2 Tbsp. water

½ c. nuts
¼ lb. butter or margarine
1½ c. chocolate chips
3 tsp. vanilla

Bring sugar and milk to a boil in a heavy pan over low heat. Boil 8 minutes. Add the water to the marshmallows and melt in the top of a double boiler. In a large bowl, put butter, chocolate chips and vanilla. Add sugar, milk mixture, and melted marshmallows. Let cool, then beat until thick enough to hold its form. Fold in nuts. Pour in 8"x8" buttered pan. Place in refrigerator until firm.

Diana Hanna

Peanut Butter Fudge

2 c. sugar
2 Tbsp. light syrup (Karo)
Dash of salt

¾ c. milk
⅓ c. peanut butter
1 tsp. vanilla

Mix together in a skillet, preferably the old iron one. Bring to a boil over low heat. Stir constantly. Cook to soft ball stage. Cool, then beat until candy loses its shine. Pour into buttered plate. Let stand until firm.

Mary Keller

Peanut Butter Fudge

2 c. white sugar
1 c. brown sugar
½ c. white syrup

¼ tsp. soda
½ c. milk
3 tsp. peanut butter

Bring all ingredients, except peanut butter, to hard boil stage. When almost done, add peanut butter. Take off stove and beat until it begins to harden. Add nuts if you like.

This is good and simple to make.

Louise Olive

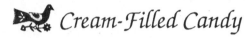

Cream Cheese Mints

1 (8 oz.) pkg. cream cheese
1 lb. powdered sugar
Food coloring

Vanilla or other flavoring
Granulated sugar

Let cream cheese soften at room temperature. Mix in flavoring and coloring. Add powdered sugar to mixture, a little at a time, until it is a heavy dough. Mint dough can be rolled into little balls and mashed flat to form a mint patty. Nuts can be added as a garnish for the patties. Balls can be rolled in granulated sugar and can then be pressed into candy molds to form shapes and immediately unmolded.

Great for showers.

Judy Seikel

Cream-Filled Candy

2 lb. powdered sugar
1 can sweetened condensed milk
½ lb. butter
2 small pkg. chocolate chips

½ sq. paraffin, shaved
Flavoring (such as vanilla, rum, maple, etc. to taste)

Mix in large bowl until creamy. Divide into separate small bowls for different flavors. Put flavoring such as vanilla, rum, maple, etc. in small bowls to taste. Let cool in refrigerator. Roll into balls. Let cool thoroughly in refrigerator again, preferably overnight.

Melt chocolate chips in double boiler with paraffin. Dip cream balls into chocolate and place on wax paper to cool. For thicker chocolate covering, dip again after cooled.

Kay Brown

New! Turkish Delight Candy

4 c. white sugar
1 c. water
6 envelopes plain gelatin
1½ c. orange juice
3 Tbsp. grated orange rind

3 Tbsp. lemon juice
¼ lb. chopped candied cherries
¼ lb. chopped candied pineapple
Pecans
Powdered sugar

Cook 4 cups white sugar and one cup water until clear syrup — about three minutes. Soak six envelopes of plain gelatin in 1½ cup of orange juice. Add to syrup, cook 20 minutes by the clock.

Soak three tablespoons of grated orange rind in three tablespoons lemon juice. Add this to ¼ pound each of chopped candied cherries, pineapple and pecans. Cook five minutes longer. Let stand until cold. Pour in pans rinsed of cold water. Let stand over night. Cut in squares and roll in powdered sugar.

Pauline Piotrowicz

Holly Wreaths

½ c. butter or margarine
1 bag marshmallows
½ tsp. vanilla

2 tsp. green food coloring
4½ c. corn flakes
Red hots

Melt margarine and marshmallows in double boiler or in microwave. Stir until smooth and creamy. Stir in food coloring and vanilla. In a large bowl, pour mixture over corn flakes. Stir to coat all corn flakes. Spoon about 1 tablespoon of the mixture onto wax paper. Dip finger in cold water and make a hole in the middle. Put 3 red hots on each of the holly wreaths. Let stand in a cool area for 24 hours.

Judy Seikel

🐦 Strawberries

Cookies or candy.

1½ small pkg. strawberry Jell-O
2 (7 oz.) pkg. coconut
1 large can sweetened condensed
    milk

1 tsp. sugar
1 tsp. vanilla
Red sugar sprinkles

Mix all ingredients and roll into the shape of strawberries. Roll in red sugar. Put leaves on the top of strawberries with green decorator frosting.

Kids love them as they taste like candy and they are beautiful to decorate a cookie plate with.

Kay Brown

🐦 **New!** Chocolate Christmas Mice

Maraschino cherries with long
    stems
Chocolate candy coating
Hershey's Chocolate Kisses

Cake decorator's icing, green and
    red
Small pkg. sliced almonds

Lay cherries out on folded paper towels to dry. (Chocolate will not stick to wet cherries.) Melt the chocolate candy coating. Dip each cherry to coat, including stem, and lay out to dry on wax paper.

Unwrap a Hershey's Kiss for each cherry. When cherries are dry and set, use a little dab of melted chocolate to "glue" the top of the cherry to the flat bottom of the Kiss to form the mouses' head and body. Stick two sliced almonds between the candy Kiss head and the cherry body to form ears. Dip one end of the almond slice into chocolate if the mouse body and head are already set together.

Using a cake decorator's tip, make green dots for eyes on the Kiss and a red dot on the tip of the Kiss point for the mouse's nose.

The Christmas mice may be used as a garnish on Christmas platters or set out on a platter by themselves with the desserts.

Judy Seikel

Chocolate Dessert Plates

Melted chocolate   **Small paper plates**
Spray cooking oil   **Pastry brush**

Use chocolate chips, candy bars or candy making chocolate, as desired and melt. Spray small paper dessert plate with cooking oil, coating well. Using pastry or basting brush, brush melted chocolate on backside of paper plate. Place in freezer until set. Peel paper plate away carefully. Use chocolate plate for serving fruit salad or ice cream. Eat the plate too!

Judy Seikel

New! Chocolate Leaves

rose leaves   *squares of chocolate*

Tools:

paint brush or basting brush   **wax paper**
knife

Wash and dry rose leaves and pat dry. Melt squares of chocolate in a small pan over low heat. Chocolate can also be melted in the microwave, but use small increments of time to avoid overcooking. The chocolate will tend to hold its shape and may not look melted. If overcooked, chocolate becomes dry and grainy.

Use a small paint brush or basting brush to paint the underside of the leaves with the melted chocolate. Refrigerate to set. After they are chilled, carefully peel the chocolate from the leaf by using a knife to lift the leaf. Set chocolate petals on wax paper and chill until ready to use on cakes or single-serving desserts such as pudding or ice cream.

The Cookbook Committee

Gumdrop Flowers

Use a rolling pin to flatten gumdrops between two sheets of wax paper. Cut the flattened gumdrops into shapes of petals and leaves. Arrange into flower on a cake.

🐦 CDA Popcorn Balls

A Harrah community Halloween tradition.

1 lb. powdered sugar
1 c. white Karo syrup
1 c. miniature marshmallows

¼ c. oleo
1 tsp. vanilla
2 Tbsp. water

Bring all ingredients to a boil. Boil until marshmallows are melted. Pour over large pan of popped corn. Mix well and form into balls. Makes 30-36.

Barbara Dull

Editor's Note: We increase this recipe 40-fold to make 1,200 popcorn balls for the community Halloween party.

🐦 Marshmallow Popcorn Balls

8 to 10 c. popped corn
1 (10 oz.) pkg. marshmallows

½ c. margarine
1 tsp. vanilla (optional)

Melt margarine and add marshmallows. Stir until dissolved. Add vanilla if desired. Pour mixture over popped corn. Mix well. Make into balls.

Pauline Haynes

🐦 Peanut Butter Popcorn

½ c. unpopped corn
2 Tbsp. butter, melted
Salt to taste

⅓ c. white corn syrup
½ c. brown sugar
½ c. peanut butter

Pop corn and season with melted butter and salt. Combine sugar and syrup in saucepan and stir over medium heat until bubbly. Add peanut butter and cook over low heat until mixture is smooth. Put popcorn in large, buttered bowl or pan and add syrup mixture. Mix well. With well-buttered hands, form into balls.

The Cookbook Committee

Popcorn Nuggets

2 c. sugar
⅔ c. water
¼ tsp. cream of tartar
2 Tbsp. molasses

1 Tbsp. butter
Few grains of salt
5 qt. popcorn

Place sugar, water and cream of tartar in a saucepan and bring to the boiling point. Boil, without stirring, to 280° or until syrup will crack when tried in cold water. Add molasses, butter and salt. Boil, stirring constantly, until candy becomes brittle, being careful not to let it burn.

Have ready a pan of freshly popped corn. Pour candy over it, mixing thoroughly. Spread lightly on a buttered slab or platter and when firm, cut into pieces or break up into little bunches of 3-6 kernels.

Recopied from "Harrah Herald," Friday, October 20, 1944.

Rosie L. Klimkowski

Baked Fruited Popcorn

7 c. popcorn
¾ c. candied red cherries, chopped
1 c. pecan pieces
¾ c. brown sugar

6 Tbsp. margarine
3 Tbsp. light corn syrup
¼ tsp. soda
¼ tsp. vanilla

Use a 17"x12"x2" baking pan to combine popcorn, cherries and pecans. Combine brown sugar, margarine and corn syrup. Cook over medium heat until margarine is melted and mixture comes to a boil. Cook 5 more minutes, stirring constantly. Remove from heat and stir in soda and vanilla. Pour mixture over popcorn. Bake in a 300° oven for 15 minutes and then stir. Bake 5 or 10 minutes more. Cool in large container.

The Cookbook Committee

Popcorn Hints

Popcorn will stay fresh and you will eliminate "old maids" if you store it in the freezer.

Running ice cold water over the kernels before popping will also eliminate "old maids".

Caramel Corn

6 qt. popped popcorn
2 sticks (1 c.) margarine
2 c. brown sugar
½ c. light corn syrup

½ tsp. soda
½ tsp. vanilla
Can of roasted peanuts

Make caramel sauce by combining margarine, brown sugar and syrup in a saucepan and heat to boiling. Add the soda and vanilla. In a roasting pan, drizzle caramel sauce over the popcorn and peanuts and mix to coat, using Teflon rather than metal tools. Spread into 2 (9"x13") pans or onto cookie sheets and bake in 250° oven for 1 hour.

The Cookbook Committee

Fruit & Nut Popcorn

⅓ c. popcorn, popped (yields 2½ to
    3 qt.)
1 c. dried apricot pieces
½ c. raisins
1 can mixed party nuts

¾ c. light corn syrup
1 Tbsp. vanilla
¼ c. brown sugar
½ tsp. salt

In a large bowl, mix popped corn, fruit and nuts. In a small bowl, mix syrup, vanilla, sugar and salt. Pour mixture over popcorn, fruit and nuts and toss to coat well. Spread into a buttered sheet cake pan. Bake in preheated 250° oven for 30 minutes.

The Cookbook Committee

No Salt Seasoning

5 tsp. onion powder
1 Tbsp. garlic powder
1 Tbsp. paprika
1 Tbsp. dry mustard

1 tsp. ground thyme
½ tsp. black pepper
½ tsp. celery seed

Mix ingredients and store in covered container or shaker.

Judy Seikel

Putter's Doggie Biscuits

3 c. all-purpose flour
3 c. whole wheat flour
2 c. bulgur wheat (or cracked
   wheat such as used for tabouli)
1 c. corn meal

½ c. instant nonfat milk
4 Tbsp. salt
3 c. chicken broth or water
Milk

In a very large bowl, mix flours, bulgur, corn meal, dry milk and salt. Add 2 cups of the broth. Mix well with hands until very stiff, about the consistency of bread dough. Add more broth if necessary. Preheat oven to 300°.

On lightly floured surface, with floured rolling pin, roll out dough to ½-inch thickness. Use cookie cutters such as dog bones, fire hydrants or cats to cut out biscuits or simply slice into about 1"x3" strips. Place on ungreased cookie sheet. Brush each lightly with milk. Bake 45 minutes. Turn off oven, but leave biscuits in overnight. Makes about 3½ dozen.

Judy Seikel

Fire-Proofing Christmas Tree

3 oz. boric acid crystals
Hot water

2 qt. hot water
7 oz. borax

Mix boric acid crystals and enough hot water to make a paste. Into the 2 quarts of hot water, mix in 7 ounces of common household borax by stirring or shaking until dissolved. Do not use metal container. Add boric acid paste and stir well. Put mixture in a household sprayer and spray tree. Wet all branches. Top side and underside thoroughly. Let stand and dry.

The Cookbook Committee

Windshield Wash Mixture

1 qt. rubbing alcohol
1 c. water

2 Tbsp. liquid detergent

Mix ingredients in a ½ gallon jug and shake well. Put into car's windshield washer container.

The Cookbook Committee

Guest Soap Balls

2 c. Ivory Snow
Powdered food coloring

¼ c. water (approx.)
Floral oil

Mix the soap powder and a little of the powdered food coloring to get desired shade. Color will be darker when water is added. Add the water to the powder a little at a time. Use fingers to mix. Add a few drops of oil. When enough water has been added, shape the soap into balls. Make balls and set them on wax paper to dry and harden.

Powdered food coloring can often be found with candy making supplies. Floral or spice scented oils can be found with crafting supplies such as candle or potpourri supplies.

Judy Seikel

Applesauce-Cinnamon Ornaments

¾ c. ground cinnamon
1 Tbsp. ground allspice
2 Tbsp. ground cloves

1 Tbsp. ground nutmeg
1 c. applesauce
Wire

Mix cinnamon, allspice, cloves and nutmeg. Blend in applesauce until mixed thoroughly to form a stiff dough. Roll out on a metal cookie sheet to about ¼-inch thick. Use cookie cutters to cut into shapes. Peel away the excess dough. Cut a short piece of wire and insert through the dough at the top of the design so that a hole will be maintained for a hanger. Christmas ornament hangers can be used in place of regular wire. The wires can be replaced with ribbons once the ornaments are dried if desired. Let the cinnamon dough ornaments dry, uncovered, for 4 to 5 days. Ornaments may be decorated with ribbons, painted or stenciled. Store in a sealed container to retain fragrance until ready to use.

Judy Seikel

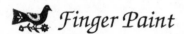 Halloween Make-Up

White Grease Paint:

3 Tbsp. white shortening
5 Tbsp. cornstarch
1 Tbsp. white flour

Glycerin
Food coloring

Brown Grease Paint:

2 tsp. white shortening

5 tsp. unsweetened cocoa

Blend shortening, cornstarch and flour on a plate using a rubber spatula. Add several drops of glycerin and blend. Add drops of glycerin one at a time, until a creamy consistency is reached. Add food coloring if desired.

Brown Grease Paint: Blend as for White Grease Paint. Apply to face with fingers, using short upward strokes.

To remove, use shortening, cold cream or baby oil.

The Cookbook Committee

Finger Paint

½ c. laundry starch
1 c. cold water
1 pkg. plain gelatin

2 c. hot water
½ c. mild soap flakes or detergent
Food coloring

Place ¾ cup cold water and the starch in a saucepan. Soak the gelatin in the remaining cold water. Add hot water to starch mixture and cook until clear. Remove from heat and add gelatin mixture and soap. Tint with food coloring. Makes 3 cups.

The Cookbook Committee

 Mold-Your-Own Crayons

Broken crayon pieces
Small tin cup

Plastic candy molds

Peel paper wrapping off crayons. Sort broken crayon pieces by color. (Similar shades can be combined.) Melt over low heat in tin cup or can nested in larger pot of hot water. Pour into plastic candy molds and refrigerate. Pop out when cooled.

Use caution. This gets very hot.

Microwave: Heat in small glass microwave safe container on HIGH until melted, about 4 to 5 minutes. Stir with toothpick.

Judy Seikel

Play Dough

2½ c. flour
½ c. salt
1 Tbsp. alum

3 Tbsp. corn oil (no substitutes)
3 c. boiling water
Food coloring

Mix flour, salt and alum together in large bowl. Add boiling water (really boiling), corn oil and dry ingredients. Mix well and knead. Add food coloring as desired. Kneading helps fine motor coordination so let the little ones help you knead!

Vicki Dimmer

Household Helps

To get crayon marks off plaster walls, use lighter fluid.

Get ink out of shirt pockets by spraying marks with hair spray before washing.

To keep blades clean on your electric can opener, run a paper towel through the cutter periodically.

Use a small paint brush sprayed with furniture polish to dust wicker furniture. It gets in the little places.

References

In addition to the general traditions and stories handed down by those of Polish descent in Harrah about their heritage, the following sources were used in compiling information about customs, history and general information.

"St. Teresa 1925-1975, Golden Anniversary," 1975.

"The Poles in Oklahoma," Richard M. Bernard, University of Oklahoma Press, 1980.

"Song, Dance, and Customs of Peasant Poland," Sula Benet, Roy Publishers, no date.

"The Land and People of Poland," Eric Kelly, J. B. Lippincott Co., 1972.

"Family Circle" magazine, 1988.

"The Polish-American Journal," newspaper, 1986.

"The Daily Oklahoman," newspaper, Oklahoma City, Okla., 1987.

"Webster's New World Dictionary of the American Language," The Southwestern Co., 1965.

Index

T

Weights & Measures

(All measures are level)

1 Tablespoon	*3 teaspoons*
1 cup	*16 Tablespoons*
½ cup	*8 Tablespoons*
¼ cup	*4 Tablespoons*
½ ounce butter	*1 Tablespoon*
½ pound butter or sugar	*1 cup*
1 pound butter or sugar	*2 cups*
1 stick in 1 pound butter, packaged in 4 sticks	*½ cup*
1 pound molasses	*1½ cups*
1 pound corn syrup	*1⅓ cups*
1 pound chocolate	*16 squares*
1 pound peanuts	*2⅔ cups*
3¾ ounces English Walnuts	*1 cup*
1 pound coconut	*8 cups*
6 ounces brown sugar	*1 cup*
5½ ounces confectioners' sugar	*1 cup*
4½ ounces cocoa	*1 cup*
4 ounces almonds	*1 cup*

ORDER FORM

Spizarnia Kosciol — The Parish Pantry,

Keepsake Edition

Court Christ the King, #1586, The Catholic Daughters of the Americas

Please send: _____ copies of "Spizarnia Kosciol –
The Parish Pantry, Keepsake Edition" @ $16.95 each = _____

Oklahoma residents add appropriate city and state
        sales tax @ .0875 = _____

Postage and packaging @ $3.00 = _____

                       Total = _____

Name   _____

Address   _____

City   _____State Zip _____

Make checks payable to:
The Catholic Daughters
Mail to:
"Spizarnia Kosciol – The Parish
Pantry, Keepsake Edition"
St. Teresa of Avila Church
1576 N. Tim Holt Dr.
Harrah, Okla. 73045

ORDER FORM

Spizarnia Kosciol — The Parish Pantry,

Keepsake Edition

Court Christ the King, #1586, The Catholic Daughters of the Americas

Please send: _____ copies of "Spizarnia Kosciol –
The Parish Pantry, Keepsake Edition" @ $16.95 each = _____

Oklahoma residents add appropriate city and state
        sales tax @ .0875 = _____

Postage and handling @ $3.00 = _____

                       Total = _____

Make checks payable to:
The Catholic Daughters
Mail to:
"Spizarnia Kosciol – The Parish
Pantry, Keepsake Edition"
St. Teresa of Avila Church
1576 N. Tim Holt Dr.
Harrah, Okla. 73045

Name   _____

Address   _____

City   _____State Zip _____

This Cookbook is a perfect gift for Holidays, Weddings, Anniversaries and Birthdays. To order extra copies as gifts for your friends, please use the Order Form on the reverse side of this page.

This Cookbook is a perfect gift for Holidays, Weddings, Anniversaries and Birthdays. To order extra copies as gifts for your friends, please use the Order Form on the reverse side of this page.